NESTLÉ USA
JOE WELLER
CHAIRMAN & CEO

JOE,

BEST WISHES FOR
FUTURE SUCCESS.

GREAT GETTING TO
KNOW YOU.

I HOPE YOU
ENJOY THE "BLUE-
PRINT."
                                    Joe

DECEMBER 2005

A Blueprint for Success

By

Joe Weller

Table of Contents

Acknowledgments

The idea of writing a book intrigues many of us at one point or another. Yet the ultimate decision to put pen to paper—or in today's day and age, fingertips to keyboard—rarely comes easily. Although it is challenging to find the time to write and organize a life's worth of insights and memories into a succinct manuscript, writing this book has been a cathartic process. It has allowed me not only to record the memories of a truly wonderful life, one for which I am very grateful, but also to thank publicly the people who have impacted my career and personal life.

Growing up in Chattanooga, Tennessee, I met many people who helped shape my values and work ethic. My first boss, Dr. Paul Pryor, a pharmacist and owner of Pryor's Pharmacy, exposed me to a variety of jobs as I worked after school and on weekends for him as a delivery boy, stock boy, and later a short-order cook. I learned about hard work and discipline from excellent football coaches like Tom Clary at Notre Dame High School in Chattanooga, who nurtured my athletic talents, and Coach Bill Murray at Duke University, who was one of the finest men I ever met because of how deeply he cared about his players. Throughout school, I benefited greatly from many competent teachers, especially Father Francis Schilling and Sister Mary James, who built my self-confidence in the areas of academics and leadership. At the University of Tennessee, my good friend and resident hall counselor Tim Carini served as an inspirational role model and was always available to give good advice.

Once my professional career began, I was fortunate to meet and work with a host of talented people, many of whom served as mentors throughout my career. It began with Timm Crull, who hired me for Carnation Company in1968. He became my mentor for some twenty-five years, teaching me a lot about empowerment along the way. As an entry-level supervisor at Carnation Company, I had one of the greatest bosses ever in Pete Haynes. Pete taught me more about selling and leadership than anyone for whom I have ever worked. In fact, many of the things I learned from him I still use today. Pete was not only my boss, but he was the best man in my wedding. Finally, Henry Arnest, who was ninety-three when I began writing this book, was the top commercial executive at Carnation Company during much of my tenure with company. He was a great leader and mentor and importantly a lifelong inspiration.

Once Nestlé S.A. acquired Carnation Company in 1985, I became a member of the Nestlé family and part of the largest food company in the world. Since then, I have had the honor of working with some of the most talented people in the food industry. I owe a debt of gratitude to Nestlé S.A. executive vice president Rudi Tschan, for whom I worked when I was managing director and CEO of Nestlé Australia Ltd. A special thanks to Carlos Represas, executive vice president of Nestlé S.A., for all the support given by Zone Americas to Nestlé USA during the ten years that Carlos and I worked with each other. When it comes to international business issues and leadership, Nestlé CEOs Helmut Maucher and Peter Brabeck taught me a great deal. These men, both of whom were instrumental in Nestlé USA's growth in the United States, are great leaders with great visions for global leadership in the food industry. I need to extend special thanks and acknowledgement to Peter Brabeck for his confidence in me and my Nestlé USA team to make the necessary investments for growth and profit improvement. His decisions in this area took vision, courage, and foresight, and without his support, it would have been difficult for Nestlé USA to achieve its consistent level of performance during the past twelve years.

My final role at Nestlé would be as chairman and CEO of Nestlé USA, a position that has rewarded me and challenged me at the same time. During my time as leader of this fantastic organization, I've met some amazing people, whom I would like to thank for their invaluable input over the years. First and foremost, thanks to Brad Alford, president and CEO of Nestlé Brands Company, for his significant contribution to Nestlé USA's success and for simply being the best operations manager I have ever worked with. I have had the privilege of working with Brad for twenty-five years in various important positions both in the United States and Australia. In 2003, Brad took on the most difficult portfolio of brands in the group and has consistently achieved superior performance. He and his team of outstanding leaders are some of the best in the entire food industry. Thanks also to Cam Starrett, executive vice president of human resources, who virtually became my alter ego and confidant over the past thirteen years. Under Cam's leadership, the Nestlé personnel department became a first class human resources organization. Additionally, thanks to Cam for her insights and suggestions about this project; I am forever grateful for her input and support.

I also want to thank Ed Marra, executive vice president of Nestlé S.A., one of the best marketing minds in the food industry, for his contributions while he was on the Nestlé USA team and later when he moved to Switzerland and became head of the Strategic Business Units. Al Stefl did a great job in the area of communications by working with marketing and our agency partners to importantly improve our advertising creative. A debt of gratitude is also owed to a group of senior marketer-leaders at Nestlé USA who executed brand innovation and renovation consistently during the past ten years. Rob Case, Dave Hubinger, Paul Bakus, Angelo Iantosca, Ernie Strapazon, Tim Connor, Brian Young, Cindy Vallar, Frank Higgins, Chris Lewis, and Bryan Badger are some of the best commercial minds in the food industry. Nestlé Purina also has been blessed with a great group of commercial leaders under Pat McGinnis—Terry Block, John McGinty, Bob Watt, Steve Crimmins, and John Vella just to name a few. Special thanks also go to Laurie MacDonald and

Molly Dell 'Omo, who guided me through eleven State-of-the-Company meetings and numerous public relations events with unmatched dedication and professionalism. Most recently, I would like to thank Nestlé S.A. executive vice president Paul Bulcke for his leadership and support during my transition into retirement.

Special thanks and appreciation go to the following people who have been vital in the successes achieved at Nestlé USA: the late John Hubbell and Mike Mitchell, two of the greatest sales leaders in the food industry; Bob Flaherty, who achieved superb results with Wal-Mart International; Chris Djernes, who has been a key sales leader for many years; Pat McGinnis, president and CEO of Nestlé Purina PetCare, who led one of the most successful acquisition transitions in the history of the food industry; John Harris, who unselfishly volunteered to move the Friskies PetCare business to St. Louis in 2001 to be part of Nestlé Purina PetCare Company; Denis Aba, who worked with me in Australia and currently manages the PetCare Strategic Business Unit; Stephen Cunliffe, CEO of Nestlé Prepared Foods Company, who led the Stouffers brand turnaround in 2004; Dan Stroud, who made significant contributions to change at Nestlé USA and will continue to have great impact as president of Nestle Business Services; Kristin Adrian, general counsel, who kept Nestlé USA's legal exposure to a minimum; Kim Lund, CIO, who led the company into the twenty-first century in information technology; and unsung hero Alex Spitzer, who along with his team of tax specialists, have made major contributions to the overall success of the company. In the finance and control area, we experienced excellent teamwork lead by Rock Foster at Nestlé USA, Kevin Berryman at Nestlé Purina PetCare, Glenn Lee at Nestlé Prepared Foods, Ray Thu at Nestlé Brands, and Bob Gatto in M&A.

We have been blessed over the years with some of the finest technical minds in the food industry. Martin Holford, executive vice president of manufacturing, has led the company to record performance in manufacturing efficiency. Critical to this success were operation executives Jim Riley at Nestlé Purina PetCare, Alan Diener at Nestlé Brands, and Jay Weaver at Nestlé Prepared Foods, along with Neil Dorfman in FoodServices and John

Joe Weller

Brocke and Bob Clark at Nestlé Purina PetCare. These executives were backed up by very strong factory managers including: Chuck Dries, Pat Emrich, Dave Klamforth, Mike Nelson, Curt Norpell, John Younger, Louise DeFalco, Jeff Weaver, Ingolf Nitsch, Ken Thompson, Don Nodtvedt, Jean Marc Garnier, Cheryl Hansen, Stephanie Hart, Dave Lighthiser, Bill Reiley, and others. Supply chain specialists Jeff Kurtenbach at Nestlé Brands Company, Marty Tendler at Nestlé Purina PetCare, and Dale Morsefield at Nestlé Prepared Foods made significant contributions to our success.

We made great progress with our human resource and community affairs roles in the company. Special thanks go to Bill Eichelberger, Claudia Horty, Judy Moon-Cascapera, Steve Degnan, Jeff Ertel, and Phil Ray. Additionally, much appreciation to Ken Bentley and his team for all their work in the community, and to Louise Hilsen and her team in the Washington office.

Finally, there are those who help me execute what needs to get done each day. A debt of gratitude is owed to two of the finest assistants that I have ever worked with: Margaret Lewis in Sydney, Australia, who could do just about anything, and Linda Hughes, whom I have worked closely with for almost fifteen years in Glendale. Linda's organizational skills have saved me thousands of work-hours and have allowed me to accomplish more than should have been possible. Her sacrifices on my behalf were often beyond the call of duty, and I will always be grateful to her. A special thanks also goes to John Bevan, who was much more than a corporate driver—he became a friend and confidant over the years. Thanks also go to Tina Lundgren, who worked with me on this manuscript and helped make this book become a reality.

I would also be remiss if I did not thank a group of loyal and dedicated executives that were both associates and friends for as long as thirty-five years prior to their retirements. Dick Ramage, Jim Walsh, Nino Cristofoli, Jim Dintaman, Dick Matthews, Peter Argentine, Rupert Gasser, the late Norm Berkness, Lou Carlo, the late Jim Heerwagen, Pete Haynes, Jim Ball, Morry Faulkner, Jack MacDonald, Frank Arthofer, Don Fuhrman, Lou Rivers, Mark Gupton, Frank Cella, Fred Hull, Bob Jessel, the late Floyd Goettge, Harlan Croston, Tom Caston, Frank Rich, Jerry Cohen,

xiii

Glynn Morris, Dwight Stuart, Jr., Jack Mulhern, Paul Stone, Bob Mason, Jerry Barringer, and Nick Riso. These individuals not only made significant contributions to our business, but also made the journey enjoyable for me.

Thanks to longtime friends Chuck Reid, Pete Brockett, Bill Matthews, Fred Zuker, and Chuck Reed. Thanks also to Rob Iverson for his friendship and for always being available for advice and counsel.

As I look back over the past sixty years, I marvel at how God has so richly blessed my life. As the hundreds of people and events flood my thoughts and I realize events flood my thoughts, and I realize that nothing I ever achieved would have been possible or would have had as much meaning had it not been for my family. I was fortunate to have two courageous parents who believed in me and encouraged me and four brothers and a sister who have always provided me with a solid familial support system. To them, I will always be grateful. But my greatest thanks of all goes to my wife Carol, who has been by my side for over thirty-five years. Without her love, encouragement, sense of humor, commitment, and inspiration, my life would be almost meaningless. Her insightful wisdom and perspective on people and events was always an invaluable asset. Together, we have been blessed with two wonderful children, Robin and Jeff, who have loved me unconditionally, and who have taught me many lessons about love and relationships. They have brought to our family a terrific son-in-law, John McMonigle, and a great daughter-in-law, Christine, who both took an interest in this project from the beginning and were a big source of encouragement.

During my life, I have worked for many wonderful leaders and have had the privilege to lead thousands of fantastic employees. There are so many people that I should call out by name, but if I did, the list alone would fill a book. Suffice it to say that Nestlé people have been my inspiration and great joy. I am so proud of what they have accomplished as a team aligned behind Nestlé USA's vision and values. They are all an integral part of the *Blueprint for Success*. Their passion to win the competitive fight each and every day has been a great source of strength for me. Nestlé Associates, you are indeed the "Very Best"!

Peter Brabeck-Letmathe, Chairman and CEO, Nestlé S.A.

As a corporate leader, I believe it is vitally important to surround myself with great people. In the end, we must have people to match our principles, rather than principles that match our people. Joe Weller is a great example of this concept. He is someone to whom I've been able to turn for sound input, and he in turn has surrounded himself with talented people with the ability and ethics required to grow our company.

I met Joe Weller for the first time in Australia, shortly after he became managing director of Nestlé Australia. I had worldwide responsibility for Culinary Products at the time, with twenty years of international experience at Nestlé under my belt; Joe on the other hand was embarking on his first job outside of the United States.

Even during our first meeting, I knew Joe was different. I recall having dinner with him, just the two of us. The issues we discussed, which I'm sure were important at the time, were secondary to the impression he made on me that evening. Interestingly, Joe would not have an aperitif, wine, coffee, or a cigar, which was quite unusual in those days for someone who had built a career at our company. It didn't take long to see that Joe Weller, while a rather private man, displayed great values and strong leadership skills.

These leadership skills served him well as he transitioned from Australia back to the United States to become CEO of Nestlé USA. By this time, I had become a member of the executive board of Nestlé, which led to our second and then subsequent meetings. My initial impressions of Joe were confirmed. He showed great loyalty to his boss and his colleagues as well as profound respect for Carnation (the company for which he had previously worked) and Nestlé. I also left this meeting with an appreciation for how hard Joe worked, how honest he was, and how committed he was to his beliefs.

Since then, we have spent time together, sharing our thoughts on business and values and how the relationship between the two would impact the future of our company. When I became CEO of Nestlé S.A., I turned to Joe for input on how to prepare our company for the future. Consequently, he helped shape the content for my first "Blueprint for the Future" by making significant contributions in two areas specifically—size versus strength and people. Joe believed strongly in the concept of moving our company "from big to strong," a process he describes in detail in this book. After discussing this concept in a global context, I encouraged him to implement this strategy at Nestlé USA by divesting weak businesses in order to invest where we were already strong. As a result, Nestlé USA streamlined its business portfolio and gathered strength in the market. Joe's greatest contribution, perhaps, was his unrelenting belief that people were our greatest asset, and at his insistence, this value was incorporated into the Nestlé S.A. "Blueprint for the Future."

The new company mission was well received, and I was very pleased that Joe became the first market head to adapt the "Blueprint for the Future" to his company and corporate culture, thereby creating the Nestlé USA *Blueprint for Success*. In my mind, this book is a natural extension of Joe's outstanding career, highlighting the strategies that have not only increased market share for many of our Nestlé brands but also increased profits at Nestlé USA. But this book goes one step further. It provides insight into how Joe used simple principles, such as respect for people, strong values, and an overwhelming belief in teamwork, to become a successful leader.

In the end, I believe leadership is a privilege, which is given to the leader by the people and, therefore, carries big responsibilities. A leader has to develop strong beliefs, which he needs to be able to articulate and communicate. Above all, however, he has to act on these beliefs, maintaining a consistency between message and behavior, because he will be held accountable for the results.

As such, it is clear to me that Joe Weller is a great leader. I learned a lot from him over the years, and I think he would say that he learned a lot from me as well. As Joe moves on to the next stage in his life, he can rest assured that he greatly impacted Nestlé during his tenure. And while his talents, passion, and leadership will be missed on a daily basis, his legacy will be present in a stronger, more unified Nestlé USA that is poised to flourish further and build upon the blueprint for success Joe put in place.

INTRODUCTION

A Word from Joe

I have read numerous articles and books over the years about leadership. Invariably, they discuss in depth the characteristics great leaders display in their professional and personal lives. Some take the position that true leaders are born with some kind of innate ability to get people to follow them, while others believe leaders are developed over time.

I believe in the second school of thought, dismissing the idea that leadership is inherited through DNA. Based on my personal experience, I am convinced that certain principles of behavior learned early in life can guide and nurture success in almost any business or personal endeavor.

I like to think of these principles as a blueprint for success. The problem is that by the time you have it all figured out, it is just about time to retire.

The true value of these life lessons, therefore, lies in how they are passed on to others, helping people avoid some of the mistakes the rest of us have already made. That is the primary reason that I have written *A Blueprint for Success*.

My life story mirrors to a certain degree the stereotypical American dream. I was born and raised in a small, relatively poor neighborhood in Chattanooga, Tennessee, along with my four brothers and my sister. Growing up, we didn't have much. In fact, you might say we were economically poor; but we were very rich in terms of life experiences, which ultimately helped shape my leadership skills.

Because of our economic reality, I began my "professional career" more than fifty years ago. Granted, my first official job was stocking shelves at Tipton's Grocery Store when I was eight years old. Nevertheless, my work ethic began to take shape inside that store. From jobs as simple as a paper route and delivering prescriptions for a local pharmacy to jobs as complex as leading a $12 billion corporation, I have learned that no job is too insignificant to teach us something. Each responsibility, challenge, and decision in life is a unique opportunity to develop a skill that can be used later, including in the area of leadership.

Foundational Lessons

One of the great rewards of serving as a corporate leader is being asked to speak to various groups about business, leadership, and success—it is my chance to pass on what I have learned during my career. Whether they are college students, MBA candidates, industry members, or fellow Nestlé employees, their questions focus on similar topics, including:

- To what I attribute my success.
- The most influential people in my life and how they affected my success.
- The most important lessons I've learned during my career.

My thoughts on these and many other topics are summarized in *A Blueprint for Success*. First and foremost, I like to remind people how fortunate we are to live in a country (and in my case work for a company) where regardless of your ancestry or pedigree, a person of average intelligence and a passion to win can succeed. We are responsible for our own success—we just have to work hard and be dedicated to persevering even when life serves up an unexpected blow. I learned early on, when I left Duke University, that failure can be a great motivator.

I also believe it is important to always give 110 percent effort on every task we are assigned in life. God has blessed each of us with several talents; the key is identifying them and using them to our greatest ability, regardless of our aptitude. (This was always my personal goal, even though at times I felt better about myself in this regard than I did at other times.) Because every responsibility or job, no matter how small, is preparing us for a future opportunity, it is important to perform it with enthusiasm. Besides, the feeling of pride in a job well done is something a paycheck won't give you.

Throughout my life I have also learned valuable lessons about teamwork and leadership. At first glance, you might not think of them in the same breath, but I believe being a team player makes you a better leader. Remember, teams always outperform individuals; therefore, understanding how to be an effective team member is important to achieving success.

At the same time, I encourage people to strive to become leaders as opposed to becoming managers. Great leaders often come from great teams, armed with the knowledge and support of the team members with whom they have worked. But the real difference between leaders and managers is that leaders have a vision for the future and an understanding of what intellectual and capital resources are necessary to direct an organization to that vision for the future. As you will see in this book, vision is critical to the success of an organization. Harnessing the collective energy, effort, and enthusiasm of twenty-two thousand employees and focusing on the same goal was the purpose in developing the Nestlé USA *Blueprint for Success*. With seven consecutive years (1998–2004) of record sales, profits, and market share, Nestlé USA's goal of becoming the Very Best Food Company In The United States has largely been realized.

They say that with age and experience come wisdom, and at this point in my career I believe that to be true. I have a different perspective on some areas of my life today than I did when I was starting out. After having met many amazing mentors and business leaders, I now know that all the professional success in the world cannot compensate for an unfulfilled personal life. In fact, I believe that balance in the areas of personal relationships, spirituality, hobbies, community, and career is absolutely essential to having a highly productive professional life.

Although I have been extremely lucky to have my wife Carol and our two children, Robin and Jeff, by my side throughout my climb up the corporate ladder, I wish I would have understood this concept better earlier in my career. Some years ago when Jeff was in college at Southern Methodist University (SMU), I flew to Dallas to discuss our relationship. We had not been as close as I would have liked during his late teen years. I told Jeff that, unfortunately, when he was born the doctor did not give me a handbook on precisely how his mother and I should raise him. Our parenting, for better or worse, was basically a result of on-the-job-training and I had obviously made a few mistakes along the way. I asked Jeff for his forgiveness for the ways he felt that I had let him down as a father, and from that day forward, Jeff and I began to build a stronger relationship that has blossomed into a wonderful friendship.

Life's Next Chapter

My former boss at Carnation Company, Timm Crull, strongly felt that no CEO should stay in the position more than ten years. He felt this was the proper amount of time to set a vision and make a real contribution to a company's success. Anything less was too brief, and anything more would create stagnation in the company. Timm also felt strongly that room should be made for others in the organization to have an opportunity to serve as CEO. I thought of Timm's philosophy as I completed my tenth year as chairman and CEO of Nestlé USA. From my perspective, he was right on target.

A Blueprint for Success is my life story. Although it highlights what I have learned in my more than thirty-seven years with Carnation and Nestlé, it also chronicles some of the most important personal events in my life, from childhood to parenthood. One important area in my life is my spirituality, and therefore, I have included some Biblical principles in this book. My goal is not to offend anyone with my personal beliefs, but rather to explain further why I may approach personal and professional issues the way I do.

Joe Weller

Most important, however, *A Blueprint for Success* is my way of recognizing and thanking the wonderful Nestlé and Carnation employees with whom I have had the honor of working over the years. In 2004 as I contemplated retirement, I felt the need to thank and pay tribute to the terrific professionals who have supported and helped me over the years. After all, my career and professional accomplishments were directly influenced by the outstanding teams, leaders, customers, and mentors I met along the way.

Now it is my turn to try to help others achieve their desired level of success. If through this book I can give just one person a jump-start on his or her career or personal life, I will consider it a success.

Joe Weller
Beverly Hills, California
June 2005

CHAPTER 1

Building Blocks

I grew up in Chattanooga, Tennessee, a typical southern town steeped in Civil War history and lots of southern charm. I was one of six children born into a working class family of very modest means. We lived in a four-room, one-bathroom rental house in East Lake—a Chattanooga neighborhood that was home to a mixture of poor and blue-collar families.

From a geographical standpoint, Chattanooga sits on the Tennessee River in the southeastern corner of the state and nudges up to the Georgia state line. It was first settled around 1835 and was initially known as Ross's Landing. From our neighborhood we would often walk across the state line for a mile or two to Rossville, Georgia, a town with many small shops, including drug stores, five-and-dime stores, and pawnshops. We entertained ourselves for most of the day, generally doing more window-shopping than buying, but taking our time, especially when we were looking through the pawnshops. Our day would end with a walk home that always seemed much longer than the morning's trip.

No Silver Spoon

My family never had much money. Growing up poor was our reality, but it was something that I believe ultimately shaped me in a positive way. I learned the value of a dollar, and I learned how to work hard. None of the Weller kids were ever spoiled, and we all appreciated even the smallest "luxury." After watching my family struggle financially throughout my childhood, I knew that I wanted a different life when I grew up. Changing my circumstances, however, would be up to me. No one was going to give me anything.

I learned about hard work from my father and my mother. My dad's work ethic was unparalleled, and he took great pride in what he did and how well he did it. From him I learned about the limitations of jobs based on physical labor, and therefore I also learned about the value of an education in finding a career with broader opportunities. My mother's attention was focused on raising six children—a job which required perhaps even more diligence, energy, and commitment than most any job she could have performed outside the home. Together, my parents worked to provide the best they could for their children.

Working On The Railroad

My father, William Tiernan Weller, worked hard to support his family, but his is not a story of good fortune, apple pie, and the American dream. His adversities began early. Dad was raised without his father during the Great Depression. He also suffered a ruptured appendix as a youngster, which almost killed him. He overcame those trials and graduated from Notre Dame High School, where he played basketball, was a star guard on the football team, and was editor of *The Clarion,* his school newspaper. Even though he excelled in school, he had no real chance to go to college because of financial constraints.

Bill Weller worked as a dining car steward on the Southern Railroad. He was "blue collar" by economic and social standards but actually wore a white collar, tie, and vest with big, shiny SR (Southern Railroad) brass buttons on it as part of his dining car steward uniform. Today a dining car steward of the passenger railroad era would be the equivalent of a restaurant maître d' or headwaiter.

My father came by his love for trains and his subsequent profession honestly. Both his mother and father had worked for the Southern before he had, and his father's father, who migrated from Germany in the 1840s, was also a railroader. Not only was the railroad in his blood, but work with the railroads had always been plentiful in the Chattanooga area. In fact, the city's history can't be told without reference to the railroad industry, which developed during the Civil War. With battlefields such as Chickamauga, Lookout Mountain, and Missionary Ridge all located in the immediate area, Chattanooga became the railway center of the Confederacy during the Civil War and remained an important railroad center in the South until the early 1950s.

Dad spent many hours in the old Southern Terminal Station, in the heart of Chattanooga, preparing for trips or returning from runs to various destinations, including New Orleans, New York, and Miami. The Southern Terminal Station was built in 1908 and had a unique dome that was the centerpiece of the structure. The station operated fourteen tracks, and in its heyday in the 1930s and 1940s nearly fifty passenger trains passed through the Southern Terminal Station on Market Street every day. But by the time I was a child in the 1950s and remember my father working there, service was down to ten to fifteen passenger trains per day. Today, the old station is a hotel and restaurant complex, hustling and bustling again, but with a whole new purpose and for a new generation.

Being a dining car steward would have been a good job, except for the fact that many of the stewards worked into their seventies and were reluctant to retire. There was never enough work to go around for those stewards like my dad who had less seniority. The railroad passenger business was in significant decline by the early 1960s, as cheaper air flights and bus travel became the primary methods of transportation in the United States. Southern Railway was down to two or three passenger trains per day by the time my dad reached fifty years of age. With twenty-five years of service, Dad was still often working on the "extra-board" (part-timer) much of the time, filling in for the older stewards who wanted time off.

Taking Pride in Your Work

My father supported a family of eight in the early 1960s on a salary of six thousand dollars per year. Granted, it was more than he made when he and my mom were first married in 1934, when he worked as a desk clerk for the Key Hotel making two to three dollars per week and would put cardboard in his shoes to cover the holes in his soles. When work was plentiful he would travel eight or nine days in a row and be home for three days between trips. Dad would sleep on the train in a sleeper car at night and work breakfast, lunch, and supper on the dining car each day. We always looked forward to seeing him get off the bus after one of these long trips. One of the boys would meet Dad at the bus stop after a trip to help him carry his grip (suitcase) the one-block journey from the bus stop to home. He would often bring mom a five-cent bag of Tom's peanuts from the train station, much to her delight. Needless to say, he had a devoted and enthusiastic welcoming committee of family members waiting for him both at the station and at home after each trip.

Dad took great pride in his work and performed it with true professionalism, yet he lacked the ambition and self-confidence to look for other job opportunities over the years. Thus, being a dining car steward became his lifelong career; and I must say he did it extremely well. At home, my father was somewhat of an introvert, but when he was at work, he became a charming, outgoing master of service and conversation. It was as if putting on his uniform and stepping onto the train transformed him into a man with a personality that most people did not forget. In essence, my father was on stage when he entered the luxurious dining cars of the Southern. Filled with white tablecloths and sterling silver service that was unmatched by any other mode of transportation of that day, the dining car became his theater. And at that time, each train and each trip had its own personality. The Miami train, for example, was named the *Royal Palm*. The train to New Orleans was the *Pelican*. They provided the perfect backdrop for my father to "perform" his job and project just the right personality to make his customers feel comfortable in their surroundings.

My dad would bring home many stories from his train trips. In those days he would serve numerous stars of stage and screen and many political celebrities on his dining car. He met greats like Humphrey Bogart and Mickey Rooney and even got the autograph of Edward Arnold, a star in the age of black and white movies. My father would continue to relive many of his stories until his death in 1987 at the age of seventy-six.

My Inspiration

My mother, Carol Pocus, was born and raised in Palmer, Tennessee and in a small coal-mining community in Grundy County not far from Chattanooga. Although her name was Carol, my dad called her Mickie and her sisters called her Cleo, which was her middle name. She was raised in a large household as one of eight children, with four sisters and three brothers. Although my mother's family tree is less certain than my father's, we do know that her father, Henry, worked in the mines and died when he was fifty years old, while her mother, Nora Seitz, raised the children. Not much is known about the family history, other than that Henry's father, John, had migrated from Sicily, Italy in the 1800s and her mother's family, which was of Swiss-Austrian descent, had lived in the Palmer and Grundy County area since the 1860s. It is entirely possible that the Seitz family was part American Indian, either Cherokee or Chikamaka. Granny Pocus, as we knew her, had many traits of the Cherokee, with her high cheekbones and beautiful long braided coal black hair. She would visit us on occasion in Chattanooga, but she was never that comfortable away from her rural home in Palmer.

My mother was a thin and frail person physically, but robust in spirit and values.

She suffered from the complications of tuberculosis, which was diagnosed in her early twenties and likely contracted during her teenage years when she cooked for the coal miners in her small hometown. She exuded positive energy and encouraged us in whatever endeavors we undertook. She always made "her boys" feel like they could do anything. But the one thing she couldn't tolerate was laziness. I remember well one of her favorite sayings: "There are some people who would not take a job tasting pies in a pie factory." Goodness knows, with six children, there wasn't a lazy bone in her body.

Mother most likely did not go to school beyond the fifth or sixth grade, but was gifted with wisdom that no amount of formal education could give. She was the inspiration and motivation of the family and played a key role in each of my brothers' and my sister's lives. My mother died at barely fifty-two years of age. Her lifelong battle with TB and heart disease finally consumed her one night as she slept.

Growing Up Poor

Our childhood years in East Lake were financially trying times, with five boys and one girl comprising the Weller family. I was born in 1945, the third of six children. Age-wise, I was sandwiched almost in the middle, with two older brothers (Bill and Jim, who were ten and three years my senior) and three younger siblings (Don, eleven months younger; Carol, four years younger; and Dan, seven years my junior). Frugality was a requirement to survive, and part of my mother's job was to figure out how to make ends meet. For example, meat was a delicacy and many times we would have meals without it. Corn, tomatoes, beans, and potatoes were staples. When we did have meat, however, it was usually fried chicken, hamburger, or an occasional round steak.

One low point for our family was when my father, due to an extended illness, was not able to work. At that time we lived from paycheck to paycheck, and missing several in a row forced my father to declare bankruptcy. In small town America, word got around fast, and the whole family was embarrassed. But there was never a doubt that my father would make good on his debts, and eventually, he paid every creditor dollar for dollar.

Our concerns, however, weren't just over our constant financial crises. The fear of polio was prevalent in poor neighborhoods like ours. Kids went barefoot and bareback all summer long, and potentially contaminated open streams often ran through the landscape, which just added to the danger. Naturally, we had just such a stream that ran behind our house. The image of rows of iron lungs in hospitals all across the country haunts me even to this day, and contracting polio was constantly part of my mother's worry list.

I learned early on that success is relative. For example, some East Lake families owned an automobile and a television set. Even though these automobiles seldom were new models and most of the television sets were black and white, they were symbols of success in our neighborhood. The Weller family, however, had neither car nor television in those early years. Our family mode of transportation was city bus, thumbing, bicycle, or just walking, and our in-home family entertainment was sitting around our radio to listen to sports events like college football, Friday night fights from Madison Square Garden, and *Gunsmoke*.

The neighborhood kids, the Weller clan included, entertained themselves outside by playing games. Touch football, tackle football, kick-the-can, and hide-and-go-seek were our favorites. Since most of the neighborhood kids were at roughly the same socio-economic level, we found many ways to enjoy ourselves without feeling deprived. We made soapbox derby carts from scraps of wood and old wagon wheels. These carts were used to race down Dead Man's Hill, the nickname we gave to the street that ran adjacent to our back yard. The name came from the fact that we had to have a "watch" at the bottom of the hill to make sure that an automobile was not en route to the intersection as we pushed off from the top of the hill. If we were really bored we would take a homegrown watermelon, cut it in half, clean out the fruit, and make an army helmet to play war games.

As I think back to these times, I realize how different things are for many children growing up today, especially with the advent and prevalence of today's computers and video games. But when we were kids, we had to invent ways to entertain ourselves, using our creativity and ingenuity. One of our favorite pranks usually took place at dusk, when we would place a woman's handbag with a string attached to it in a street intersection. We would then hide behind a nearby bush, with the other end of the string in hand, ready to pull it when a car stopped to examine the "lost bag." We were always poised to run when necessary. In many ways, these were the best times of my life, and it helped to have a sense of humor.

Learning the Value of Hard Work

The Weller boys were always busy. If we weren't outside playing, we were working. Jobs were a necessity for all of us at an early age. They provided our spending money and lunch money when finances became tight, usually toward the end of the month. Our jobs also generally kept us out of trouble, which was easy to get into with some of the characters in the neighborhood.

My mother took the lead role in finding jobs for her boys. I often heard her on the phone singing the praises of our work ethic to prospective employers. At seven years old, I worked for Mrs. Hamby, a widow who lived on our street, breaking large pieces of coal into smaller pieces for her coal-burning stove. I made fifteen cents each time I worked for her. By eight, I was helping to stock the shelves at Tipton's Grocery, a mom-and-pop corner grocery store located one block from our house. The pay was twenty-five cents per hour, which I considered excellent. When I was ten years old, my brother Jim and I had a paper route. Our papers were dropped off five blocks from our house at five-thirty a.m. every day. We learned responsibility at a young age. We had to set our alarm and get to work on time ourselves. This is probably the reason I remain a morning person to this day.

We learned a lot from these jobs, including the value of hard work and the responsibility of contributing to the welfare of our family. One of the greatest lessons from our paper route was that not all people are honest. We always had a certain percentage of people that would read our newspapers each day but not pay their bill at the end of the month. We were shocked that some people would not even come to the door when we knocked on collection day. We could actually hear them whispering inside their homes.

The funds generated by our paper route were combined with some of our dad's earnings to buy the family's first black and white television, which was on sale to make room for the new color models arriving at the store. By today's standards, programming was greatly limited and for many hours of the day and night all that could be seen, even with our trusty rabbit ears, was the test pattern for the local CBS and NBC stations. Many nights Jim and I would sit and stare at the test pattern just so we felt we were getting our money's worth out of that TV!

By my tenth birthday, Jim and I had become a work team. I was always tall for my age so I looked older than I actually was. Our next team experience was pushing an ice cream cart for Liggett Ice Cream Company in Highland Park, a slightly more "up-market" section of town, located two neighborhoods away from East Lake. We would catch an early bus to the ice cream plant each morning in time to pack dry ice and various novelty ice cream products into our three-wheel cart. We used the early morning hours, when sales were slow, to push our cart to the far end of our territory and the rest of the day to sell our way through the neighborhood back toward the ice cream plant.

We had one rather unorthodox customer who would meet us each day at the same place and same time. In order to continue our route we would have to bribe him with an ice cream sandwich, or else he wouldn't let us pass by. This non-paying customer was a rather large boxer bulldog that would force my brother and me to jump on top of our ice cream cart until we could pull out a partially unwrapped ice cream sandwich and throw it as far as possible in the opposite direction from where we were headed. While the boxer was entertaining himself with the ice cream, we would beat a hasty retreat to safety.

Our goal was to arrive back at the plant at the end of the day sold-out of ice cream, pushing only the dry ice. Because we were pretty successful salesmen, the last half-mile of our six-mile route was usually a very easy push. The final thrill of the day was counting our money, paying for our ice cream, and tabulating our profits, which we shared fifty-fifty. Typically we each made between three and four dollars per day—a tidy sum we felt was well worth our effort.

Many of our foundational life lessons were learned at a very young age, and many of them came directly from the early jobs that Jim and I performed. I learned that a good name, a reputation as a hard worker, honesty, and dependability were all critical in getting and keeping any job. We had absolutely no sense of entitlement; we never felt that anyone owed us anything. On the contrary, we felt extremely blessed and lucky to be able to work and make a little money. We also learned that we had to develop good interpersonal skills in order to sell our products, and sometimes even to stay out of harm's way. The unfriendly bulldog wasn't the only customer who tried to bully us. Even older kids and sometimes adults would try to trick us into giving them free products or too much change.

By the time I was twelve years old, the "Joe and Jim team" had moved up the ladder, with the help of a few well-placed phone calls from our mother, of course. Mom had talked Dr. Snodgrass, the head pharmacist at East Lake Drug Store, into giving the Weller boys a chance to demonstrate their work skills. We began alternating as delivery boys for prescriptions, and it wasn't long before word about our work ethic got out, and I was approached by Dr. Paul Pryor of Pryor's Pharmacy to work for him in Highland Park. The job was a bus-ride away from home, but close to my paternal grandmother's (Mama Rose's) little apartment, where we could always depend on a gourmet lunch of Vienna sausage sandwiches with mustard. For the first time in my work life, at the tender age of twelve, I began paying taxes and paying into the Social Security System. A few years ago my wife was astonished when the recap of Social Security taxes paid each year arrived in the mail, and she noticed that my contributions started in 1957. She thought it must be a mistake, but I assured her it was accurate.

The Weller Boys Go to Washington

With work came the kind of freedom that only money can buy. Jim and I splurged when we were sixteen and thirteen respectively, taking some of our earnings and planning a week-long trip to Washington, D.C. by ourselves. It was an adventure we would talk about for years to come. I am sorry to say that I cannot imagine parents today allowing their young teenagers to travel to Washington, D.C. without adult supervision. But in 1958 two boys traveling alone seemed very safe. My dad arranged for passage on one of the Southern Railroad's sleeper cars, and unbeknownst to us at the time, would have his waiter friends keep an eye on us. When we arrived at the train station for embarkation, a very pleasant black man around sixty years old welcomed us aboard. He looked me square in the face and said, "Are you Mr. Bill's baby?" This struck me as a rather odd question to ask a thirteen-year-old who was almost six feet tall, but I knew exactly what he meant. I told him that Dan was the baby, as he was the youngest in the family. We hit it off right away.

Dad had arranged for Jim and me to stay at a small, economical boarding house in Washington D.C. that he often used on his trips. The boarding house was located directly across from the old Ford Theatre, where Lincoln was shot. This was a great central location and staging area for our daily adventures. We rode on the streetcars, walked a lot, and once even took a taxi, which we later regretted because the cab driver greatly overcharged and took advantage of us. We walked to the top of the Washington Monument and back down, visited the Lincoln and Jefferson Memorials, and spent time in the Capitol Building and the White House. We spent an entire day in the Smithsonian Institute and were particularly fascinated with the *Spirit of St. Louis* and the original Wright brothers' airplane. Jim was an avid aviation fan, so we spent an entire afternoon on the observation deck at Washington's National Airport, watching flights land and take off. We also took a boat trip to Mount Vernon to visit George Washington's ancestral home, which was quite an educational experience.

On our final day in Washington we rose early and made our way to Union Station for our trip home. We had had a great time, but we were practically broke, so it was indeed time to leave. During our trip, we had stayed on budget, spending only the money we had allocated for each day. And because breakfast at the boarding house had been free, we had eaten three meals each day for no more than four to five dollars.

We got to Union Station early, so we checked our bags in and decided to walk around the big, beautiful train station. As we walked we noticed an older gentleman, who we guessed to be in his late sixties or early seventies, but clearly in bad health. He was trying to get the attention of a porter because he needed help with his two large bags. Jim and I immediately went to him and asked if we could help. He told us that he was going to Walter Reed Medical Center for treatment and could not carry his bags to the taxi stand. He said he would give us each twenty dollars if we would assist him. Almost simultaneously, we told him that we would be happy to help with his bags, but we could not accept the money. As we put him in the cab, he tried to hand each of us a crisp new twenty-dollar bill, but again we strongly declined. He was so grateful for our help that he insisted, and after several minutes and an impatient taxi driver, we agreed to accept one of his twenties to split between the two of us. The old gentleman seemed very relieved at our decision, and ten dollars each was still a lot of money to us.

Jim and I were quite sure that our parents would not have approved of us taking the money, but at the time we did not see an easy way out of the dilemma. Our values told us that we should not take money for an act of charity, and we were later sorry that we did not follow our conscience. I have often thought about that gentleman, who was likely a military officer, and wondered about his war story.

Family Values

I grew up in a house in which my father's beliefs were important, and he was not ashamed to make his convictions known. Dad was a strong union advocate who was proud of his membership in the Brotherhood of Railroad Trainmen and supported this group wholehcartedly. He was also a devotee of Franklin Delano Roosevelt and was a staunch Democrat whose party affiliation never wavered. But when I think of my father, most of all I think of him as a devout Catholic.

From a very early age, religion was a part of my life. I admit, its importance and role have changed and evolved over the various stages in my life, but it has always been a part of who I am. The Weller family was one of only two Catholic families in East Lake. Chattanooga was situated in the Bible Belt, where people were either Baptist or Pentecostal or they did not go to church at all. A large Nazarene Church was situated less than a block from our house, but we were forbidden from even peeking through the door. Even when we were at our house, however, we could hear the music and singing anytime a service was held.

I also grew up in a time where prejudice was commonplace in the United States. In our area of the country, prejudice against Catholics, Blacks, and Jews was strong in the 1950s and 1960s. I remember one Friday night when we heard that there was going to be a Ku Klux Klan rally in the lumberyard that was near the bus stop where we often met our dad when he returned from a trip. My mother wanted us to understand what prejudice was, so she allowed Jim, Don, and me to witness the rally, under the strict supervision of Bill, who was then fifteen years old. My mother gave us all specific instructions not to tell anyone in the crowd that we were Catholics. Bill, Jim, Don, and I watched the proceedings from a safe distance, across Dodds Avenue.

Over a period of an hour or so, groups streamed into the lumberyard's large open field in cars with Tennessee and Georgia license plates. The KKK members were all wearing pure white robes—some with hoods that hid their faces, others with their faces uncovered. They soaked a large wooden cross that must

13

have been at least fifteen feet high with kerosene, placed it up-right into a hole in the ground, and then one of the hooded men set it on fire. It burned intensely. As it burned, one hooded man after another climbed onto a makeshift stage to address the crowd with a megaphone so they could be clearly heard. As I lis-tened, I became more and more frightened, despite the fact that we were away from the crowd and I had my older brother, whom I thought was a physically imposing figure, beside me.

The messages that resonated from the hooded men behind the megaphone were about hatred, yet the key speaker held a big Bible in his hand and often invoked the name of God in between his words of hate. The hooded speakers made it clear that the number one enemy on the Klan's list were African Americans, whom they called the N-word. That word was never used in my home as a child; I cannot even write it or say it today. Next on their hate list were the Jews, with third place reserved for Catholics, whom they called Papists. I had never heard that term before, but I knew they were talking about my family and me.

Mother's objective had been achieved. I would never forget this experience with the KKK. I realized from that day forward that as a Catholic in East Lake I was as much a minority as a Black or a Jew was. Not only did I begin to feel a moral superi-ority about what I knew was wrong about the people who had gathered that night in that open field, I also felt a moral kinship with Blacks and Jews, even though at the time I did not know any individuals of either group. I knew that the KKK represented a small minority of the people in my community, but I'll always remember knowing of its existence. It wasn't until later in life that I learned that the KKK's interpretation of the Bible and God was a perversion of Protestant Christianity and had no place in true Bible-based Christianity.

As Catholics, the Weller kids attended Notre Dame School on Eighth Street in downtown Chattanooga, which was one of only two Catholic grade schools in the city. Chattanooga was to-tally segregated in the 1950s, so no Black students attended Notre Dame. Catholics were required to attend a Catholic school or to attend Confraternity of Christian Doctrine (CCD) meet-ings after school each day. My father and my grandmother had attended Notre Dame School, so there was no question as to where we would go. From my father's point of view, public school was out of the question for any of his children; he valued a Catholic upbringing and for that reason insisted his children go to Catholic school.

Notre Dame School was a dark brick building built circa 1929 that housed all twelve grades, from first to twelfth. Notre Dame was the only Catholic high school in Chattanooga, or in the southeastern section of Tennessee for that matter. Students from the other Catholic grade school would transfer to Notre Dame School when they were ready for high school. Even so, the entire school had a student body of around four hundred and fifty students, which was smaller than most three-year high schools in the Chattanooga area. Every morning, the Weller family would ride the city bus about thirty minutes from East Lake to downtown Chattanooga and Notre Dame School. When money was tight at home, the school provided us and a few other kids in similar financial straits with bus tokens so that we could make the daily journey to school.

Students from all socio-economic levels attended Notre Dame School. The common denominator, of course, was their Catholic faith. A few non- Catholics paid a high tuition to get a Notre Dame education, but this was rare. In comparison, our neighborhood East Lake Public Grammar School consisted of students who were almost entirely at the same socio-economic level, but unlike Notre Dame, few would aspire to go on to college after high school.

Students suffered few social disadvantages at Notre Dame because the staff was very discreet and everyone was required to wear the same uniform. If a student could not afford a uniform, the school would discreetly provide one. I learned the importance of appearance from my father, who always took great pride in how he looked. His uniform was always in perfect condition, his shoes always shined, and his brass buttons were always polished. My mother taught me to iron my shirts and polish my shoes during the first grade, so few people would have known my family's socio-economic standing, except for the fact that East Lake was a poor neighborhood. My mother and father taught us that just because we were poor, we didn't have to look poor—a lesson that is still valuable today.

One advantage that the students from more affluent areas had over those of us from poor neighborhoods was the degree of preparation they received before attending school. Kids from affluent families arrived at Notre Dame for first grade either directly from pre-school or from a home in which they had been heavily tutored. I didn't have the benefit of either, so I started the first grade academically behind the vast majority of the class. I remember how embarrassing and humiliating it was to be the last person in class academically, so I studied as long as it took to get it right. But it wasn't until the fourth grade that I caught up and attained above average academic status in the class—a real turning point in my life.

It was during the fourth and fifth grades that my academic self-esteem was established for the first time. I would never fall behind again. I certainly was not the brightest kid in my class, but no one worked harder than I did, at least in my mind. And it wasn't because my parents pushed me or checked to see if I had done my homework. They had other priorities and bigger worries on which to focus. Doing well in school was *my* decision. So I decided to work just as hard at school as I worked on my various jobs, and I found that the effort always seemed to pay off.

One event, while insignificant upon reflection, seemed at the time to make a world of difference in how I felt about myself. My fifth grade teacher selected me as a patrol boy (traffic monitor), which was her way of giving recognition for being a responsible student. This honor was never given to students who were struggling academically. I was one of three or four out of fifteen to twenty boys from my class to be appointed. (Unfortunately, in those days no girls were even considered for this assignment.) I performed my duties with distinction for several years and was rewarded in the eighth grade by being selected by my teacher, Sister Loretta, as captain of all the school's patrol boys. I was honored by the recognition, but suspected that my tall height probably also played a role in my selection. Regardless, I was thrilled.

In retrospect, I realize that this was my first taste of leadership. I can remember that my badge was distinguished from the others by a United Nations light blue background, while the others were solid silver. This honor signified that I had arrived academically and proven myself as socially responsible by eighth grade graduation, which I admit bolstered my self-esteem.

Developing Pryor Experience

I worked for Dr. Pryor from the sixth grade all the way through high school, progressing from delivery boy to short order cook. During those seven years, I learned a lot about people and life and almost every aspect of the drugstore business, from making deliveries to taking inventory to mopping the floors. By the time I was a senior in high school, I had been around so long and Dr. Pryor knew me so well that he trusted me with the keys to the store, and I would lock up after closing.

I had some great adventures making deliveries for Pryor's Pharmacy. McCallie Avenue divided the area we served into two very different neighborhoods. North of McCallie was a blue- and white-collar section, which was a relatively safe area for bicycle deliveries during the day or night. South of McCallie was a different story all together. This was a very troubled neighborhood with high unemployment and groups of young men with nothing to do but stir up trouble; today, they would be called gangs.

I grudgingly made deliveries after dark to homes in this area. Several small gangs of two or three teenagers each thought it entertaining to let their dogs, usually Chows with black tongues, chase and sometimes actually take down delivery boys. Situations such as these forced the Pryor delivery boys to improvise and find creative solutions to our problems. We eventually perfected a defense weapon to ward off these dog attacks. We took the ammonia solution that we cleaned the hamburger grill with each night and diluted it with water. This solution of 50 percent ammonia would then be loaded into a toy water pistol. This water pistol was always in the pharmacy delivery bag for any trip south of McCallie Avenue, ready for quick use should we be attacked. Our routine was to wait until the dog was released by its owner, then allow it to chase us until it was about two or three feet from us. Then we would pull the water pistol out and spray one or two shots of our solution as close to the dog's nose as possible. This usually stopped the dog in its tracks just long enough to allow us time to escape.

Had we not been armed with our ammonia pistols, making deliveries to that side of town would have been too dangerous. I am not aware of any real harm that ever came to the dogs, only some momentary discomfort. Unfortunately, on one occasion I forgot to put my ammonia gun in my bag, which I did not realize until I was frantically reaching for it to ward off another attacker. As a consequence, the large brown and black chow that was chasing me bit my leg, sending me over the handlebars of my bike and tumbling onto the pavement. Luckily I suffered only cuts and bruises, but I still carry the scars from the four puncture wounds on my calf. Eventually, at the ripe old age of fourteen, I learned to drive Dr. Pryor's '55 blue Plymouth station wagon and after that I made my deliveries by car.

Much of my seven years at Pryor's Pharmacy was spent inside the store. In order to take inventory, another one of my many tasks, I had to know the wholesale price of each item in the drugstore. So as we brought each item into the inventory during the year, part of my job was to code each unit with the wholesale price, which needed to be kept separate from the retail price. Each drugstore had its own easy-to-remember code words to symbolize wholesale prices for every product. Pryor's code was "GOLD WATCH" plus X for zero. So, the G stood for one, the O was two, the L was three, and so on. For example, an item that cost the drug-store a dollar-fifty wholesale was coded on the unit with a grease pencil as GWX for reference during inventory time. This code was used so customers could not calculate the profit being made on each item. It wasn't high tech, but it was effective.

Another common job that I performed at Pryor's was helping Dr. Pryor fill gel caps with the prescription powders that he had carefully blended and measured. Under his close supervision I filled the measured amount of drug powders into each capsule. When I wasn't the pharmacist's aid, I cleaned the grill, cleaned out the grease traps, and worked the cash register. With all of these responsibilities, I met a lot of people. I was exposed to many wonderful ones, but I was also exposed to the seamier side of life. I saw the panhandlers, the alcoholics, and the people addicted to all sorts of prescription drugs like paregoric and codeine cough syrup. These people were always looking for a handout from anyone with two nickels to rub together.

We had many humorous experiences at Pryor's Pharmacy. One occurred during my days as a short order cook. We usually had a big lunch business on Mondays through Fridays, when people from nearby businesses would converge on our fifteen counter stools and fill our ten booths. The rush always occurred from eleven-fifty a.m. to twelve-ten p.m.; it was a short time frame but extremely hectic. My job as short order cook was to have the hamburgers ready to be served as customers placed their orders. The grill would accommodate exactly twenty hamburger patties at one time, and we would also prepare twenty "set-ups," which were the buns complete with lettuce, tomato, onion, and pickle. The set-ups were ready by eleven-forty-five a.m. and the hamburgers would be on the grill frying, ready to be placed on the buns as customers placed their orders. As soon as the waitress shouted out an order, I would immediately add the mustard or mayonnaise to the bun, place the patty on it, and serve the hamburger as quickly as possible. On this particular day, in all my haste, all the set-ups had been served, but one patty remained on the grill. Obviously someone was eating a hamburger with no meat on it. In the hundreds of lunch shifts I had worked at Pryor's, this had never happened to me before. I casually walked the counter to see if I could spot the customer who had been shorted. I noticed one of my regular lunch customers eating the set-up without the meat, so I asked him how he was enjoying his burger. He responded that his hamburger was excellent. He and I had many laughs about this episode in the months following. Like the meatless hamburger, my experience has been that often life is not always as it seems.

Some jobs were more interesting and educational than others. During my senior year in high school, I took a job as a surveyor's assistant for the Tennessee Department of Highways. Our summer project was surveying roads that were atop the Missionary Ridge

Civil War battlefield, very close to my home. I spent many afternoons over that summer eating a quick lunch from a brown bag and "catching a few winks" beneath a Civil War monument dedicated to those who had died at that historic site on November 25, 1863. I could not help but be in awe of what had occurred on that hilltop ridge only a hundred years earlier, as almost seven thousand Confederates and almost six thousand Union troops were killed, wounded, or declared missing. More than a hundred thousand soldiers from both sides took part in this battle, which became the beginning of the end for the South in this devastating civil war. I could almost hear the musket balls being fired when I closed my eyes; in fact, it was not uncommon for one of our crew to find an old musket ball on occasion

Understanding the Value of Sports and Education

One of the things my father loved was sports. He always encouraged us to play whatever sport we desired, and he became our biggest fan. Sports were an outlet for him—something he just really enjoyed. He didn't, however, value education as much as perhaps he should have. This became apparent when my oldest brother, Bill, decided to go to the University of Tennessee instead of doing what my father wanted, which was to work for the railroad and help out with the expenses at home. But Bill understood what I would come to learn—the importance of an education.

By the time Bill was a junior at UT, however, my dad had accepted that a college education was the right thing for his oldest son. He entered a co-op program in combustion engineering for several years, which allowed him to work for a quarter and go to school for a quarter in order to be able to afford the tuition and room and board. Bill always had a job at the university faculty club or elsewhere on campus to make ends meet. Very little support could be expected from home other than a care package of snacks that our mother would put together occasionally and send up to Knoxville.

Bill graduated from the University of Tennessee in 1958. Not only was he the first family member to ever graduate from college, he would go one step further by going to law school at night and earning his law degree. He later became an assistant district attorney in Atlanta and finally established a successful legal practice on his own in Atlanta.

Bill became my role model for his persistence despite the odds mounted against him. Bill helped my dad buy our first family car in 1960. It was a 1950 Studebaker, priced at three hundred dollars, which they split fifty-fifty. So when I was fifteen years of age, my family had transportation other than the city bus for the first time, and we were able to move to a nicer neighborhood and attempt to buy our family's first modest home.

A true turning point in my life arose when Notre Dame High School football coach Tom Clary asked me to try out for the football team, just prior to the tenth grade. I was playing basketball and running track, but wasn't sure I could play football and find time to work and carry a full academic load. The only football experience I had was as a young kid playing pick-up games in the back yard with neighborhood kids in East Lake, but I did love the game. So I decided to follow my brother Bill's footsteps and join the team. Bill had played football at Notre Dame ten years earlier and went on to become head cheerleader at the University of Tennessee. We almost always listened to Tennessee football each Saturday in the fall. The radio announcer would say, "Vol fans, welcome to Tennessee football, and your Tennessee Vols will be coming to you from left to right on your radio dial." For the next two hours we would be glued to the radio set, "watching" the UT Vols move from left to right and right to left across that radio dial. I found that I really had a passion for football and wanted to be the best that I could be at the sport regardless of my lack of experience. I asked Coach Clary if I could have my brother Bill's old number—88-as we were both ends. He agreed and I was off and running. Dr. Pryor was kind enough to allow me to work after football practice and on the weekends, and he always gave me game nights off.

My brother Don joined the team my junior year, when he was a sophomore. We played two years together on the same side of the line—he was a tackle, and I was an end. I think we played well together and were an asset to the team. Despite our school's small student body, our NDHS team was quite successful during my three years in high school. In 1961, 1962, and 1963, our record was a combined twenty-two victories, nine defeats, and two ties. The fact that several of the high schools that we defeated had large student bodies of one to two thousand students, versus Notre Dame's two hundred and fifty students, made these victories even sweeter. Two of the losses occurred in the last two games of the 1963 season, games that Don and I did not play. This was due to a dispute between the principal of NDHS and my father over an insurance claim for an injury I had received while playing football. The school had refused to pay the medical-related insurance claim, which was customary at that time, but the issue was miraculously resolved shortly before a Bowl game that year against state powerhouse Bradley County. Don and I played, and we won the game.

Sports became a bond between my dad and me. He was a big man physically, but beneath that large exterior and even larger personality lived a gentle heart. He always had a word of encouragement before and after each football or basketball game that he was able to attend. Often I would spot Dad at a distance out of the corner of my eye at football practice after he returned home from a long trip. I knew he must have been exhausted from the trip, but that never kept him away.

I received several honors my senior year at Notre Dame High School. My senior class elected me president of the class, which meant a lot to me. I was pleased, but the truth of the matter was that it was more of a personality contest than a campaign of substance. I realized afterwards that a number of very deserving classmates could have been elected. I was also extremely honored to be selected All-City my junior year, and Most Valuable Player my senior year. I was most proud of being elected co-captain by my teammates my senior year in 1963. As a result of my efforts on the football field, Duke University offered me a full grant and aid four-year scholarship to play football for the Blue Devils in Durham, North Carolina. Football had opened a door for me which otherwise would have seemed too intimidating to open.

Team Building Blocks

The experience of team sports would serve me well later in life and would be a great building block for my future in business, where teamwork is so critical for success. I learned from playing football that a team depends on each player to execute his assignment to perfection in order to achieve success. If you fail in your assignment and let the team down, you feel much worse than when you just let yourself down. Teamwork is about trust and commitment and personal sacrifice. It is clear that even the best of athletes can be relegated to mediocrity without support from their teammates. Teamwork takes practice, practice, and more practice, but the pay-off is always very rewarding for each member of the team.

From the time I was seven to the time I was eighteen years old, I tried to give 110 percent effort to each experience that I had, whether in sports, work, or in the classroom. I learned early that my happiness depended upon the satisfaction of knowing that I had done the very best job that I was capable of doing. It made me happy to make the most of the talents that the good Lord had blessed me with. Little did I realize at the time that each of these experiences, whether mopping the floor at Pryor's Pharmacy, bringing an A+ effort to each football game, or studying extra hard to ace a test would be a pattern that was establishing building blocks for the future.

CHAPTER 2

If It's Going to Be, It's Up to Me

"I am glad to inform you that the committee of admissions to the College of Engineering has reserved a place for you in the freshman class, which will enter in September," read the letter I received from the dean of admissions at Duke University. It was almost impossible for me to believe that a poor kid like me from East Lake, Tennessee could have been accepted at such a highly respected institution as Duke University. But there it was in black and white. A separate letter from the athletic department granted me a full four-year athletic scholarship that would be honored even if an injury made it impossible for me to continue playing football. With that, in the summer of 1963 I headed to Durham, North Carolina and became a Duke Blue Devil.

Arriving at Duke and moving into the Freshman Quad, at old house C, where I would room with one of my high school teammates, was the highlight of my life up until that point in time. The campus was the most beautiful place I had ever seen. The Sarah P. Duke Memorial Gardens were always in pristine condition. It seemed as if its beautiful flowers, vivid plants, and perfectly placed trees had been painted onto a canvas of green grass. Throughout campus, the gothic architecture was clean and orderly. Among the most breathtaking was the Duke Chapel, which stood right in the middle of the campus between the library and the student union. From old house C, I could get a clear view of Duke Chapel's twin spires—they just seemed to reach all the way to heaven.

Unfortunately, I was certain that my parents would never get to see the beauty of the Duke campus, as we had never traveled as a family and financial considerations would certainly prevent any trip across the Smoky Mountains from Chattanooga to Durham. Still, I knew in my heart that they were proud that their number-three son had achieved this level of success, regardless of their own personal situation.

My years at Duke would not be smooth and easy, however. Rather, they would test me in ways I could not have anticipated. I would face the physical challenges of playing college football, the academic challenges of attending a top university, and the personal realities of my family situation. However, this was a turning point for me—a time in which I took control of my future and charted the course for my life.

College Football—A Whole New Level

Clearly, attending Duke would have been impossible without the athletic scholarship I received. My family would not have been able to afford the tuition, let alone the other incidental costs of an education at a school like Duke. Had it not been for his love of football, it's unlikely that my father would have encouraged me to attend college at all. But I had been selected as one of only nineteen boys from all fourteen high schools in the Chattanooga area to be awarded a college scholarship to play football. Three of us were from Notre Dame High School. One of us chose to attend West Point, and two of us decided on Duke, which meant I would be playing college football with one of my high school teammates. The others were going to Georgia Tech, Vanderbilt, Georgia, Mississippi, Memphis State, and the University of Chattanooga. Many of these players, like me, had been All-City or All-State during their high school playing days.

Two primary conditions had been set by the Duke University Athletic Association (DUAA), however, that would need to be honored to maintain the scholarship in good standing. They were:

1. Conduct myself as a gentleman in keeping with the standards of Duke University
2. Acquit myself scholastically to a degree that I could be eligible for intercollegiate athletic participation each of the four years that the scholarship would run on the basis of work done during the regular academic year

As long as I met these requirements, my tuition, fees, room rent, board, books, and supplies were all paid for, and I also received fifteen dollars a month for laundry and incidental purposes allowed under the Athletic Award Program of the Atlantic Coast Conference, of which Duke is a member.

Football at Duke, like at all universities, was a full-time job. The two-week preseason consisted of two exhausting daily workouts, each two to three hours long, in the hot, humid August sun of North Carolina. During the football season, we had practice each day except Saturday and Sunday. Saturday was usually a game day, and Sunday was a healing day. During the off-season, the Duke athletic department required its scholarship athletes to lift weights, wrestle or box, and stay in good shape for the coming year. I had a thirty-eight-inch reach, so boxing was my sport of choice during this period. The athletes always ate well, too, because staying in shape also meant maintaining body weight, which was critical to performance. With the overall regimentation of the athletic department, I never had enough time to get everything done that was necessary to lead a full life.

One of the great thrills for any Duke football player was game day at home. It was an experience that made all of the hard work worth it. You always knew when it was game day because the campus began to fill with fans who created a buzz of enthusiasm that settled over the stadium. The entire team, dressed in crisp, clean blue on white uniforms, would listen to our coach give his pre-game motivational talk. With adrenaline running through our bodies, we would wait for the blast of the school cannon and then dash through the tunnel leading from the locker room into Duke Stadium. Then, to the roar of forty thousand fans, we would spill onto the field through a cloud of heavy smoke. The daily practices were work, but this was show time. If you didn't feel an emotional high after all of that, then you certainly did not belong on the field.

The man who got us fired up before every game was Bill Murray, one of the greatest men ever to coach football. Coach Murray had the leading active major college coaching record based on the twenty-year average at that point in time. Coach Murray's name was often mentioned along with coaches like Rip Engle of Penn State, Bud Wilkerson of Oklahoma, Frank Howard of Clemson, and Jess Neely of Rice, among others. If there was one thing he taught everyone on the team, it was the importance of preparation.

Coach Murray was a teacher-coach. He never had to raise his voice to get a point across because he had the ability to motivate his team in a very professional manner. He was highly respected by his players and believed in winning with pride and character. I have often thought back to Coach Murray's ability to motivate his team and the role his pre-game ritual played in getting the team psyched up to play to win. In my role as the CEO of Nestlé USA, I have tried to create a similar feeling during our State of the Company meetings, although I've never actually started our business meetings with a cannon.

One of the real perks of being on the Duke football team was having the opportunity to meet and get to know many talented people and having the honor of being on the same team as several great football stars. One such player was Mike "Mad Dog" Curtis. Mike had entered Duke as a high school All-American from Rockville, Maryland and left as one of Duke's finest full-backs of all time. I was introduced to Mike my freshman year, when Mike was a senior. The freshman squad, where I was playing defensive end, was called up to scrimmage the varsity team,. The ball was snapped to quarterback Scotty Glacken, who handed off to Mike Curtis, who slanted off the left end of his offensive line. The only object between the six-two, two hundred twelve pounder and the goal line was me. All I can remember, as they carried me off the field half-conscious, was his knee hitting me in the helmet. This was my very painful initiation into college football. On a happier note, Mike went on to be an All-Pro linebacker for the Baltimore Colts.

Another star player on my freshman team was Bob "Boone" Matheson, a two hundred fifteen pound, six-three halfback from Boone, North Carolina. Bob's father had been a Duke athlete in the 1920s, making Bob's career at Duke even more special. After college, Bob became an All-Pro linebacker for the world champion Miami Dolphins during the Don Shula era. Bob's jersey was number 53 to signify the Miami 5–3 Defense that he made famous. (For those who are not football aficionados, this refers to a defense of five down linemen and three linebackers, which left three players to cover the secondary and safety positions.) I knew Bob better than I knew Mike because we were the same age, and I fondly remember visiting him in Miami when he was still playing for the Dolphins. Bob was one of the sweetest and finest gentlemen I have ever known. He always put others first, and his kindness and sense of humor were like a beacon to all around him. Sadly, Bob died from Leukemia before his thirtieth birthday.

I learned some valuable lessons from these Duke football heroes, which I would remember later as a manager and corporate leader. Both men were great athletes individually, but they were even better team players, often sacrificing themselves for the good of the team. One of the things I most liked about both of these athletes is that they left it all on the field. They gave 110 percent effort every moment they played. This was something I tried to emulate in business. I have always believed the saying "Failing to plan is planning to fail," something Coach Murray reinforced. I realize that in order to be successful, you have to play the game of business with 110 percent effort, just like football. Practice hard and play hard, and work hard to have a team win.

College Life off the Field

Perhaps all of the physical hard work helped take my mind off the reality of my personal plight, which became obvious on my nineteenth birthday—my first birthday at Duke. I remember making several trips to the post office in the student union that day, thinking that I might get a birthday card from home. I had helped my mother send care packages to my older brother when he was in college, so I had hopes of receiving something myself. But when no card and no care package arrived, the truth became clear. I knew my parents loved me, but with their other priorities, I was out of sight and out of mind. The bottom line was that three younger children were still at home, my mother was not well, and my dad traveled to make a living. While they had their life struggles, they knew I was getting a free education and doing something that I really loved.

I knew I was a great distance away from home, both literally and figuratively. Sure, I had always had a lot of independence growing up in a large family and hadn't had a lot of personal attention. But for the first time in my life, I realized that I was basically on my own. No one was going to check up on me. No one would make sure I was doing what I was supposed to do. No one would guide my future and help me make decisions. I realized that if it was going to be, it was up to me.

I did find a family-like camaraderie during my sophomore year, when I joined a fraternity. Unlike at most universities, Duke students were integrated into the general student population during their sophomore year, which made it an exciting time for us. Fraternities were integrated into the gothic quads, which were without differentiation except for the Greek letters affixed to their particular section of the quad. Because the athletic scholarships covered fraternity fees, even the poorest athlete could join a fraternity or sorority if he or she so chose. Most of the athletes who did join opted for what were known as "jock fraternities." The most noted was Kappa Alpha, which boasted a larger-than-average number of athletes as members. The next tier, with around 10 percent to 15 percent athlete membership, consisted of the Phi Delta Theta and Alpha Tau Omega fraternities. I joined Alpha Tau Omega, or the ATO's as we called ourselves. I had many great times with my fraternity brothers, and they would go on to help me later during a difficult period in my life.

By the end of my freshman year, it had become obvious to me that the number of hours required by DUAA coupled with a demanding academic major, engineering, were taking a toll on my grade point average. While a majority of my seventy teammates majored in liberal arts, I was one of only a handful who chose to study engineering. This should have been my first clue that I was perhaps biting off more than I could chew. I selected engineering primarily because I had been good in math and chemistry in high school. But the truth was that I had no guidance on these matters from home or high school and was left to decide my major on my own. I approached my academic counselor for advice about switching to general business, but he felt strongly that I should stick with engineering at least one more year. I did not have enough confidence academically to argue the point, as I knew my counselor had my best interest at heart. Because I was not a starter on the football team, the chances of getting extra tutoring were slim, so I just had to tough it out.

I learned about the importance of setting realistic goals the hard way. At the end of the first semester of my sophomore year I failed my physics final exam, causing my grade point average to slip below C for the first time. I had violated one of the conditions of my scholarship, which made me ineligible to play football. Coach Murray called me into his office with a plan for me to attend a small college in North Carolina to get my grades up to the necessary average for reinstatement. Coach Murray told me that he would be happy to hold my scholarship for me until my grades improved. Unfortunately, I had no money or means of support for extra classes. My parents certainly could not help me financially. I knew I would have to leave Duke. Coach Murray did his very best to be encouraging, but I left his office totally dejected.

Facing the Music

When I left Chattanooga to go to Duke, I left as something of a local hero because I had received some attention in the local press for my success in football during my high school years. I was well liked by classmates and teachers and was considered the local kid who had "made good" by getting a scholarship to Duke. In less than two years, I had gone from feeling like I was on top of the tallest mountain peak to knowing I was in the lowest point in the valley. The most difficult part was that I had to face my failure totally alone. My teammates and fraternity brothers were sympathetic to a degree, but they all had their own individual battles to fight, and I soon became persona-non-grata. I had not shared much about my life at Duke with my parents, and I felt that the less said to them, the better.

I left Duke with my pride and my ego wounded. My family had not made me feel like I had let them down—that was a feeling I generated all by myself. My parents were in no position to help me, nor did I have extended family that could help. Besides, even if that had been an option, I would have had too much pride to ask.

This was a defining moment in my life; it was time to face the music. I could either crawl into a hole and sink into depression, or I could summon up the courage and strength to figure out what to do next. I chose to start the game of life all over again.

A New Game Plan

After my experience at Duke, I accepted the fact that I had failed this test in my life; but I was not going back to Chattanooga to face the disappointment from others—that was too much for me at that point. I had no money, so I began to look for a job in Durham. As I left Duke to interview for possible jobs, I noticed for the first time the contrast between the beauty of the campus and the unsightliness of the city of Durham, an old tobacco town that was struggling for survival. The contrast may have been exaggerated to some degree by my outlook at the time, but the difference was still quite visible.

After a few days, I took a job as a salesman at a Chevrolet dealership in downtown Durham on a 100 percent commission deal. I worked from nine a.m. until nine p.m. on the used car lot and slept on a portable cot that I placed in the commons room of the ATO fraternity house. After a while, I wore out my welcome there and moved around until I made enough money to buy an old car to make the dreaded trip home to Chattanooga. My manager was nice enough to sell me a banged-up 1952 Chevrolet that had been taken in on a trade for $50.00, which was exactly what it was worth. It was in such bad shape that I had to carry a case of motor oil in the trunk to replace the quart that was burnt every hundred miles or so.

The drive across the Smoky Mountains from Durham to Chattanooga was slow, long, and lonely, but it gave me ample opportunity to resolve in my mind and soul the game plan I needed for my future. My plan was to work as hard as I could to save enough money to go back to school. I had grown up in a family where finances were always an issue, and I didn't want to live my life fighting one financial battle after another. I knew getting an education was still the best way out of the circumstances in which I grew up.

My dad and mom were pleased to see me when I arrived, but frankly, I was an inconvenience at that point. The only place for me to sleep was on an old bed in the garage. Although it was attached to the house, my new "bedroom" was without heating or air conditioning and therefore was hot in the summer and cold in the winter. I shared it with a number of critters that found their way inside through numerous cracks around the big aluminum garage door. It was unusual to wake up to a few friendly cockroaches scampering across the concrete floor or moving slowly across my bed covers. Believe it or not, these fine accommodations were not free. My dad insisted that I pay him a monthly rent in order to help him make the mortgage payment.

I secured a job in a matter of a few days making Coke bottles at the Chattanooga Glass Company. I went immediately back to what I knew best—hard work. It had not been enough to get me through Duke for a whole host of reasons, but I knew hard work would serve me well at the glass company as I entered phase one of my game plan, which was to make and save enough money to be able to afford to go back to college.

After several months, all the foremen knew me and wanted me to work on their shifts. Because everything over eight hours paid time and a half, I took every opportunity to "double-over." Doubling-over meant working sixteen consecutive hours, which was no easy task even for the hardiest soul. I had various jobs over the years at the glass factory, from stapling boxes together on a giant Bostich staple machine to packing bottles to changing glass molds on the "hot-end." The hot-end, which could easily reach 120–130 degrees Fahrenheit, was where the gas furnaces melted the special green Georgia sand into molten glass. The molten glass drops would form from a flow of molten glass rope from the melting vessel that would be systematically cut into small drops. This would then be sequenced into a number of molds formed in a circle directly below the large glass tanks. Air would be forced into the mold, blowing the classic Coke bottle. My job at times was to change the molds in between sequence because the flow of glass could not be stopped. I had less than thirty seconds to change the mold or else I could have molten glass drop on me. This was a dangerous job that required focus and steady nerves.

In the summer, the hot-end required workers to take salt tablets before starting the shift to replace salt lost through perspiration. Doubling-over on the hot-end was never a good idea. The best scenario was to work the hot-end on the graveyard shift that started at eleven p.m. (the coolest shift) and double-over into the first shift that started at seven a.m. I made my own lunch each day, which always consisted of a fried bologna and mustard sandwich, which would not spoil in the heat and humidity of the factory, regardless of shift or mealtime.

Other than the money I paid to my dad for rent or spent on gas and food, every dollar I earned went into my college fund. I was building up a reserve that would enable me to attend three quarters at the University of Tennessee (UT), assuming I would be accepted. This was phase two of my strategy—getting accepted at UT.

After I saved enough money, I applied to the College of Business Administration there. I was hoping that the admissions office would understand my unusual circumstances at Duke and overlook my problems there. Much to my disappointment, however, my application was rejected. I still have a copy of the rejection letter from the dean of admissions explaining that my grades from Duke did not meet Tennessee's requirements. Every so often I take it out and reread it just to keep my ego in check and occasionally revisit the humility I felt that day.

I have always had a difficult time taking "no" for an answer. So in May of 1965, I got behind the wheel of my oil-burning 1952 Chevrolet and headed for Knoxville, Tennessee, determined to plead my case in person to Dr. Truman Pouncy, dean of admissions. I was completely at his mercy. He must have been impressed with my persistence, however, because he allowed me to meet with the admissions committee. My meeting was successful, and I was admitted into the College of Business Administration for the winter quarter of 1966, subject to academic probation. I was so grateful to Dean Pouncy and the committee for accepting me, that I was determined to prove to them that they had made the right decision. I proceeded to make the Dean's List each of my first three quarters at UT and all but two quarters until I graduated.

Finances were still a consideration for me, however. I was fortunate to become a residence hall counselor at Hess Hall in order to help defray my school expenses. I learned several skills at Hess Hall, including the art of listening. Many of the students who came to me for advice just needed someone to listen to their problems; they usually arrived at their own solutions after the chance to talk them through with someone who just listened. Hess Hall also taught me a lot about how to conduct successful negotiations. As you can imagine, students were constantly testing the system to see how much they could get away with without getting into serious trouble. It was important for me to be flexible and bend the rules without breaking them so that I could keep order in the dorm but also keep the respect of my dormmates. This job was a great exercise in developing interpersonal skills, which would come in handy throughout my career.

Overcoming Personal Adversity with Work

One of the darkest days of my life came while I was traveling in central Florida for a job I had taken selling and delivering Webster's Dictionaries for Southwestern Publishing Company, during the summer of my junior year at UT. On June 30, 1966 I received a phone call that my mother had died unexpectedly in her sleep. She was only fifty-two years old, too young to die, and I was twenty-one, too young to lose a mother. As difficult as it was for me, however, it was even harder on my two teenage siblings who still lived at home. The saddest part for me was that I did not have a chance to say good-bye. I bought a ticket on a Greyhound Bus to start the lonely trip home for the funeral. It was a reflective time for me. My oldest brother Bill, in later years, penned a poem that described our mother better than any words that I could ever write. It is seldom that I read this poem and am not brought to tears.

Reflections

A fragile body slightly bent,
With slender hands oft rough and rent.
A gentle face that life had aged,
Yet hazel eyes with tender gaze
Revealed a heart that brimmed with love.

This was the Mother of my life,
Whose body brought me forth in strife;
Whose hands did hold me as a babe;
Whose eyes, when she was hurt, forgave;
Whose heart of love did give me up
To manhood and its awesome cup.

And now O Mother of my life,
Who longed to listen to my dreams;
Who tried to help me find the means;
Who urged and pushed me on the way,
To you, I owe the most today.

The world you left is richer too,
Because you passed so quietly through.
And though I miss your precious touch,
And love and care that meant so much,
I know some day we shall unite
In mystic forms and brilliant light.

February 1985
William Weller

My mother had always been a hard worker; with so many children, she had to be. But she also knew how to delegate responsibilities to the kids. By the age of nine, I was making decisions for myself and solving little problems that others may have gone to their parents with. I was also working by then, learning basic life skills like being on time and showing up when I was expected. From the time I was little, I always found myself being thrust into leadership positions. My peers always looked to me to lead various projects, perhaps because I had been independent from an early age. Now I can look back on how my mother raised me (with an unusual level of independence but also with love) and say that it affected my affinity for leadership and my management style.

The loss of my mother was very difficult, but I was able to cope with her passing by losing myself in my work. It wasn't long before I returned to Florida to finish the job I had begun earlier that summer—selling door-to-door for Southwestern Publishing.

Before heading out to our sales territories across the United States, we had met in Nashville for training. The key message was clear—although door-to-door selling was hard work—you were likely to close one out of ten sales calls, if you followed the sales methods that Southwestern was teaching us. I learned these techniques very well and could virtually demo a book by reading it upside down without missing any words. It took me about thirty calls on my maiden sales voyage before I made a single sale. But when I made my first sell, I was thrilled. After that, I averaged a little better than one sale in ten demos. I was focused. I would literally make sales calls from dawn to dusk, seven days a week. With every sale of a set of two Webster's books for $19.95, I got to keep $9.95, which was a pretty healthy profit. All summer long we reps would take orders and collect down payments. The last two weeks of summer we would deliver the books and collect the final payment. It was not unusual for a rep to make three to five thousand dollars during the summer, which was a lot of money for a college student in those days.

The job was rich with "once in a lifetime" experiences that required quick thinking and thick skin. It also required a lot of energy, which is why I always carried a jar of honey and a spoon to energize myself between sales calls. Many people slammed the door in my face, and some even cursed at me. I learned that I had to approach the very next call in less than sixty seconds with a positive mental attitude, which became a very useful technique when I went to work for Nestlé, calling on grocery store managers or grocery buyers. In essence, Southwestern Publishing taught me the importance of training, hard work, and discipline, and the value of maintaining a positive mental attitude at all times. I also learned not to take insults personally; doing so is just a waste of energy and an unnecessary focus on negative experiences. Interestingly, I have met many business and political leaders over the years who developed solid interpersonal skills selling door-to-door for Southwestern Publishing.

Starting a New Life

My senior year at UT was an interesting time for me. During the job-recruiting season, I had the opportunity to interview with a number of companies in the region, but also some from out of state. I approached the job search process much like a job itself. I did my own research about each company with which I was going to interview prior to the first meeting. I then continued to analyze each company during the recruiting process. I was thorough because I did not want to be in a position of second-guessing my decision after I accepted the job. Of course my expectations were not unrealistic. I knew from past work experiences that even the perfect job would likely bring with it a period of difficulty and uncertainty, but I wanted to give myself the best chance of success. I felt that the new job I would choose would require a high level of commitment, and commitment was not new to me. I was ready for the challenge of finding the right position to start my career.

I interviewed with many companies. The most memorable recruiting trip, however, was my first off-campus interview with Carnation Company in New York City. It was my first time visiting New York, and I was in awe of the size of the buildings and the number of people on the streets of Manhattan. I flew into New York the day before my interview, which was thrilling in and of itself. I must have walked ten miles, starting at the Park Lane Hotel, and going up and down 5th Avenue, Park Avenue, Lexington Avenue, and Madison Avenue, and along Central Park. But when I got to Times Square, I stopped in amazement. It was even more impressive and unusual than I had imagined it would be. I am sure that any New Yorkers who saw me taking all this in knew by the look on my face that it was my first New York experience. My trip to New York was also one of the first times I had been on an airplane, other than my initial recruiting trip to Duke in 1963 and a short flight from Chattanooga to Knoxville as a young teenager, which had been as a paid traveling companion for a former employer's daughter who was afraid to fly.

I was impressed with Carnation for many reasons, but what made the biggest impression on me was Bob Stevens, the recruiter. He made me feel special. He took a lot of time with me and made me feel like I would fit in there. After our initial meeting, we met again, and he introduced me to a number of Carnation executives. He called me to follow up, letting me know that the company really wanted me to come on board. With seven firm job offers under my arm, I chose to start my career with Carnation Company. It was not the job offer with the biggest starting salary, but it was the one that I felt would give me the greatest sense of synergy and belonging. I didn't feel like I would be just another new recruit; I felt like I would be joining a group of people with whom I could identify—a group where I could make a difference.

I graduated from the University of Tennessee on a beautiful Saturday in September of 1968. Finally, I had done it! Lyndon

Johnson was president of my country, and H. E. Olson was CEO of my new employer, Carnation Company. On the Monday following graduation I moved to Memphis, Tennessee and began to work for Carnation Company. I can honestly say that I have never looked back, and I have never seriously considered working for another company, other than Nestlé who acquired Carnation in 1985.

I learned a lot of important lessons during this time in my life. I learned about overcoming adversity. I learned about humility. I learned that there is little value in looking back. I learned about the value of hard work, especially when it is coupled with a game plan. But most important, I learned that each of us is in control of our own destiny. It is our responsibility to figure out how to make things happen in our lives. The decision to do whatever it takes to take control of your own situation isn't always easy, but in the end, it is worth it.

CHAPTER 3

Pluck Wins!

When I joined Carnation upon graduation, I knew I was joining an outstanding company with well-performing brands—such as Coffee-Mate, Friskies, and Carnation Milk—and a strong reputation in the marketplace. With 1968 sales of $930 million and leading market shares in evaporated milk, instant milk, Coffee-Mate, and instant breakfast, I was confident that I could learn a great deal at Carnation about marketing, sales, and operations from the managers with whom I would be working. What I didn't realize, at the time, was how much I would learn about the importance of corporate culture, diversity, and values. These would be lessons I would take with me and utilize throughout my entire career.

Carnation's Cultural Foundation

In recent years, corporations have begun to place more importance on corporate values, the topic of the best-selling book *Built to Last* (Collins and Porras, 1994). Many have even taken the steps to summarize their values, teach them to their employees, and present them in their annual reports. E. A. Stuart, Carnation's founder, was ahead of his time in this respect. From the company's very beginning in 1899, he created a culture within Carnation that valued family and hard work. Stuart recruited and developed people who reflected these values, and he continued to instill them throughout his organization during his forty-year tenure.

One of E. A. Stuart's favorite verses was called *Pluck Wins!* It embodied his beliefs about how his employees should conduct themselves throughout their careers with Carnation so clearly that he kept a framed version of it prominently displayed on the wall in his private office. If you look up *pluck* in the dictionary, you'll find many synonyms listed, from *nerve, guts,* and *courage* to *resolve, fortitude,* and *backbone.* Stuart described it as "perseverance, hard work, dedication, taking personal responsibility, loyalty, tenacity, and never quitting until the prize was achieved." I like to think of it as a hardworking and tenacious "can do" spirit that never gives up. Regardless of exact wording, *Pluck Wins!* resonated with me throughout my career and became a guiding force in my achievements over the years.

Carnation continued to evolve as E. A. Stuart's son Elbridge Hadley took over the reins in 1932 and ushered the company through the difficult Depression years. By running a very tight ship and watching costs meticulously, he led the company through what proved to be some of the most challenging economic times. Pluck won again! E. H. would go on to serve as chairman until his retirement in 1971.

In 1963, H. E. Olson took over as only the fourth president of the company. Olson had been intimately involved in most of the key decisions years before he became president. Although Carnation was a company with no formal organizational chart or vision statement, it was clear that Olson was running the show, a role that he would retain until the 1985 acquisition of Carnation by Nestlé S.A. On the commercial side of the business, executive vice president Henry Arnest—a protégé of E. H. Stuart and a tough, barrel-chested, man's man—had strong control over marketing, sales, and distribution. By Henry's retirement in the late 1970s, Carnation was known as one of the very best sales and distribution companies in the entire retail and food services industry.

My career at Carnation began in 1968—H. E. Olson was president, Henry Arnest was executive vice president, Timm

Pluck Wins!

Pluck wins! It always wins! though
    days be slow,
And nights be dark 'twixt days that
    come and go.
Still pluck will win; its average is
    sure,
He gains the prize who will the most
    endure;
Who faces issues; he who never
    shirks;
Who waits and watches, and who
    always works.

Sincerely

E A Stuart
1941

*A favorite verse of Mr. E. A. Stuart, President
of the Carnation Company. A framed copy
has for many years hung in his private office.*

Crull was vice president of sales, Bob Adams was my district manager, and I was an entry-level salesman, calling on individual supermarkets and grocery stores and small grocery wholesalers in the Memphis area. I also checked on distribution, inventory levels, and pricing, which gave me a great foundational background in the grocery business.

Fresh out of college, I was ready to tackle any assignment that would be thrown my way. My first big sale was a hundred cases of Carnation Evaporated Milk to Big Star Supermarket in Kosciusko, Mississippi for a promotion that sold ten cans for a dollar. But closing the sale wasn't easy. Most grocery store managers did not have a college education and were less-than inviting to young college types like myself. In fact, they used to call me "Joe College." I figured that in order to win their business, I had to earn their trust. And the only way to do that was with hard work. So when the store manager to whom I was trying to sell the evaporated milk was deciding whether to give me the sale, I saw a chance to win him over. He didn't expect me to say that if he bought the product, I'd be there at five-thirty in the morning to help unload the truck. That definitely broke the ice, and I got the sale.

It was a short time later that I met Pete Haynes, a steely blue-eyed thirty-nine-year-old Carnation district manager, who had come to Memphis to evaluate my readiness to be promoted to a first line supervisor as part of a new team he was putting together in Houston, Texas. Pete had recently been promoted from Pittsburgh to Houston, which in the late 1960s was the fastest growing major city in the United States. However, Houston was an area of the country where Carnation had performed poorly for a number of years.

Pete's assignment was to turn things around in the Houston area and to put Carnation on the map. Although I had been on the job in Memphis for only nine months, Pete Haynes saw something in me that he felt he could build on. (I suspect that being a fellow Tennessean did not hurt my candidacy.) I became one of three new managers that Pete would hire to become the nucleus of his Houston team. And at twenty-four years old, I was the youngest of five team managers to report directly to Pete. My own team consisted of seven salespeople who were located in Houston and Austin. We were all part of the Powerful Houston District (PHD) team and Pete was our head coach.

On-the-Job Training

In most of our business careers someone along the way stands out as a major contributor to our thinking and style. For me, Pete Haynes is that man. Although his middle name was Luther, it should have been Desire based on his tenacity and hunger for success.

As a young employee, I connected easily with Pete Haynes, perhaps in part because of our similar backgrounds. Pete's family ran a small grocery store in Nashville, Tennessee, and he grew up very quickly, moving from working in his parent's mom-and-pop grocery store to being a bellhop in the Sam Davis Hotel in downtown Nashville at age fourteen. Pete had also been an athlete his entire life. He was an All-City and honorable mention All-State football player at Nashville's Central High School, and a one hundred fifty pound quarterback for Middle Tennessee State University (in Murfreesboro) in his college days. He also was a first class water skier, tennis player, and a scratch golfer. In short, Pete Haynes was very competitive in every aspect of his personal and business life. It is that determination that kept him in top physical condition so that he could still fit neatly into his Korean War Army uniform in 1970.

Under Pete's leadership, Carnation Company became a powerful food company and a "force to be dealt with" in Houston, Beaumont, San Antonio, Corpus Christi, and the surrounding areas. By the mid-1970s, the PHD for Carnation was the only district out of thirty that ever shipped one million cases of Carnation products in a single month. The PHD would go on to compile one of the most successful year-after-year performance records in the history of Carnation Company, achieving thirteen consecutive years of top-ten performance in terms of cases sold versus previous year.

The year and a half I spent under Pete's leadership was the greatest concentration of learning experiences of my life. Under his wing, I learned valuable lessons about leadership, empowerment, goal setting and achievement, motivation, and balance.

How Management Differs from Leadership   Working with Pete was my first real exposure to leadership. Whereas my boss in Memphis was a real gentleman, he focused on managing those around him. Pete, conversely, focused primarily on empowering his team to be successful. He was a coach and a leader who provided guidance. He was not a controlling micromanager who insisted on showing his team "his way" to accomplish a task. Though impatient for performance, he was a very patient trainer for people who wanted to learn or improve themselves in any way.

I learned that as a leader, it is important to let others see the boss in action. When Pete worked with salespeople, he took his jacket off, rolled up his sleeves, and showed them how to get things done. He also set the tone for work ethic by working harder than those half his age and half his rank.

Only Promise What You Can Deliver   Pete would ask his five managers for monthly, quarterly, and yearly sales figures by account, holding each one of us responsible for achieving those sales. We always faced consequences when the numbers were not met. It was during this time that I learned one of the most important business lessons of my career: *Never, ever, promise something that you knowingly cannot or will not deliver.* Pete taught us that the time for negotiation was when the target was being established—not after it had become part of the budget plan. I learned that our reputation was built on our dependability, both individually as salespersons and collectively as a company. Promising more than what we could deliver was the quickest way to disappoint, alienate, and eventually lose a customer.

Praise in Public; Criticize in Private   True to the military training he received in the U.S. Army, General Haynes (as some called him) always praised his "troops" in public and criticized them in private. The fact is that people love to be recognized for their achievements in front of their peers, and Pete used every such opportunity to milk every ounce of motivation from his troops. For example, he recognized his people's personal accomplishments, from achieving aggressive sales goals to gaining prominent shelf space, with the entire Houston district contingency in attendance. After a meeting like that, we felt energized and motivated; it reminded me of how I used to feel during a home football game at Duke.

Pete was a master at using recognition and public praise to rally the troops against the competition. We saw our competition as the enemy, and there was absolutely no fraternizing with the enemy. In those days, competition for shelf placements or display space in supermarkets was so intense that fistfights would occasionally break out between reps from the different warring factions. Bonuses were always appreciated, but more importantly they symbolized recognition for winning a battle against the competitor—a focus that was instilled and reinforced by our magnificent leader.

Compassion Isn't Weakness   Pete was an excellent listener, communicator, and developer of people. Pete performed every task with passion and could be a very compassionate leader, but I learned never to mistake that compassion for weakness. Pete had a big heart, which he wasn't afraid to show, but that didn't cloud his judgment when it came down to doing the right thing for the organization. In fact, when I left Houston for my next assignment, he had tears in his eyes. As much as he cared for me, I know he would have fired me in a second had it been the right thing to do for the company. That's the kind of leader he was—he could be teary-eyed one moment and steely-eyed the next. Later, as a leader in my own right, I allowed myself to show emotion and compassion at times, and I found that it did not compromise my authority and effectiveness as a leader. Perhaps it even enhanced it.

The Importance of Balance in Life   One of the things that made Pete such a great leader was that he didn't just teach us business skills, he also taught us life skills that helped us grow as individuals. Pete believed in working hard, but he also believed in playing hard. We learned to play golf, tennis, poker, and liar's poker. We learned to fire a shotgun with the accuracy necessary to down our limit of white-wing doves in the Rio Grande Valley each year.

Regardless of skill level, everyone was expected to participate in the activity at hand. For example, whenever we had a company golf tournament, we were all expected to play a role. Just because I didn't play golf or drink beer at the time, I wasn't off the hook. Although I didn't play in the tournament, I drove the beer cart and provided my fellow teammates with much needed "sustenance" and "motivation." Being part of the experience made us a closer team and gave us a chance to enjoy time with each other.

All in all, Pete introduced us to the idea of having balance between work and play, a concept I try to instill in my employees today. I truly believe that balance in your personal life allows you to be more effective on the job, whether you are an hourly employee, a manager, or a leader.

The Importance of Giving to the Community   In words and in action, Pete taught us about the responsibility we all have to give to our communities and help others. In 1972, Pete Haynes founded the Houston Grocery Manufacturer Rep Association (HGMRA), where he served three terms as president and is now a permanent board member. In the first year, Pete and the HGMRA gave three, seven hundred dollar college scholarships to deserving students in the retail grocery industry. In 2003, the HGMRA distributed twenty-five scholarships of three thousand dollars each to help outstanding students attend Texas universities. Even though he has been retired for a number of years, Pete's commitment to HGMRA has not diminished. His goal is to help the association distribute fifty college scholarships to Houston-area high school students each year. Pete's commitment to his community also continues to thrive. At seventy-five years young, he is the treasurer of the Walker County Proud Community Association, which has planted seventeen thousand trees to date and is responsible for keeping the community's highways clean.

Pete Haynes' success as a leader could be measured several ways. In traditional circles, some might look at sales growth, market penetration, and profitability. And under those traditional measures, Pete's success was immense. But in those days, we would often measure successful Carnation leaders by the size of their alumni association—the number of managers who had been trained and developed by someone and then promoted to other areas of the company. In this regard, Pete Haynes' success was legendary. He went on to have one of the largest alumni associations at Carnation, a group which I am proud to say includes me.

Meeting My Partner for Life

Houston will always hold a special place in my heart. As significant as my business experience was, my personal life took an even more important turn during this time. It was in this city that I met a beautiful and intelligent schoolteacher by the name of Carol Hail, my wife-to-be. Both Carol and I were looking for places to live in the Houston area, which led us to a chance meeting at the sales office of the Andrew Jackson Apartments complex. We spoke that day, but it wouldn't be until six months later that we would actually go on a date.

Carol and I had dated for all of three months when I was promoted to area manager for Carnation in Miami, Florida. When I told Carol about my new assignment and the imminent move to Florida, she asked, "What about me?" Of course I had thought from the first time I met her that she was vivacious and very cute, but more important, I recognized that her extraordinary personality and good sense of humor would make her a great partner. So on Saturday, September 26, 1970, we were married in Carol's hometown of Crockett, Texas, a small East Texas town named in honor of Davy Crockett, who slept there on the way to the Alamo. It was the luckiest day of my life. I went to work in Miami the following Monday, and Carol has been my closest friend and biggest supporter for thirty-five years.

To complete the picture, you need to know that Pete Haynes was my best man and that all of my four groomsmen were Carnation managers and part of our team. No members of my immediate family were able to travel from Tennessee to Texas for the wedding, so the Carnation family was a great source of support for me that day. The PHD had become a high-performance team in Houston that impacted every aspect of our lives, integrating the personal with the business.

After our wedding, Carol and I set up our first household in Miami. From the beginning, we tackled challenges together, turning to one another for advice and help when we needed it. Carol was not only beautiful, but she had many qualities and talents that would later make important contributions to our married and career life together. Carol was a gifted seamstress who could design and make beautiful clothes for the family, and even drapes for the numerous homes we were to occupy over the years. Carol was a good artist, a teacher, a writer and poet, a good interior decorator, a very capable fundraiser, a superb community volunteer, and a wonderful homemaker. But most importantly, she was a terrific mom, wife, and now a grandmother. All of these things brought much of the balance (which Pete taught me about) to our lives and helped me become a more effective leader throughout my career.

One of my fondest memories of our time in Miami was when Carol and I worked together to get ready for the Miami Cat Show, where I was responsible for preparing a large sales booth at the convention center and selling Carnation Pet Food products. With her excellent artistic skills, Carol was able to draw and paint giant replicas of Friskies labels for my booth; she also worked the show for me. Her Friskies cat posters were a big hit on the floor. I knew then and there that I had a talented business supporter and the right partner for life.

When you are moving your way through the corporate ranks and attaining different leadership milestones, you realize that the process is not something that is easy to go through alone.

A good partner is vital. Carol was masterful at being a corporate leader's wife and for the past fifteen years, both in Australia and the United States, a top-notch CEO's wife. She and I define the person in this role as someone who must make numerous personal sacrifices, remain flexible, be a cheerleader, manage the home front (often as a single parent), be a good listener and advisor, be involved in the community, and much more.

From Miami my next career stop with Carnation was Dallas, Texas as district manager. By 1973, I was in Los Angeles as one of Carnation's seven regional sales managers. By 1978, when I was thirty-three years old, Carnation appointed me vice president of sales for all of Carnation, which by then was almost a $2.5 billion company. In 1981, I was elected a director of Carnation Company. At the age of thirty-six I was one of the youngest directors in the history of the company.

Leadership from the Eighth Floor

H. E. Olson was still CEO of Carnation Company when I was made vice president of sales and subsequently appointed as a director of the company. I learned many valuable lessons about leadership from him during the twelve years that I worked in the Wilshire Boulevard headquarters—some habits I adopted and some I didn't. That is a lesson itself. You can learn from someone even when you don't agree with him.

H. E. Olson was an autocratic leader, which was the norm for managers in the United States at the time. Olson would seldom be seen off the executive floor except when he was on his way into or out of the building. He seldom traveled to Carnation's facilities across the country, preferring to wield his power from his Wilshire Boulevard, Los Angeles office. Every decision of any consequence was made in Olson's eighth floor corner office.

Mr. Olson's office was located in the northwest corner of the building, where he sat behind a massive desk in front of six chairs that appeared to have shortened legs. Olson's desk chair was, of course, raised to its fully-extended height. I would take my seat for a meeting, and I—with my six foot, five inch frame—would actually be looking up at Mr. Olson, who was approximately five feet, eight inches tall. His physical posturing epitomized well the psychology of his leadership style. For example, at one meeting with a middle level marketing manager and the executive team, Olson dismissed the marketing manager, tore up his presentation, and told the manager's boss that he "never wanted to see that man again," and to "have him out of the building by the end of the week." I was by no means immune to this type of directive. Mr. Olson once chided me for taking a strong position against a planned price increase on pet food that I did not think was justified. I will never forget his response to my presentation at a management meeting. "Mr. Weller," he said, "take the price up this afternoon, and never be embarrassed to make a profit."

After the meeting ended, I decided to talk to Mr. Olson in private because I didn't agree with his position. Our meeting was positive; it wasn't confrontational on either front. But the result didn't change—I increased the price as requested. However, I learned something from the experience. Mr. Olson was open to discussing issues, but in private. Questioning him or disagreeing with him in committee meetings created an aura of confrontation and inevitably made things worse.

H. E. Olson was a tough and at times a brutal CEO. It shouldn't surprise anyone to learn that the most often heard phrase at meetings with Olson was, "Yes, Mr. Olson." The only top executive I witnessed challenge Olson face-to-face was Henry Arnest. Because of his tenacity and clout throughout the organization, Henry Arnest became somewhat of a Carnation folk hero to many of us. He was tough as nails, but unlike Olson, very approachable. Eventually, Mr. Olson would be the last "Mr." at Carnation Company, outwardly signifying a change in the company's style of movement.

During his tenure at Carnation, Olson created an atmosphere where his intellect was pitted against the rest of the company's. This had the surprising effect of creating a certain cooperation and esprit de corps among the groups below him. I was never sure if this was by design on Mr. Olson's part or just coincidence, but there was real value in the united spirit and co-operation of the employees. He managed by intimidation and fear. It worked for him.

In those days, board meetings at Carnation were somewhat a perfunctory exercise. Eleven of fifteen board members were inside directors, guaranteeing Olson's control. All documents that we needed for the board meeting were bound in a red book with each director's name on it and placed at the assigned seat of that director. At the end of the meeting, all documents were to be left in the boardroom as the directors exited. I'll always remember the red book and what it represented during that period in the history of the company. In fact, Olson's assistant, Pat Costello, was kind enough to give me the red board book with my name embossed in gold as a souvenir following our last board meeting. I still have that book today as a reminder of those very interesting times.

Today, however, the corporate environment has changed dramatically, as have the roles and responsibilities of board members. With the passage of Sarbanes Oxley, the pendulum has swung all the way to the other side, leaving today's directors with an overwhelming sense of liability for every result of their decisions, perhaps to the point of overkill. Gone are the days when executives actively sought to serve on numerous boards. The increase in both perceived and actual personal liability has instead caused many executives to turn down board seats, when in fact they could really be of help to a variety of companies. But our old Carnation board meetings took place in another time. We would always break for lunch and dine at Perino's Restaurant on Wilshire Boulevard, which stands vacant today, a reminder of that very different corporate world.

Because of his toughness and intimidating demeanor, when Olson praised someone, which was never routine, it had real meaning. Unlike Pete Haynes' method of public praise, Olson's favorite method of praise was a one- or two-line note about a particular accomplishment, written on a half-page of paper, and always signed with the initials H.E.O. These notes were treasured by their happy recipients—a fact to which I can attest by pointing to the small collection of these notes I still have from my days as a young Carnation executive. For a number of years I used a similar method to recognize individual accomplishments of people who worked for me. Voice mail and e-mails, however, have changed all that and have given us an opportunity to reward individual accomplishment in "real time."

In spite of the autocratic management style of H. E. Olson, or maybe because of it, the company prospered and grew due to the plethora of solid managers, leaders, and teams positioned throughout the company. No one could ever question his dedication to Carnation—it was his life's passion. H. E. Olson retired on December 31, 1985 at the age of seventy-eight, and he died a few months later. Under his leadership, the values established by E. A. Stuart and E. H. Stuart were preserved and they still define Carnation and Nestlé people today. "Pluck" was still alive and well long past E. A. Stuart's days.

Nestlé S.A. Buys Carnation

On the Saturday of Labor Day weekend in 1984 the directors of Carnation Company assembled in the Wilshire Boulevard world headquarters to learn for the first time that the company had been "put in play," as they say. Nestlé S.A. was the prime suitor. Emotions ran rampant after the announcement. Surprise. Disbelief. Denial. Anger. Concern. Anxiety. As the youngest member of the board and with hopes of a long future with the company, I experienced them all. Needless to say, I was not happy.

A group of directors, including H. E. Olson, explored a leveraged buyout (LBO) as an option to an acquisition. With interest rates at 18 percent and forecast by some in our group to go to 21 percent, it was clear that we could not service the debt required to buy our company ourselves, while at the same time making the necessary investments to run the business properly and effectively. It was also clear to most of us in the group that we could not out-bid a company like Nestlé S.A.

By 1983, Carnation Company had achieved increased net income for thirty-one consecutive years, reaching $3.4 billion in revenue, compared with Nestlé's $14 billion in revenue worldwide for that same period. In January of 1985, Nestlé received approval from the Federal Trade Commission (FTC) to acquire Carnation for $3 billion cash or eighty-three dollars per share. In essence, Nestlé bought a company with relatively low debt and around $250 million in cash, and overnight doubled its size in the United States. When the deal was done, it was the largest non-oil acquisition in history at the time.

From the acquisition, Nestlé also received many assets that didn't formally appear on the balance sheet, most notably a significant position in the U.S. market. It also acquired one of the best sales organizations in the industry, armed with leading brands such as Carnation Evaporated Milk, Carnation Coffee-mate, and Fancy Feast Cat Food. Although Nestlé didn't recognize at the time the gem it had inherited with the pet food business, it did recognize Carnation's outstanding management and leadership team, which would go on to lead Nestlé in the U.S. market. Between the sales and marketing skills, the brand leadership, the talented management group, and the fact that Carnation had been much more profitable than Nestlé Enterprises, Inc. had been, Nestlé S.A. made a wise strategic acquisition.

From my personal standpoint, the times were a bit uncertain, because none of us in Carnation management were very sure of our futures with our new parent company. We were all too familiar with the typical scenario of massive management changes following a majority of acquisitions. Most often, the acquiring company moved quickly to take control by putting its own key executives in charge. To our surprise, we soon learned that Nestlé had a much more enlightened approach to acquisitions.

During their first visit to Carnation in early 1985, Helmut Maucher, chairman of Nestlé S.A., and Carl Angst, head of technical for Nestlé S.A., held a large meeting in the seventh-floor auditorium on Wilshire Boulevard, where shareholder meetings normally took place. All managers of the company were invited. The entire group of inside board members and top executives was seated in the very first row, where you could cut the tension with a knife. Even as people filed into the auditorium, prepared to hear preliminary announcements regarding their future careers and the future direction of Carnation, you could hear a pin drop. As Carl Angst began to speak, in very good English but with a distinct Swiss-German accent, the tension increased. We had to listen very carefully, as we were not used to being addressed by people with foreign accents. As Angst made a sweeping motion with his right arm to make a point, he accidentally knocked a full glass of water all over Helmut Maucher. He did not even break stride as he commented, "Well it's a good thing that you don't serve wine here at Carnation." With that, he continued his remarks unshaken, and everyone in the room immediately relaxed.

Shortly thereafter, Dr. Angst introduced Helmut Maucher, whose German accent was even more pronounced than his colleague's. Maucher started by welcoming all of us into the Nestlé family, and he set everyone at ease by telling us that Carnation people would continue to run Carnation. He also indicated that Nestlé was willing to invest whatever capital was necessary to improve and update Carnation's manufacturing facilities, a move that was long overdue. But our new leader really broke the ice when he told the group that he bought Carnation because he thought we shared many of the same values as Nestlé S.A. He further commented that he felt Carnation was more like Nestlé S.A. than its own U.S. operations at the time. With that, he immediately won over the entire Carnation management team.

Fast forward to January 16, 2001, to a meeting near Purina's headquarters in St. Louis, Missouri, where Peter Brabeck was formally announcing to Purina employees the acquisition of their company by Nestlé. As I sat in the rear of the audience listening to Peter's comments, I could not help but flash back to the meeting at Carnation in 1985. Peter welcomed the Purina employees to the Nestlé family and announced that former Purina CEO Pat McGinnis had agreed to be the CEO of the new and larger Nestlé Purina PetCare Company. Not only would the company stay in St. Louis, he also announced that we would move our Friskies PetCare business from Los Angeles to St. Louis. With these words I could sense the audience relaxing, and I knew that Peter had won over the Purina team with the sincerity of his message. It was déjà vu. I was fascinated by how consistent the message was from two different Nestlé CEOs, discussing two different deals, but separated by sixteen years.

A similar message would again be delivered in May 2005 at the Cronk Conference Center in Oakland, California to the Dreyer's Ice Cream company's top leaders. Peter Brabeck welcomed the Dreyer's folks to the Nestlé family, talked about the importance of the Dreyer's culture, and affirmed that Dreyer's top management would stay in place.

On March 1, 1985 Nestlé released a formal announcement of management changes at Carnation, listing the top twenty management positions beginning with the CEO. A Carnation employee filled each spot. Not only did Carnation executives get their opportunity to manage the newly acquired Carnation business, but also many of them would get valued international experience that would have been unlikely prior to the acquisition. Additionally, Carnation would report directly to Helmut Maucher, just as Nestlé's other operations in the United States did. Maucher had indeed delivered exactly what he had promised during that first meeting at Carnation headquarters, thereby establishing a foundation of trust among company leaders on both sides of the Atlantic.

In the next five years, Carnation's senior executives would mostly lead Nestlé's management team in the United States, proving that Nestlé was no respecter of pedigree. In other words, you were not given preferential treatment because you were a long-term Nestlé employee. The U.S. headquarters for Nestlé was relocated to Carnation's hometown of Los Angeles in 1990 and reorganized into a new company called Nestlé USA Inc., which resulted from the consolidation and reorganization of all Nestlé food and beverage businesses in the United States. Timm Crull, the former CEO of Carnation, took the reins as CEO of the newly formed Nestlé USA. As with its initial management assignments, Nestlé S.A. continued to exhibit respect for the value of human talent acquired when buying a successful business. This strategy and culture would pay large dividends as Nestlé's market shares and profits improved dramatically in the United States in the 1990s.

In my mind, Nestlé had an unusual approach to acquisitions, which would be very useful to me during the late 1990s as Nestlé USA approached companies like Powerbar, Chef America, and Purina as potential acquisition candidates. I could present myself as living proof of Nestlé's veracity when it came to making commitments to current managers and executives about their continued role in running the business after acquisition. Because of my career path at Carnation and then at Nestlé, I became a "poster child" for the possibilities available to senior management should Nestlé acquire their company. Not only was I made CEO of Nestlé USA approximately ten years after the acquisition by Nestlé, but thirteen of my seventeen direct reports were former Carnation employees. Chef America, Purina, and other companies would be successfully acquired and integrated into Nestlé USA in a manner similar to the Carnation acquisition. Managers from all of these companies could be sure that if they performed well, their future was just as secure as if they had been Nestlé employees from the beginning of their careers.

Building on Company Similarities

When Nestlé acquired Carnation I was struck by how closely the values of the two companies matched. Henri Nestlé established Nestlé S.A. in Vevey, Switzerland in 1866. Nestlé's first commercial product was a baby food formula he invented named Farine Lactee, used as a breast milk substitute to save the lives of infants who were unable to breast feed. Carnation Company was founded thirty-three years later and had since its birth had a significant presence in the milk products business.

In addition to having been started in similar business markets, both companies valued loyal long-term employees. When visiting either company, it was not unusual to find many thirty-plus year veterans with valuable experience and a wealth of knowledge in every aspect of the company's activities. And because of their family orientation, you would often find several generations of a family working for the company. This was true even in the top leadership ranks of both Nestlé and Carnation. Helmut Maucher, chairman of Nestlé S.A., had more than thirty-five years of service with Nestlé at the time of the Carnation acquisition in 1985. His association with the company went back a generation to when his father was the manager of a Nestlé factory in a town close to the Swiss-German border. Carlos Represas, who became my boss in 1994, followed his father, Jose, as head of Nestlé Mexico. Their stories were not unique; many Carnation families have given multigenerational service to the company. The similarity of the cultures of Nestlé S.A. and Carnation would greatly facilitate the smooth integration of these two companies in 1985.

As much as the cultures of Carnation and Nestlé were alike, the two CEOs were very different from each other. As mentioned earlier, Mr. Olson was an introvert who seldom visited Carnation facilities. In fact, he rarely traveled much in the United States at all. During the Nixon administration, Olson was called as a witness by a Senate sub-committee conducting hearings on illegal campaign contributions. After his testimony, Olson asked his driver to show him around Washington, D.C., so he could see the various sites. He drove by the Washington Monument, the Lincoln Memorial, and the White House. He had never visited the nation's capitol.

On the other hand, Mr. Maucher was an extrovert who managed by traveling around the world and visiting key Nestlé markets. He knew each market head on a first name basis and spent at least 50 percent of his time traveling outside Switzerland. Mr. Maucher's successor as CEO, Peter Brabeck, follows an even more demanding schedule of international travel and involvement, which is greatly enhanced by his command of a half dozen different languages. Peter often travels to the most remote locations in the world to observe Nestlé people and Nestlé products.

The evolution of management culture can be seen today by examining the leadership style of Helmut Maucher's successor as chairman, Rainer Gut. He followed the example of both Helmut Maucher and Peter Brabeck by visiting all of the major Nestlé operations in the world during his first few years in office. Mr. Gut, former chairman of Credit Suisse First Boston and Nestlé board member since 1981, brings to the job a personal management style that is more American than any of his predecessors' due in part to the years he lived in New York working with CSFB, Lazard Fieres, and Swiss American Corporation, and I think due to his American wife, Josie. These personal and professional experiences have developed his acute understanding of the United States and its people and values system, which make him an effective worldwide leader. And similar to his predecessor, he is fluent in several languages, including English, French, and German. Rainer Gut may be Swiss, but he is just as comfortable in St. Louis as he is in St. Moritz—or Paris or Frankfurt for that matter. Mr. Gut will be missed as he officially retires in mid-2005.

Diversity as a Corporate Strength

All of us at Carnation would eventually learn that one of Nestlé's greatest strengths is her diversity. As with many European firms domiciled in countries with limited sales growth potential, Nestlé's diversity was born out of the necessity to understand the local customs and cultures of promising markets outside the Swiss borders. Nestlé has been a Swiss-based company for more than 135 years, yet by the early 1900s more than 90 percent of Nestlé's sales turnover occurred on foreign soil. The company, therefore, did not have the luxury of being politically partisan. Rather, she had to blend into the local culture of each country in which she operated or sold products.

This diversity is still evident in the origins and foundation of the general management of what has today become the largest food company in the world. At this writing, the Nestlé executive team consists of two general managers of Spanish origin, two Americans, one Belgian, one Dutch, one Swede, one German, one British-Australian, and one Swiss-Austrian. To top off the top management roster, our CEO is Austrian and our chairman is Swiss. I believe one of our true competitive advantages, among all other global food companies, is the uniquely diverse background of our leadership group.

Although I believe that the diverse makeup of Nestlé's leadership was (and continues to be) a clear advantage, we, as Americans, had adjustments to make. To many of the U.S. constituents, Nestlé S.A. appears to have somewhat of a split personality. In spite of the diversity among the company's general management, a distinctively Germanic culture exists within Nestlé S.A. From a business standpoint, the growth of the company has been more Anglo-Saxon and Asian, with the United States alone now accounting for almost 25 percent of Nestlé's worldwide sales.

The more formal Germanic personality of the parent company can at times be at odds with the impetuous American "can-do" personality of key U.S. leaders. A great illustration of this point was made by one of the top leaders in Vevey, who once said, "I know if I ask an American to climb a mountain, he or she will be determined to find a way to get to the top, but unfortunately it will likely be the wrong mountain." Perhaps an exaggeration, this analogy accurately reflects the general tactical focus of many American managers, which some business gurus like Tom Peters have described as having a "ready, fire, aim" management mentality.

Americans are also often seen by Germanic cultures as being too nationalistic and overly motivated by greed and capitalism. On the other hand, Americans often see the Germanic culture as formal, inflexible, not patriotic, and somewhat socialistic. As the saying goes, Europeans (socialists) work to live, whereas Americans (capitalists) live to work. I've also noticed that in America, people are likely to praise others in public, while in the Germanic culture, reprimands are more likely to be made in public. Furthermore, praise at any level is less common in Germanic management cultures. Doing a job well is expected; it is what people get paid to do. Praising an employee because they have fulfilled what are considered to be normal expectations and job requirements seems frivolous.

The CFO of Nestlé USA deftly described the differences between the Germanic and Anglo-Saxon cultures in the mid-1990s. Being Swiss, he explained it from a Swiss military training perspective. Swiss males, he pointed out, all have to enlist in the military after they finish their formal education for a specified amount of training and active duty. Following that period, they are required to stay in the military for most of their adult lives and are constantly trained in the art of strategic warfare. "In the Swiss Army," he said, "you are trained that the most important priority is to save the equipment at all costs. The horses are second, and the troops come last." He went on to contrast that with the U.S. philosophy by adding that "In the American Army, you are trained to save the troops at all costs, with the horses being the second priority, and the equipment being the least important." I am not sure that he had it exactly correct, but he did capture a certain flavor of the difference between the two cultures.

My personal observations after almost twenty years of serving under Germanic leadership differ somewhat from this military analogy. The leaders of Nestlé S.A., unlike many of their American counterparts, are not cheerleaders, but rather are more concerned about adding real value than raw motivation. Real value would be defined in this instance as recognizing a specific fault or defect and giving specific advice on the solution. Without this type of immediate critique and instruction, these leaders would not feel like they were doing their jobs properly. American managers typically spend more time motivating the organization, praising the troops, and reinforcing good behavior as opposed to finding faults and areas of improvement, which in our culture is seen as focusing on the negative. The net result is that the Germanic management style often focuses on the 10 percent of the work being done incorrectly in an attempt to attain perfection. The American management style focuses on the 90 percent being done correctly, assuming that praise and reinforcement will result in individuals feeling encouraged to strive for perfection. In other words, the 10 percent will resolve itself in the process. The truth is that either approach can be successful if applied in a consistent manner over time in a certain cultural setting. The trick is to know which approach to use when and where. Much of the success that Nestlé USA has achieved in the past fifteen years can be attributed to this blending of two cultures to realize the best of both worlds.

The Importance of International Experience

Understanding the differences in management cultures that exist within global companies is the first step to creating a leadership style that will be effective throughout the organization. I have found that the emphasis on international experience among managers is much greater in European companies than in their American counterparts. Because many European companies have done business across international borders since near inception, understanding cultural differences among their customers and management teams has been a minimum requirement for sales growth and even survival. American companies, on the other hand, were often able to delay and even avoid international expansion because of the size of their domestic market. But the global nature of today's marketplace and multinational corporations has changed that, even for U.S. firms. I believe that living and learning to think in a different culture is absolutely necessary for understanding the many nuances of any multicultural company, including Nestlé S.A.

The logical next step in developing an effective global leadership style is to gain international experience. That's why an international assignment for high-potential leaders is a must in today's global economy. Nestlé believes in this philosophy as well, increasing dramatically over the last few decades the international assignments among its executives. By late 2003, more than one hundred American Nestlé associates were serving in Nestlé international assignments around the world. In fact, over a ten-year period ending in 2003, one thousand Nestlé employees had served in international assignments, either as ex-pats from other countries working at Nestlé USA or as Americans working in foreign countries. Although the numbers constantly change due to reassignments, at one point over the past few years, over 50 percent of my direct reports at Nestlé USA had international work experience.

In early 1988, Helmut Maucher approached me about relocating to Sydney, Australia and assuming the position of managing director and CEO of Nestlé Australia Ltd. I informed him that I appreciated the offer, but felt that I could be more useful to the company in my current position. Mr. Maucher asked to see me the next time I was in Vevey. At that meeting he convinced me that an international assignment with Nestlé in Australia would benefit both my family and me, despite the advice from others and the anticipated family sacrifices.

At Mr. Maucher's suggestion and before accepting the position, the entire Weller family made its first six thousand–mile trek from Los Angeles to Sydney in July 1988-the middle of the Australian winter. It quickly became clear that relocating would present personal challenges for all of us. Relocation to Sydney would mean leaving our daughter Robin, then a senior in high school, to begin her freshman year at Southern Methodist University. It would also mean separating Jeff, our thirteen-year-old son, from his friends in L.A. and from baseball, a sport that he not only loved but at which he excelled. We knew from our family visit that Sydney had no American school and no baseball. And further culture shock was in store for our son, who was used to attending school in shorts and a T-shirt. In Sydney he would have to don a full school uniform, complete with straw "boater" hat and Doc Martin shoes. Jeff was quite vocal in his desire not to leave his friends and his home for parts and customs unknown. Needless to say, this was a major family decision for parents with two teenagers at home, each at critical points in their personal development.

Back at Carnation, my personal advisors were not very encouraging either. Because of my senior level in the organization, they reasoned that I had little to gain professionally from the assignment and that my family would likely pay an unnecessarily high price for the relocation. They also felt that I was in a good position to be considered eventually for the CEO position in the United States, with or without the Australian assignment.

I knew I would be taking a risk with a one-way ticket to Sydney, especially if things did not go well. My entire twenty-year Carnation experience had been domestic—managing Carnation products and dealing with American retailers. Almost 80 percent of Carnation's sales were domestic, making its international business a relatively small part of its total sales. Only a small number of its senior executives had ever been involved in the company's international operations, and I only had limited exposure to Carnation International, which was as a director. In contrast, Nestlé was the most international of any food company in the world, with less than 5 percent of its total sales being domestic (Swiss).

All things considered, relocating would mean taking serious personal and professional risks. I knew that my return ticket to the U.S. would depend on my performance in a market that I did not know and marketing many brands, like Milo and Nescafe, with which I had no prior experience.

Bottom line, I accepted the assignment because I trusted Helmut Maucher and because I trusted that my wife would support my decision. The next step would be discussing the details with my new boss Rudi Tschan, who had responsibility for all of Asia, including China, Japan, and Australia. I actually had to refer to a map to see which countries were in the general vicinity of Australia to gauge the true scope of my new responsibilities. One of my territories, as an example, would include Papua, New Guinea, a country located almost due north of Sydney in the Coral Sea.

As I contemplated our move to Sydney, I had a flashback to my first big culture shock some seventeen years earlier. Relocating from Dallas, Texas to Los Angeles in 1972 was a big step for someone who had spent his entire life in the South. Miami was certainly different than Chattanooga, Memphis, Houston, or Dallas, but all of these areas had a familiar southern culture. My brothers and sisters could not believe that I was moving all the way to California—the land of "fruits and nuts," as they would say. If California represented the other side of the world to them, Sydney certainly existed in another galaxy.

During my time Down Under, I would learn invaluable lessons about management styles and cultural differences, which would shape the way I would ultimately lead Nestlé USA. As is the case with the many American Nestlé executives who have lived overseas for two or three years, I attribute some of my management success to my international experience. It helped me understand, firsthand, the importance of high-potential executives having international experience, and as a result, I have since encouraged as many high-potential American mangers as possible to accept international assignments, despite their hesitations. My tenure Down Under would become one of the most critical factors in my success as a leader at Nestlé USA— my subsequent assignment.

CHAPTER 4

The Transformation Down Under

A s a teenager flipping hamburgers at Pryor's Pharmacy in Chattanooga, I could never even have fathomed the idea of moving to Sydney, Australia. Yet in September of 1989, the Weller family, minus Robin, arrived in Sydney for our new assignment. I knew I was ready to take on the challenges that went along with becoming the managing director of Nestlé Australia, Ltd. (NAL), and Carol was ready to take on her responsibilities as corporate wife and partner in a completely new country. I knew that as parents we would have to help our teenage son adjust to a new school, new friends, and a new country. We ourselves would have to adjust to living without our daughter, who was beginning her freshman year at SMU in Dallas, Texas.

What I didn't know at the time was that I was embarking on one of the greatest adventures and learning experiences of my career. My time in Australia gave me a chance to both affect the thinking and management style within my new corporate home and be affected by it—making me a more well-rounded and effective leader. But there were many unknowns as I began my stint Down Under. Would I be accepted by my new associates or would I be cast as an outsider? Would I learn enough about the Australian culture and marketplace to increase market share and profitability? Could I achieve the goals expected of me? But beyond the questions about my effectiveness on the job were concerns for my family's happiness.

Sometimes fear of failure can be the greatest motivator. So with many questions, some answers, and a great deal of motivation, I arrived in Sydney ready to tackle the challenges that awaited me.

Determining My Early Priorities

One of my first steps in preparing for my assignment was to discuss the details of my responsibilities as managing director and CEO of Nestlé Australia, Ltd. with my new boss, Rudi Tschan. Because everything was much more formal in Switzerland than in the United States, I visited with him personally to get his instructions on our new relationship. He did not seem too pleased that I had been assigned to him and spoke for thirty minutes on Americans' lack of success in Australia. Although I was never certain, I suspect that somewhere in his career Mr. Tschan had had a bad experience with an American, which left a lasting negative impression. I would need to overcome that. But things would change during my time in Sydney, and Rudi and I would go on to develop a wonderful and gratifying working relationship.

As is true in most major markets of the world, Nestlé (pronounced "Nessels" by many Aussies) is an important part of the Australian economy and the Australian culture. With operations that began more than one hundred years ago and brands such as Milo, Nescafe, and Maggi—all mainstays of the Australian diet—it isn't surprising that many Australians consider Nestlé as a distinctively indigenous Australian company. But that brings with it challenges for any American trying to create significant organizational change.

Rudi Tschan had been a former market head himself in Australia years earlier, and he suggested that I take it very slowly and not make many changes until the Australians accepted me. Rather than leaving his office fired up about my new assignment, I left wondering why I had even accepted the job. But I would not go back on my commitment to Mr. Maucher, so I decided that I would make the best of the situation and strive to deliver a good result. Going against Rudi Tschan's advice to "not rock the boat," I began a process of change that would be both welcomed by Nestlé Australia employees and refreshing to me.

My first course of action would be to identify areas and company practices that I could affect quickly, in order to set the tone for things to come during my time at NAL. Increasing communication among top management and then with their direct reports would be a key factor to working together as a team. Only then could we achieve any of the corporate objectives that were set, regardless of their size or scope. But I would have to do this in a corporate culture that was different from the Carnation culture to which I was accustomed. The Nestlé Australia corporate culture was clearly Anglo-Saxon, as opposed to Germanic, but it also incorporated a European socialistic twist that called for a different style of leadership. The Aussies were not buying into the typical "gung-ho" American approach to hard work and fervent loyalty. Therefore, I had to take into consideration the cultural mind-set of my new team of employees while setting my early priorities. Any changes I instigated early on would make lasting first impressions, which would chart the course for how effectively NAL would work as a team to achieve the goals I set for the company.

Opening Doors and Talking to People Believe it or not, the process of opening up the channels of communication began with something as simple as opening office doors, talking to people, and socializing with them. During the first week in my new assignment, my executive assistant, Margaret Lewis, a terrific woman who stayed on from the previous managing director, asked me what I would like to have for lunch. The custom had been that most executives either brought their own lunch or their assistants would go out and buy a sandwich, which would be eaten in their offices alone and behind closed doors. I told Margaret that I would be taking different people to Darling Harbor, a restaurant and shopping complex several blocks from our Bathurst Street offices, and that I would be buying them lunch several times a week. Hardly revolutionary, this sent a signal about my management style through the office very quickly. Not only were these lunches a treat for our people and a lot of fun for me, I always learned a great deal about what was going on with the business in this relaxed environment, away from the formality of our offices.

People began to speak freely with me on many subjects, and before I knew it, they opened up and told me how they really felt about the company, their customers, Nestlé associates, and even me. I learned who the "movers and shakers" were, who the real players were, who the weak links were, who could be trusted and who couldn't, and who had hidden agendas. People told me what they thought about NAL, our headquarters in Switzerland, and various individuals in the organization. I learned which factories had problems, which departments were considered weak or strong, and which customers were either easy or difficult to work with. I also learned what the real issues in the organization were—not the ones my direct reports told me about, but the ones they failed to bring to my attention. Even my direct reports shared more with me during these informal lunches. In formal settings, they had the tendency to deliver the good news but seldom bring up the problems. Going out to lunch had never been so profitable. In a short period of time, I had a good idea where the strengths and weaknesses of the organization resided.

A domino effect began. We began to leave executive office doors open in the Nestlé building so the atmosphere was more conducive to communication. We also started a project to remodel the workspace floor-by-floor for all employees. The building was relatively old and had aged poorly. It was in definite need of updating and lots of paint. Employees were pleasantly surprised, and they appreciated the fact that we cared about their work environment. And by showing them we cared about their working conditions, we showed them that we cared about them. All of these little things began to change the mood in the building.

Movers and Shakers   Within the first five months of my time Down Under, we created the Movers and Shakers forum. This forum, which was made up of the top forty Nestlé managers across Australia, including my direct reports and their direct reports, met twice a year to review our progress as a team and provide ideas and input on what changes we needed to make to create a better company. I told them they were hand-selected by me to attend because they touched the greatest number of people in the organization.

But the forum did much more than provide me with information about the company and its strategic initiatives; it gave me legitimate access to the key leaders one line removed. In these meetings, I could interact with the company's top leaders without the limitations imposed by command structure. I was also able to ask a lot of questions without the answers being filtered through the bosses. All of a sudden, the reports to my direct reports had firsthand access to the CEO. It was their first taste of real empowerment.

The Movers and Shakers forum was held in a meeting room specifically set up to encourage open communication. The tables were arranged in a rectangle so that there was no head of the table. Nametags were placed on the tables before the meeting began so that I could break up cliques and sit close to "high potentials" as opposed to my direct reports whom I saw daily. I had microphones placed every two seats to send a strong message that this was a forum and that I wanted everyone to discuss the issues. The truth was that most people could be heard without a mic, but this "prop" was very effective in encouraging participation. It wasn't long before everyone felt like they had a real *voice* in the company.

The Movers and Shakers forum was a real success, yielding dramatic results in employee attitude, actions, and performance. Not only did everyone feel valued, important, heard, and empowered, they felt like they had equity in the direction of Nestlé Australia. Although nothing like this had ever been done at NAL prior to this, it became the precursor to the Leadership Forum we would later institute at Nestlé USA.

Setting the Goals for Nestlé Australia

The changes that were occurring in the areas of communication and corporate culture were positive signs, but the real challenges loomed ahead. As the new leader at NAL, I had to set my priorities and goals for the organization for Year One. The major goals included:

- Identify and begin the process of factory rationalization
- Merge two independent operations into Nestlé Australia to improve focus and efficiency
- Explore new distribution options for existing brands
- Deliver the 1990 Operating Plan

On a personal level, my own goals were to lead NAL effectively and develop my skills as an effective CEO. Achieving all of these tasks would undoubtedly ensure my return ticket to the United States.

Project R   When I first arrived at NAL, Nestlé had twenty factories in Australia, which was nine too many. But in the past, management had been reluctant to close factories due to union considerations. One of my first priorities was to begin analyzing which factories were performing well and which ones were redundant. The process was dubbed Project R, which stood for rationalization—the term used to describe the process of eliminating redundant or excess production capacity.

Resistance to closing factories started at the top, with my boss Rudi Tschan, who had been market head in Australia earlier in his career and had acquired some of the factories that needed to be closed. His key concern was that we would not be able to supply our customers should we have a strike or a disaster. This was a legitimate concern due to Australia's geographical distance from any reliable source of supply. Many of my subordinates knew and shared Rudi's sentiments. However, we had two frozen food factories, for example, making many of the same products. Neither was more than 50 percent to 60 percent utilized. Yet Rudi believed that if we had a strike or even a disaster (such as a fire) in one plant, redundant factories would make it possible to continue operating and supplying the market. The reality was that this was much too high a price to pay when we could limit those risks in other ways. The overriding feeling was that we would be vulnerable with single-source factories.

Against the advice from many quarters, we announced our plans to close nine factories between October 1989 and June 1991. Among the plants closed were those inherited from the Friskies and Arnott Harper acquisitions, including the Friskies Pet Care factories at Campsie, Shepparton, Ballarat, Blacktown, and Sumner Park. Additionally, Maryborough confectionery, Rooty Hill frozen food, Castle Hill Andronicus coffee, and Abbotsford Nestlé Foods factories were closed as part of this production-restructuring program.

Naysayers argued that we would experience strikes, bad publicity, and even serious labor incidents should we proceed with the closings. In fact, at one point during this period, a local member of parliament challenged me to a debate at one of the factory locations, but I figured an American would not fare as well as a general manager of the affected division. I delegated this task to the appropriate division executive, and he handled the situation brilliantly. In the end, we did not experience any of the problems the non-believers had forecast because we treated people in a decent way. We tried to relocate them whenever possible and gave them generous redundancy packages and long lead times, so they could plan their lives accordingly.

Project R involved more than just closing factories, however. We also had to move production lines from one facility to another and integrate machinery when possible. My head of technical, Tom Higgins, was invaluable during this process. He was a genius at saving and using equipment that had any useful life left. When others would not relocate holding tanks with only a few years of useful life, for example, Tom would move them. He would also save the wiring and anything else that might be salvageable. He was frugal but not to the point where production and efficiency were sacrificed. Imagine the cost savings associated with consolidating two factories, each requiring its own equipment and management infrastructure to produce the same product. Tom helped us make an inefficient operating structure more efficient and cost effective.

Nestlé Australia experienced many positive results during 1990 and 1991, beginning with a dramatic improvement on its return on invested capital because of the factory closings. During this time, nearly one thousand positions were eliminated, for a total reduction of 23 percent of the total factory workforce. Additionally, some 14 percent of all office staff at NAL was reduced. Although the media's interpretation of these types of facts usually focuses on the number of jobs lost, we focused on the number of jobs we were able to save in the long term because of these necessary, but controversial, cutbacks. With these reductions, the remaining staff and factory personnel had greater security with our businesses because we shaped them into strong, competitive, and viable units.

Company Consolidation   During January 1990, NAL underwent significant restructuring. The Confectionary division, along with the new Friskies Pet Care division, was consolidated into the new Nestlé Australia, Ltd., making it the fourth-largest food manufacturer in Australia. Prior to 1990, NAL was actually three separate operations—Allen Lifesavers, the newly-acquired Arnott Harper Pet Food, and traditional Nestlé businesses which included brands from the 1985 acquisition of Carnation. Lifesavers had reported directly to zone management in Switzerland, while Arnott Harper was being integrated into the Friskies Pet Care Division. (Arnott's pet care business was acquired in September of 1989.) However, with the consolidation of these entities into one new Nestlé Australia Ltd., all operations now fell under my realm of responsibility. The only food and beverage companies in Australia larger than NAL at the end of 1990 were Goodman Fielder, which was primarily a canned foods manufacturer; Petersville, which was primarily ice cream; and Coca-Cola Amatil, which was less than $100 million larger than Nestlé.

Brand Growth   While it had been a difficult year for Australia, as the country had been pushed into a recession, we found several successes among our Nestlé brands. KitKat, our largest confectionery brand at the time, achieved record market share and became the number one candy bar brand throughout the country. We decided to leverage our LifeSaver distribution base to increase the presence of KitKat wherever there was a cash register. Whereever there was a LifeSaver display, KitKat would soon be available. We created a new merchandising piece—a KitKat tree that was smaller than the normal display and the perfect size for the cash register area. It didn't take long to catapult KitKat sales dramatically. In addition to our successful chocolate bars, the soluble coffee business—which includes Nescafe—hit record sales with market share exceeding 70 percent. Food for our four-legged customers also did well. Friskies successfully rolled out Buffett brand canned dog food nationally, achieving results beyond our expectations. Lucky Dog followed suit by extending its brand into national distribution.

We continued to grow our brands in 1991. Maggi 2 Minute Noodles led sales growth by posting a 30 percent sales increase for the year, while KitKat, Smarties, LifeSavers, Minties, and all therapeutic brands also performed well. Following formulation and packaging changes, Go-Cat, which was Friskies cat food brand, achieved excellent results during the year. We improved the packaging by incorporating better graphics and increased the quality of the food with better-quality ingredients, as competitors continued to cheapen their products. As a result, Go-Cat's sales and market share climbed steadily through the year.

Operating Results   January 1990 began a new era for Nestlé Australia—one characterized by consolidation and renewed focus. We tightened our belts and increased sales at the same time, and overall, we achieved outstanding results. Nestlé Australia, Ltd. group sales turnover exceeded $1 billion for the first time in 1990, as sales increased more than 11 percent over the pervious year. Operating profit showed marked improvement at a 34 percent increase over 1989, exceeding the goal set for the year. In addition to becoming the fourth largest food supplier in Australia, NAL became Australia's leading food exporter in 1990. In 1991, NAL had another record year, with increased sales and a 37 percent increase in operating profits. On the marketing front, 70 percent of Nestlé Australia's key brands held or grew market share during the year.

One of the primary contributors to our success in Australia was a young marketing executive named Brad Alford, whom I consider a personal mentee of mine. Brad was from Cincinnati, where his dad was in the used car business. He did his undergraduate work at Miami University (in Oxford, Ohio) and received his MBA from Indiana. Brad is a Midwesterner with great Midwestern-values who I thought would fit very well into the Australian landscape. I was right. Shortly after I relocated to Australia, I asked Brad to join me, which he did without hesitation. Brad is a gifted leader, and it did not take him long to make a difference. He became a major force in developing the pet care business for Nestlé in Australia.

Brad's success continued over the years. Following his tour of duty in Australia, he went back to the United States, only to return five years later to Australia, this time as managing director of Nestlé Australia, Ltd. Today, Brad is back in the United States as CEO of Nestlé's largest single business in the world, Nestlé Brands Company—home of a number of Nestlé's major U.S. grocery brands, including Nesquik, Coffee-mate, Nestlé Crunch, and Butterfinger. I am proud to say that Brad has developed into the best operator with whom I have ever worked. He is what I like to call a long-ball hitter—when he gets up to bat, you can depend on him to score runs and help win the game. His no-nonsense approach to leadership is legendary at Nestlé, where today he co-chairs the high-energy monthly operating meetings at Nestlé USA. He does it masterfully, which is a real tribute to his leadership talents.

Learning from My Australian Colleagues

As with any assignment to a new territory, it took time and research to get a clear understanding of the corresponding retail landscape. The Australian market was comprised of four major retail customers, Woolworth's, Cole's, Franklin's, and David's Holdings, which accounted for approximately 90 percent of Australia's grocery sales. Australia's retail trade was much more concentrated than that of the United States, where the top four customers controlled only around 20 percent of total grocery sales in the early 1990s. The highly concentrated nature of the Australian market afforded us the opportunity to know personally the retail customers that controlled a vast majority of the country's grocery business. During my time in Sydney, I was able to meet and develop relationships with many of these market leaders. I valued the personal relationships we built, and I also learned a lot from them in the process.

One of the influential and knowledgeable people I met during my time in Australia was John David, manager of David's Holdings, Australia's largest wholesaler. John's father had founded the business, but John was successful in his own right, leading the company to a sales turnover of more than $2 billion by the early 1990s. He was also a major voice in the food industry and developed the Australian Supermarket Institute, which he chaired. Socially, John and Patti David were wonderful hosts, often entertaining suppliers in their home and always making us feel welcome in our new "homeland."

John wielded his power at David's Holdings from an old stone cottage, The Judge's House on Kent Street in Sydney, about two hundred meters from Nestlé's offices on Bathurst Street. It was very easy for me to walk over to have a discussion with John on short notice. These discussions were always educational as John was a very knowledgeable and affable individual. He loved to talk about the business and was very approachable. He was always selling something.

Another valuable relationship I developed during my Australian assignment was with Paul Simons, chairman of Woolworth's. With $9 billion of grocery sales turnover, Woolworth's was Australia's largest grocery retailer and Nestlé's largest retail customer. But Woolworth's had not had a trouble-free corporate history, experiencing a period of slipping sales and declining market share. Paul, however, turned around Woolworth's business. He was considered to be the official unsung hero of the

Australian retail industry and was named Australia's Business Man of the Year at the end of 1989.

Similar to John David's office, Paul's was also located just a short walk from mine. He led his company from a small, unpretentious office located above one of Woolworth's stores on George Street in downtown Sydney. I enjoyed my conversations with Paul, when he would pour over detailed statistics from each retail unit with the precision of a surgeon. Paul would site the merchandising in individual stores he visited over the weekend with a complete history of each store that was most impressive. He could also recite the dollar value done over the weekend at different stores, referring to them as Store 53 or Store 106 rather than their locations.

Paul was always very relaxed and had the ability to make suppliers feel very comfortable. But underneath all that relaxed demeanor was a hard-nosed, competitive, no-nonsense businessman, who was the consummate student of the retail industry. Paul Simons spent a great deal of his time in individual stores to understand the profile of each store. He understood the Woolworth consumer and what her expectations were. He was one of the first to recognize that there were big differences in demand for certain products depending on the neighborhood. While the advantage to a major chain like Woolworth's was the scale of buying in large lots for distribution to all stores in the chain, the trick was to understand different patterns in each store. For example, an upper-end neighborhood like Double Bay, a suburb of Sydney, might index at 180 on sales of Nescafe Gold Blend Coffee but only 50 on International Roast, which was less expensive and made with Robusta beans as opposed to the more costly Arabica coffee beans. Conversely, in certain low-end neighborhoods, International Roast might sell on an index of 200 while Gold Blend might only reach 50. Paul understood that knowing the difference in what did and didn't sell in certain stores was key to the supermarket industry, which operates on low margins.

Although I learned a lot about the Australian food business during our discussions, I think that he too gleaned something from our idea exchanges. Remember that Australian retailers, for the most part, were evolving to modern supermarket formats in the late 1980s. Consequently, they were open to U.S. merchandising ideas like in-store sampling and full-truck and full-pallet sales.

Something I learned from Paul was that what you get out of something is determined by what you put in. He was not a person to sit in the office—he was hands-on, spending time in the stores, talking to customers. He was a 24/7 kind of guy who lived and breathed the business, and reaped the rewards handsomely. Paul was one of the finest gentlemen I would have the pleasure of knowing during my stay Down Under. Even though I left Australia more than thirteen years ago, I still hear from him each year.

Mr. Maucher was right in asking me to reconsider my decision and take the job as managing director of Nestlé Australia, Ltd. after I turned him down the first time. Rudi Tschan and I developed a wonderful working relationship that was extremely gratifying. Both the career and family experience exceeded expectations in ways we could not have imagined before relocating to Sydney.

Life Down Under for the Weller Family

Australia brought wonderful times for our entire family during our twenty-eight month adventure there. It is a beautiful country, rich in natural resources but under-represented in human resources. Imagine only seventeen million people living in an area equal to the size of the United States minus Alaska. For comparison purposes, remember that approximately seventeen million people live in southern California and that the U.S. population is more than 260 million. The vast majority of Australia's population lives in the cities of Sydney, Melbourne, Brisbane, Adelaide, and Perth. Once you move inland from these coastal cities the Australia Outback becomes harsh and uninhabitable.

Australia is home to many beautiful destination points—the Great Barrier Reef, the famous Gold Coast of Queensland, Ayres Rock, and the Blue Ridge Mountains, which reminded me of my own Smoky Mountains in east Tennessee. Our family took a train from Sydney to Katoomba, situated at the foot of the mountains, for a day trip that we still talk about to this day. We also spent many a weekend on the fantastic Australian beaches—from Bondi to Palm Beach—surfing and sunning. Teams of lifeguards, who constantly practiced their rescue techniques, entertained young children almost as if on a movie set. To add even more entertainment value, Uncle Toby's, a local breakfast cereal company, sponsored a continual stream of Iron Men contests on these beaches. We also enjoyed the annual Royal Sydney Easter Show, which presents the best of rural Australia with livestock and agricultural products from all over the country. There were New Years fireworks in Sydney Harbor viewed from Point Piper Park, Annual Speech Day at the Sydney Opera House, the Annual Medici Ball, and much, much more. We also visited the many attractions that are popular with visitors to the country, such as the Tarronga Zoo, one of the best in the world, and Old Sydney Town, a recreation of early Australian history from the 1788 to 1810 period, showing the birth of the nation.

Getting to know a country, however, means more than just seeing the sights and visiting all the popular destination spots. It requires getting to know the people and the culture that make the country unique. Although understanding the culture was important for us socially, it was also very important for me from a leadership, operations, human resource, and marketing perspective. For example, Australians really value their friendships. Meeting their mates at the local pub for a cold Foster's on Friday night is a long-standing tradition among Australians. In fact, oftentimes a career promotion or step-up in business is less attractive for Australian executives than retaining relationships with friends and maintaining a constant social lifestyle. Although Americans typically live to work, Australians clearly work to live.

I learned about something called the Tall Poppy Syndrome. In short, it means that when someone achieves excellence or rises above others because of exceptional performance, their mates "chop" that person down to size. In Australia, people don't admire individual achievement, symbolized by the tall poppy. It is not uncommon for an employee to turn down a promotion because he or she doesn't want to be shunned by friends and wants to make sure the Friday night invitation to the pub still stands.

But don't kid yourself; the people of Australia are a very competitive lot, especially from a sports perspective. You can observe this phenomenon every four years at the Summer Olympic Games, where Aussies are consistently over-represented. You can also observe this at rugby games—one of the things I miss the most! Rugby is much more entertaining than Grid Iron, the local name for American football, because the game is in constant motion. There are no huddles, just continuous running and movement, and every play has the potential of leading to a touchdown. I became attached to this sport quickly and felt very lucky to be among the hoards of enthusiastic fans that would fill the stadiums to watch these exciting games. As fans we were lucky that Australia always fielded one of the best rugby teams in the world, along with New Zealand's famous All Black Rugby Team. If you wanted to get a little more daring you could attend a match of the Sydney Swans "Aussie Rules" football, which in short was an even faster, more kicking-oriented form of rugby.

Unfortunately, life's good experiences are often accompanied by sad times. Our blessed time in Australia was marred by a tragic accident that would leave a permanent scar on our entire family. Our son Jeff lost his best school-friend, Courtney, or Cort as his friends called him. Jeff and Cort attended the Scot's College in Sydney, an old all-boys school with an historical reputation in Australia. Glengarry was a Scot's College second campus, one hundred and fifty miles south of Sydney in the Bush country, called Kangaroo Valley. Each Scot's College student was required to attend Glengarry for one semester during his high school years. This campus was devoted half of the time to classroom activities and half to nature activities, forming a type of outward-bound Rite of Passage for Scot's College's young men.

Cort had been instrumental in helping Jeff adjust to life in Australia. Cort had traveled with his family to the United States and even talked about going to university there. Tragically, Cort died in a rafting accident that was witnessed by many of his classmates and Jeff's friends. Jeff had elected not to attend Glengarry until the following semester, but he saw the report from the scene of the accident on the local news telecast. The loss of Cort would impact Jeff's life in many ways over the following years. In some ways, Cort's passing became Jeff's own rite of passage out of childhood. Carol and I struggled to help Jeff make some sense out of this tragedy, but it was only with the passage of time that Jeff was able to look beyond this heartbreaking episode in his Australian journey.

This terrible incident happened in 1991, toward the end of my three-year Australian tour of duty; this timing was a blessing for Jeff and Carol, as they could leave some of the pain behind as we transitioned our family back to a new Nestlé assignment in the United States. Carol and Jeff left Australia mid-year to start the new school year, and in December I joined them in Los Angeles.

Lessons from Down Under

As I left Australia, I took with me many memories and lessons about life, family, management, and leadership. Leading the significant performance improvement of Nestlé Australia Ltd. and testing a new approach to leadership were very valuable experiences for me. They gave me the background and the confidence to tackle my next assignment with vigor and authority.

Among the most valuable insights I gained from my time as managing director and CEO at NAL were:

- *Leadership is not a popularity contest.* We closed factories and laid off hundreds of people, and I realized that there was no way to make everyone happy with these tough decisions.
- *Take the advice of others but make your own decisions.* Even though my boss told me to go slowly and take no chances, I knew I would never get my ticket back to the United States punched by taking that approach.

- *Evaluate company performance against the competition and marketplace.* Making the operating plan and generating profits are good, but the performance picture is not complete unless you know how you are performing against your competitors.
- *Select the best people to be on your team* based on your instincts and not just the opinions of others. Understand that just because someone is not popular, he may be a good worker and decision maker.
- *Don't sit in the office and expect information and inspiration to come to you.* If you want to know what's really going on in your business, you have to visit factories, sales offices, and stores to get the information first hand. I call this MBWA—manage by walking around—which in Australia translates well into manage by walk about.
- *Repeat your message over and over.* You can't assume everyone will hear, understand, and retain your message after hearing it only once—or even twice. Being consistent over time helps ensure that everyone throughout the organization is on the same page and working toward the same goals.
- *Be a good listener, and people will tell you more than what they think you want to hear.* The Movers and Shakers forum showed me that in order to find out what was really happening in the company, I had to dig deeper in the organization and make myself available to people who would otherwise not have the ear of the CEO.
- *Delegate everything you can.* Remember, you are not an expert at everything. Also, there is no extra reward for trying to accomplish everything yourself.
- *Empower your employees.* Without empowerment, your employees will not be able to be successful in accomplishing what you delegate to them. If they make mistakes, help them learn from them and move on.

I also found that many valuable lessons can be learned outside the company walls that define an international corporate assignment. From my Australian friends, I learned more about balance, an idea I first became aware of through Pete Haynes, but which germinated during my time in Sydney. Australians give up a lot for family and friends, including promotions, which was a unique concept for a self-proclaimed workaholic like me. I also found that Australians typically have friendships that last a lifetime. What Americans often call friendships, Australians would describe as acquaintances.

By diving into the Australian culture—making new friends, experiencing sports and the arts, and traveling beyond Australia's borders into Asia—all of us expanded our horizons and added new dimensions to our personalities and lives. It is difficult for a family to adjust to a new culture. New things must be learned in order to fit in and old habits need to be broken. Learning how to adapt to a different culture was a valuable lesson for my entire family and an experience that I believe made me a better leader going forward.

Back in the U.S.A.

In 1992, I returned to the United States as president and chief operating officer (COO) of the newly created Nestlé USA. Nestlé had operated in the United States since 1900 as Nestlé Food Company, Nestlé Milk Products, Inc., and The Nestlé Company, and finally as Nestlé Enterprises, Inc., which functioned as a holding company based in Solon, Ohio. Carnation had operated independently since its acquisition in 1985, until 1990 when it merged with other Nestlé operations to create Nestlé USA—a new business model for the company.

After two and a half years as a successful CEO of a major Nestlé market thousands of miles from home, I had been transformed into a Nestlé man, with a deep understanding of the Nestlé S.A. values that were never truly projected by Nestlé's operations in the United States prior to the Carnation acquisition. Nestlé's values included a focus on family culture, loyalty to the company, career employees, and trust to do what is right. When I arrived in Los Angeles, I finally understood clearly what Helmut Maucher already knew. The residual benefits to me, my family, and the entire company from my experience in Australia would make me a better leader in the long run.

When I began my new job, I began the process of "taking the bandage off and looking at the wound," as my old mentor Henry Arnest would often say. I succeeded Nestlé USA CEO Timm Crull, who was a naturally charismatic leader and a master-delegator. Timm embodied positive attitude and always empowered employees to do whatever was necessary to improve the business. He was an excellent motivator of the troops. Unfortunately, I now had to play the "bad cop" to help the organization take the next steps to improving performance. Several areas needed to be addressed immediately, including the relative performance of Nestlé USA compared to its competitors, and its relationship with its parent, Nestlé S.A.

Comparative Performance   One of my first responsibilities was to explain to the organization that although we were doing relatively well versus historical results, we were still under-performing against our competitive set of food companies in key areas. The company had a false sense of security because business was O.K. The reality was that we were one of the lowest profit companies in the industry. This was a difficult message, and the organization was surprised to find out that we were not competitive. However, once understood, it made future restructuring and reorganization decisions easier to execute.

We created a "dragon to slay" by announcing to our employees that we had a $300 million operating profit gap with the competition. We went from asking "How are we doing?" to "How are we doing compared to the industry?"

Our dragon was represented by three numbers—13–30–6-something everyone in the organization would soon understand and use as a measuring stick for performance success. Our goal was to achieve 13 percent return on sales, 30 percent return on invested capital, and 6 percent adjusted cash flow. This was the industry average for each of the key performance indicators (KPIs). When we began this process our numbers were actually 8 percent ROS, 18 percent ROIC, and 2 percent ACF. Armed with goals that were clear and easy to measure, the organization had been given its marching orders. This would eventually evolve to become The Nestlé USA *Blueprint for Success,* used by the company today.

Creating Transparency During my first trip to Switzerland as a Nestlé employee, I learned that Vevey did not consider Nestlé Enterprises in the United States to be transparent—in other words, headquarters didn't feel like it knew what was going on. Unfortunately, an "us versus them" attitude existed, and management had not taken a strong position against it. It did not help that the businesses Nestlé owned in the United States prior to buying Carnation had a reputation for being secretive and under-performing. The hallway talk in Vevey was that the Americans over-promised and under-performed, as opposed to the Japanese who under-promised and over-performed. I made up my mind then and there that if I were ever in charge of the U.S. market I would live by the Japanese approach.

When I returned to Nestlé USA in 1992, I was the only senior manager from the old Carnation Company with Nestlé international experience. It struck me that there was an obvious need to create more transparency between Nestlé USA and its parent company headquartered six thousand miles away.

I had received some interesting advice from a top Nestlé Enterprises executive shortly after Nestlé S.A.'s acquisition of Carnation. He told me, "Just remember that in Vevey only one person can help you, but fifteen hundred can hurt you." I did not fully appreciate his comment at the time, but after my first few years with our new parent company, I understood the advice I had been given. In Vevey, information was power. Fifteen hundred people focused on collecting and disseminating data from the various markets around the world. Much of this was necessary for a global company with far-flung operations, but there were many instances where little or no value was added during the exchange of information.

Unlike the remainder of the world, the U.S. market reported directly to the CEO because Mr. Maucher felt that it needed his direct attention and protection. Other areas of the world reported to zone managers who in turn reported to the CEO. This special reporting relationship shaped an attitude that manifested itself into an adversarial relationship between Nestlé Enterprises executives and the fifteen hundred support advisors in Vevey.

These Vevey advisors felt that the U.S. market, Nestlé Enterprises specifically, did the minimum communication necessary with them. The U.S. modus operandi was to go directly to the CEO on most issues without vetting by the advisory groups. This resulted in the support groups believing that they really did not know what was going on in the United States. Even travel to the United States from Vevey by lower level advisors was largely restricted.

I was convinced that Nestlé USA's long-term success would be greatly enhanced by creating a new, transparent relationship between Nestlé USA and our Vevey advisors and support groups. The questions became: How could we get them on our side? How could we open up the doors to Nestlé USA?

We created several tools to open up the lines of communication with Vevey and create a new era of transparency. One such tool was our *Nestlé Very Best Times* newspaper. I made sure that the top thirty people in Vevey received a copy of this Nestlé USA company newspaper each month, so they could read about all of our important activities and ideas. During the first year, Mr. Maucher and other top Nestlé S.A. executives received our newspaper and would send me regular notes asking for an explanation of a new policy or to define a word that they were not sure about. And they did not hesitate to tell me about an idea that they did not agree with either.

The back and forth dialogue that was stimulated by the *Nestlé Very Best Times* became a great checks and balances tool to assure Vevey that the U.S. market was making huge efforts to expose everything of importance. When the notes from Vevey stopped coming some eighteen months into the process, I realized we had made great progress toward full transparency with our parent company. Trust had been established and would be the foundation of a healthy relationship with our Swiss parent.

CHAPTER 5

Making Size an Advantage in the United States

W hen I returned to Nestlé USA from Australia in 1992, I returned to a vast collection of companies that had been acquired over the past several decades and were now owned by Nestlé S.A. Although the potential for market growth and increased profits was clear, the companies were performing at a level that could be described as less than stellar.

As the new president and chief operating officer my job was to work closely with each of the seven operating companies Nestlé Food Company, Nestlé Beverage Company, Nestlé Brands (food service), The Nestlé Frozen Refrigerated Ice Cream Company, Wine World, Sunmark, and Nestlé Foreign Trade Company. My number one objective was to improve sales growth and profits.

As mentioned in the previous chapter, we started out by clearing the lines of communication throughout the organization, making sure that everyone within the company was on the same page and that Nestlé USA was communicating with more transparency with Nestlé S.A. Our next task was to analyze the portfolio of businesses that had been acquired during the previous decades and incorporated into the Nestlé holding company. While the acquisitions included many well-known brands, the companies were still managed as quasi-independent companies, which added "size" to Nestlé but detracted from its overall efficiency.

Since the industrial revolution, size has often been considered an advantage in business. The overriding assumption is that the bigger the company, the greater the efficiency. It has only been in recent years, with the advent of technology, that the idea of being "fast and focused" in business can challenge and even prevail over the advantage of size. Historically, the idea was that the big ate the small, but today the fast and the small have the ability to eat the big. And they often do. Good examples of this recent phenomenon are AOL's acquisition of Time-Warner, Yahoo!'s acquisition of Broadcast.com, and Sanofi's bid to acquire larger rival Aventis in France for $65 billion.

We came to realize that size for the sake of size was rarely a strategy that led to long-term success in the marketplace. Size had to be strategic in order for it to be an advantage. Our goal was to figure out how to transform our size into a true strategic advantage. Determining the best next step for Nestlé USA was a cumbersome task. Bottom line, we had to increase Nestlé USA's operating efficiency and her profits. This process would involve considering a variety of solutions, from reorganizing the businesses under a new operating model to acquiring new brands and selling off some existing ones.

Nestlé had not just sprung to life suddenly in the U.S. market; it had evolved over many decades, and each phase of evolution brought with it a different approach to business and a different historic perspective. Appendix A highlights the major events in Nestlé's history.

Nestlé had grown over the years under three distinct business models: functional, holding company, and divisional. Most recently, Nestlé USA has adopted a network business model (also known as a matrix business model), under which it currently operates. Throughout each of the three phases of Nestlé's existence in the United States, as seen in Figure 5.1, the company experienced various levels of success in terms of sales, brand growth, operating efficiency, and profitability, as described in the following several pages.

FIG 5.1

Evolution of Nestlé Business Models in the United States

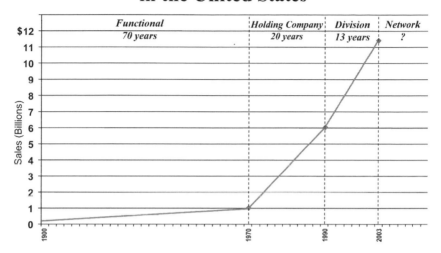

Phase I: The Early Years (1900–1970)

Nestlé began operations in the United States with the commission of its first factory in 1900 in Fulton, New York. Originally opened as a condensed milk factory, Fulton was later converted into a chocolate factory and continued to operate until it was closed in 2003. During this first phase of operations in the United States, Nestlé Food Company operated under a traditional functional business model that was managed primarily with a strong Swiss influence. The results during this period were unspectacular. It took seventy years of marketing coffee, milk, and chocolate products in the fast-growing U.S. market to achieve $1 billion in annual sales, yet profits remained negligible.

Phase II: The Acquisition Years (1970–1990)

By the early 1970s, Nestlé's senior management recognized the great potential of a market like the United States. As a result, Helmut Maucher, chairman and CEO of Nestlé S.A. at the time, implemented an aggressive acquisition strategy. During the next twenty years, Nestlé's U.S. business grew six fold by acquiring a myriad of small, medium, and large size companies, including Stouffers, Wine World, Libby, Hills Brothers, and Sunmark. Certainly the acquisition of Carnation was one of Maucher's crowning achievements, adding both size and profits to the company. In addition, it was the beginning of a new career path for me.

During the 1970s and 1980s, Nestlé used a holding company business model to manage the company's growing collection of U.S. businesses, as seen in Figure 5.2. This independent holding company operating business model, called Nestlé Enterprises, Inc. (NEI), was useful in executing a successful growth

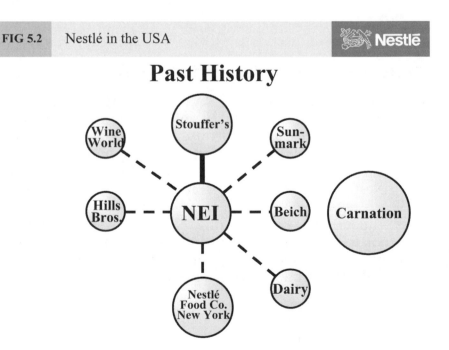

FIG 5.2   Nestlé in the USA   Nestlé

Past History

strategy over a twenty-year period. Nestlé Enterprises acted as a holding company for the old Nestlé Food Company (New York), Hills Brothers Coffee (San Francisco), Wine World (Napa, California), Stouffers (Solon, Ohio), Sunmark (St. Louis), Beich Products (Chicago), and an ice cream operation (Columbus, Ohio). Carnation remained independent under this model. Nestlé Enterprises and Carnation were managed separately and each reported directly to Helmut Maucher from 1985 to 1990.

For the most part, Nestlé S.A. took a laissez-faire attitude about the U.S. market during this period, without a lot of commercial interference. As implied by the name, the holding company business model allowed each of the operating companies to function independently, with local American management largely in control of day-to-day operations. On the technical side, however, headquarters in Vevey was substantially involved in matters such as capital investments in factories, even though these factories reported locally.

By 1990, Nestlé Food and Beverage business on a consolidated basis reached more than $6 billion in sales in the United States. However, profit margins remained low, averaging half the industry average.

Phase III: The Performance Years (1990–2004)

As Nestlé entered its third phase of operations in the United States in 1990, it faced many unknowns about how best to improve the business. The company had experienced sluggish growth during its early years and then rapid growth fueled by rampant acquisitions during the previous twenty years. Nestlé's food and beverage businesses in the United States, not including water, had become relatively big, but had realized few of the efficiencies that can potentially accompany size.

Nestlé Enterprises, a collection of companies managed quasi-independently, now faced the need to reorganize itself. The American management team's challenge in 1990 and 1991 was to take this portfolio of businesses and turn it into the Very Best Food Company in the United States.

When we combined all of the businesses and brands that fell under the Nestlé holding company umbrella plus Carnation, we definitely had size. Now we had to answer the difficult question of how to make size an advantage. The answer would not come immediately. But eventually, as we focused on performance and honed our growth and operations strategies, we began to formulate new ways to make our size an advantage in the U.S. market. The new Nestlé USA would experience unprecedented growth, as depicted in Figure 5.3.

Focusing on Performance

In December of 1990, while I was still in Australia, Nestlé changed its business model in the United States for only the third time in nearly one hundred years. The new model was a

FIG 5.3

Key Financial Figures
Nestlé USA (w/ NPPC) 1993 - 2004

	'98 - '04 Average	'93 - '97 Average	'93 Average
Sales Growth	+10.2%	+1.3%	-3.4%
RIG	+4.3%	-0.5%	-1.9%
Profit/EBITA Growth	+24.4%	+0.3%	-0.3%
Advertising % of NPS	3.4%	3.0%	2.8%
PFME % of NPS	9.1%	8.0%	7.1%

Note '98 – '04 Average includes Purina beginning 2002.

division-oriented model that started the process of taking advantage of size by consolidating NEI and Carnation. Product types were organized into business units or companies reporting into a new parent company called Nestlé USA, as shown in Figure 5.4. Each brand would be categorized into a specific product-oriented company. For example, Tasters Choice moved from Nestlé Food Company in New York to Nestlé Beverage Company in San Francisco.

The new organizationally optimized Nestlé USA included Nestlé Food Company, Nestlé Beverage Company, Nestlé Frozen, Refrigerated and Ice Cream Company, Nestlé Brands (food service), Wine World, Sunmark, and Nestlé Foreign Trade. The organization began to realize important synergies for the first time. The NEI management structure was eliminated and a new Nestlé USA corporate support group began to coordinate a number of areas, such as purchasing and parts of finance, manufacturing, and human resources.

FIG 5.4

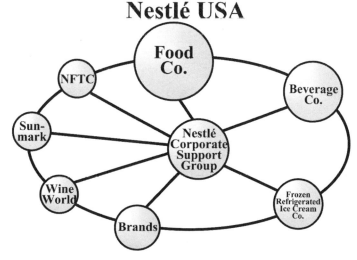

"Organizational Optimization" Nestlé USA

The headquarters for Nestlé USA moved from the east coast to the west, and was relocated to Glendale, California. Nestlé businesses that were not directly food- or beverage-related, such as Alcon, the very successful eye-care company located in Fort Worth, Texas, and Perrier of America, renamed Nestlé Waters of North America located in Greenwich, Connecticut, continued to report directly into Switzerland.

Creating a Strategic Portfolio of Brands By 1990, Nestlé's business portfolio consisted of scores of brands, but few with sales of more than $500 million. Although these companies gave Nestlé a broad presence in the market, each one did not contribute to the overall profitability or united goals of the new Nestlé USA. As each reorganization decision was executed, efficiency improved and the bottom line grew, but at the expense of focusing on certain consumer efforts. I often referred to the Speedometer Chart shown in Figure 5.5 when characterizing the effects of reorganization on efficiency and focus for our com-

FIG 5.5   Nestlé

Evolution of Nestlé
in the United States

Focus ← → Efficiency

"Optimized"

Divisions

IOCs

Integrated Divisions

Holding Company

Sharing Resources

Centralized

1994

1990
Nestlé USA

1997

70's–80's
Nestlé Enterprise Inc.

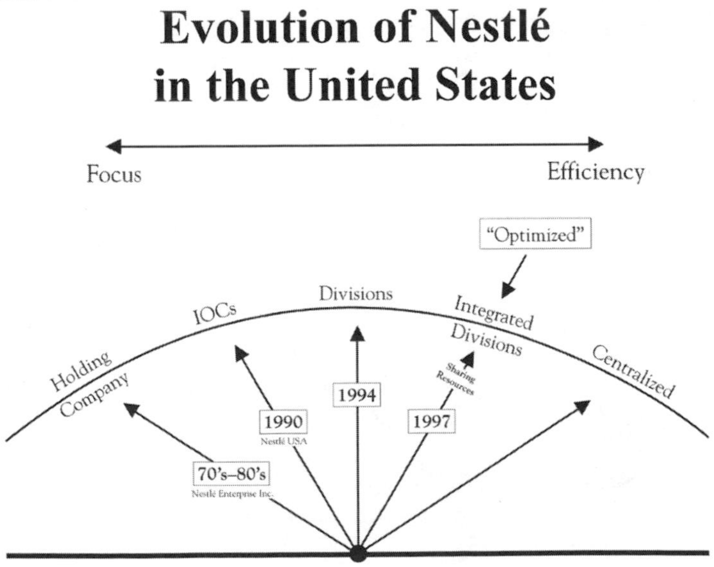

pany. Because of our broad portfolio of brands, we could not have the same level of focus that a company doing business in only one product category could. It became obvious over time that scale was the answer to maintaining and improving efficiency without losing focus.

Over the course of several years this speedometer chart helped us visually communicate our challenge to the entire organization. As we changed and improved our structure, we plotted these changes against a continuum ranging from focus on one extreme to efficiency on the other. Our starting point on the speedometer dial was the holding company structure of the 1970s and 1980s, which was very focused, yet inefficient and yielded virtually no profits. In 1990, we reorganized into independent operating companies (IOCs), reporting into a new corporate entity, Nestlé USA, which fully integrated Carnation into the Nestlé family for the first time. This reorganization improved efficiency and profits, moving the speedometer dial from left to right along the continuum, with slightly less focus but more efficiency. This was our first step toward optimizing the company.

In 1994, after divesting Wine World we consolidated Sunmark and Nestlé Foreign Trade into the Nestlé Food Company and created a structure with four major divisions including Nestlé Foods, Nestlé Beverages, Nestlé Frozen, Refrigerated and Ice Cream, and Nestlé Brands (food services). Once again this moved the speedometer dial further to the right—toward efficiency but somewhat away from focus.

In 1997, the three independent sales organizations of the three retail organizations—Nestlé Foods, Nestlé Beverages, and Nestlé Frozen, Refrigerated and Ice Cream—were merged to create one large sales organization projecting one face to the trade. This reorganization gave us what we felt was a fully optimized structure without going to full centralization, as depicted in Figure 5.6. Over seven years, we had in effect moved the speedometer dial as far to the right (toward efficiency) as we felt we could, considering the negative impact of such a move on focus.

By 2000, we began to search for a business model that would allow Nestlé USA to maintain and even improve efficiency while simultaneously improving focus. The network or

FIG 5.6

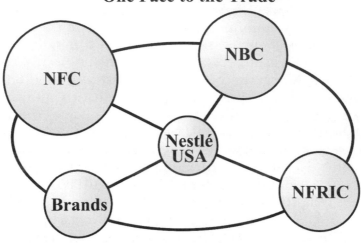

Nestlé USA – 1997
"One Face to the Trade"

matrix business model that we would launch in mid-2003 allowed us to improve efficiency *and* improve focus by capitalizing on the scale that resulted from including all of the North
American Nestlé operations in our corporate reorganization.
After adopting this business model, we officially retired our famous speedometer chart.

The company's penchant for acquisitions, indicative of the
1970s and 1980s, did not end with the establishment of the new
Nestlé USA. In fact, during the 1990s several acquisitions like
Alpo Pet Foods, Powerbar, and Häagen-Dazs were completed.
Nestlé also bought Purina and Chef America, both of which were
outstanding, large, and profitable companies. Purina made us
number one in pet care, and Chef America's Hot Pockets made
us number one in the high-growth handheld food market with
its 50+ share. Unlike some of the acquisitions of the past
decades, these were strategic in nature and were meant either to

complement an existing Nestlé business or allow Nestlé USA to expand into new and important food- or beverage-related areas.

I am very proud of the quality of acquisitions that we made in the 1990s. Equally important to our portfolio, however, was our divestiture program. Nestlé USA began to eliminate businesses that were not currently adding value, or in some cases, were actually destroying value. In fact, more than $2 billion in sales were divested over the thirteen-year period ending in 2003. Each of our businesses was evaluated on how it contributed to the company's overall profitability and strategic direction. Simply put, those that lost money were sold off. For example, Wine World Estates, including Beringer Wine, was sold in 1996 primarily because it did not cover its own cost of capital in the Nestlé structure. Many other businesses were sold as well, including Stouffers hotels, David and Sons, Kathryn Beich, Ortega, and Peter's Chocolates.

During the early 1990s, the majority of the commodity businesses that had been acquired were also divested. One of the first was Carnation Dairies, which had large fresh milk and ice cream operations all along the west coast including San Diego, Los Angeles, Oakland, Seattle, Portland, Spokane, Phoenix, and as far east as Houston, Texas. Other non-value added divestitures included Cains roast and ground coffee company in Oklahoma, and MJB and Hills Brothers coffee brands in San Francisco. Contadina tomato products, with their national distribution, were also divested, along with Libby's canned meats. Carnation's frozen potato business, which operated primarily in the food-service area, was also divested during this period.

Our new disciplined approach to acquiring and divesting businesses resulted in a strong portfolio of strategic brands that could be grown profitably into the future, as seen in Figure 5.7. Most of the support for this aggressive local divestiture strategy came from Nestlé CEO Peter Brabeck, who gave Nestlé USA the green light to clean up our local portfolio. Historically, our Swiss parent had been growth-oriented and divestitures were frowned upon. But when Brabeck became CEO, he charted a very different course in this area. It wasn't long before a divestiture was no

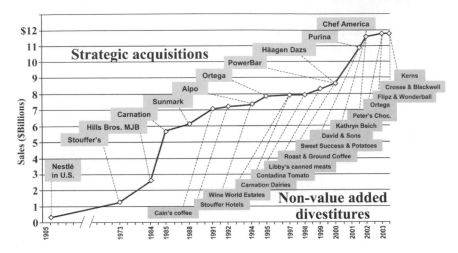

Evolution of Nestlé in the United States

longer automatically seen as a failure, but rather as an opportunity to improve the company's future by eliminating activities that generated losses. But even with this change in management philosophy, *adopting a quality-of-earnings orientation was no small task.*

Capitalizing on Business Synergies The performance potential of the divisional business model became apparent once major restructuring was completed in the mid-1990s. As the company moved from an independent operating company structure to a division structure, synergy savings were realized in many areas, as seen in Figure 5.8. For example, the consolidation improved our profits, we developed value managed relationships (VMRs) with suppliers, and we were able to save approximately 10 percent on purchases of items such as office supplies and travel. In one purchasing area—corrugated—we went from forty suppliers to just three. We also sold some factories and closed others, reducing the number of plants from

FIG 5.8

Evolution of Factories and Employees

(*$ Billions*)	**1990**	**1997**	**2004**
Total Sales	$6.1	$7.9	$12.5
EBITA Index	100	133	316
# Factories	72	49	47
# Employees	40,000	20,986	21,107

seventy to thirty-five by 2000. We also decreased the employee base from forty thousand in 1990 to twenty-one thousand by 2004, but we did not suffer from negative publicity over job reductions because most people retained employment with the new owners. In fact, more than half of the reduction in employees came from the labor-intensive hotel business.

Offering Competitive Incentive Programs I am convinced that one of the key ingredients of our success in the 1990s was the ability to have competitive short- and long-term incentive programs to reward and retain key executives. Nestlé SA was uncomfortable with these programs initially, as they were viewed as being "too American." Management in Vevey realized, however, that Nestlé USA had to compete for the best talent against other reputable U.S. companies that had stock options, elaborate bonus programs, and other longer-term financial incentives for high-performance executives. So in the mid-1990s our Swiss parent company took a bold step and approved a long-term incentive plan for Nestlé USA that allowed us to be competitive in total compensation with our American counterparts.

As a result, we launched a competitive annual bonus program called Awards for Performance Excellence (APEX) and replaced an antiquated phantom stock option plan with a long-term incentive plan that is tied to sales and profit targets. Being able to align our business objectives with these new incentive plans was a major factor in the consistency of our improved performance and the retention of top performers over the years.

Creating a Blueprint from a Vision   It was at our market heads conference in Vevey, Switzerland in June of 1997, when I heard our CEO Peter Brabeck give a speech he called "The Blueprint for the Future." He was outlining the vision for Nestlé SA, citing four pillars that were required to achieve international competitiveness. This was the perfect model after which to mold our new vision. Our American version would be called The Nestlé USA *Blueprint for Success,* and the four pillars, with slight modifications, became our four strategies. Not only did it make sense strategically, it was a great way for us to show support for Peter's vision.

Closing the Performance Gap   In the early 2000s, we began having monthly operations meetings, separate and apart from the monthly Executive Leadership Team meetings. Division CEOs, along with their key sales, supply chain, and marketing leaders, would identify gaps between their latest sales estimate and their high-performance targets (HPT). The HPT was a stretch target established by the division CEOs and me to achieve results significantly above the industry expectations. Our philosophy was to shoot for the stars (HPT) and hit the moon (annual plan).

The Proof Is in the Profits

By 1998, Nestlé USA began to hit its stride. Stripped of its commodity businesses and armed with a portfolio of strong-performing brands that made strategic sense, the company was poised to realize its full potential in the marketplace. It was aligned behind The Nestlé USA *Blueprint for Success.* During the seven-year period of 1998 to 2004, Nestlé USA had real internal growth (RIG) in core businesses alone of more than 4 percent each year, while sales growth was almost 6 percent, which was above the industry average. As seen in Figure 5.9, earnings before interest, taxes, and amortization (EBITA) in our core business alone averaged almost 19 percent, or more than triple the average of the competitive set of food companies, which are used internally at Nestlé USA to benchmark our progress on profit improvement on an ongoing basis This was accomplished in spite of investing more than $150 million per year additional in the marketing and advertising of our brands, as depicted in Figure 5.10.

In addition to sales and profit growth, increased market share was also set as a measure of success. Over the four-year

FIG 5.9

Key Financial Figures
Nestlé USA (w/o NPPC) 1993 - 2004

	'98 - '04 Average	'93 - '97 Average	'93 Average
Sales Growth	+5.8%	+1.3%	-3.4%
RIG	+4.4%	-0.5%	-1.9%
Profit/EBITA Growth	+18.6%	+0.3%	-0.3%
Advertising % of NPS	3.4%	3.0%	2.8%
PFME % of NPS	9.2%	8.0%	7.1%

Note '98 – '04 Average includes Friskies through 2002.

FIG 5.10

Nestlé USA Financial Trends

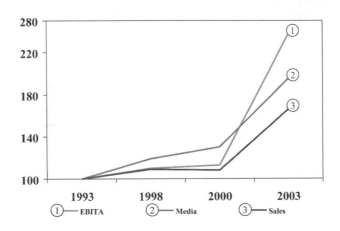

period ending March 2005, market share increased for the majority of Nestlé's top brands—Stouffers, Lean Cuisine, Coffeemate, Fancy Feast, Mighty Dog, Toll House Morsels, Good Start, Powerbar, Juicy Juice, and Purina Cat Chow. Figure 5.11 highlights the share point increases for the top-performing brands. (These share positions are exclusive of Wal-Mart. Nestlé USA's Wal-Mart sales have consistently performed above Wal-Mart's internal sales growth rates over this four-year period.)

Acquiring Ralston Purina grew Nestlé USA by one third to around $12 billion in sales. Importantly, it improved the company's overall EBITA margins. Purina was one of the most profitable companies in the food industry. Still, in spite of the excellent year-to-year performance during these seven consecutive years, overall margins exclusive of Purina were still below the competitive industry average.

The reality was that Nestlé USA had become a very large company in the United States. Only Kraft, ConAgra, and Sara Lee were larger than we were in the food-processing arena. But

| FIG 5.11 |  |

Market Share Increase Top Core Brands
(2000-2005) Dollar Share
(Excludes Wal*Mart)

	Share	Pt. Change
Coffee-mate	61.7%	+7.2
Nestlé Toll House Morsels	56.4%	+3.2
Fancy Feast Cat Food	32.5%	+7.0
Stouffer's	20.2%	+1.9
Juicy Juice	19.1%	+1.0
PowerBar	17.8%	+2.8
Lean Cuisine	16.3%	+4.5
Mighty Dog Food	13.3%	+1.2
Good Start Infant Formula	10.3%	+2.0

in many ways we were still operating with the inefficiencies of smaller businesses driven by our large portfolio of brands.

Phase IV: Network Business Model—Making Size a Competitive Advantage

The challenge for any company and for any CEO for that matter is to anticipate change, as opposed to being forced to react to it. Nestlé USA experienced great success during what we call The Performance Years. Since 1990, Nestlé USA's net sales had grown by 70 percent, net headcount had been reduced by 45 percent, and net EBITA profit had grown by over 300 percent. Yet by 2003 we found ourselves at a crossroads.

Could Nestlé USA "morph" to a new business model without suffering through a period of sales and profit decline? Could we in fact bring about change that could create even more efficiency, and actually gain focus? Or as they might say in Chattanooga or in Texas, could we change horses in the middle of the stream without getting wet? The scale brought about by the acquisition of Purina in pet care, and Chef America in frozen foods helped facilitate the business model shift we needed.

After thirteen successful years of operating under a divisional business model, it was now time to evolve into one that could accommodate ongoing industry and company change in a more efficient manner. In effect, we changed from a hierarchical business model to a network business model, as seen in Figure 5.12. The new matrix or network model, launched in 2003, allows us to take full advantage of Nestlé's size in North America by aggregating $12 billion of Nestlé USA sales with Nestlé Canada, Nestlé Waters, and Dreyer's Ice Cream to create leverage of $20 billion of total sales. Additionally, this network model, by nature of its design, could foster even greater focus,

FIG 5.12

Evolution from Hierarchy to Network Business Model

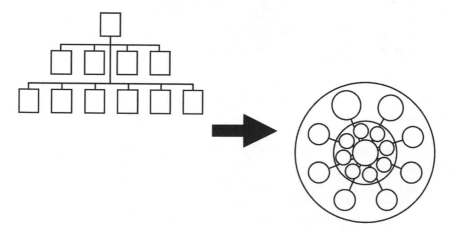

teamwork, and alignment, while driving empowerment. The center of this new business model, shown in Figure 5.13, would be a shared service center, called Nestlé Business Services (NBS).

Nestlé Business Services allows each defined business, such as Pet Care, Waters, Frozen Food, and Nestlé Brands, to focus on the most important strategic aspects of the business—marketing and manufacturing. Transactional activities and support functions would be consolidated into "centers of excellence" or shared service centers that would serve each company through individual service contracts.

With this model, the efficiencies and cost savings that Nestlé *could* experience from the aggregation of these services and activities would help transform our "size" from a competitive disadvantage into a true advantage. The trick would be to organize the company into large, highly-focused business units focused on the important strategies of the business, while aggregating support activities into "shared services."

FIG 5.13

Nestlé USA

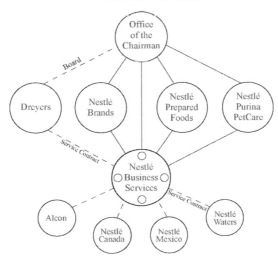

The goal of the shared service center concept was to leverage the size of Nestlé USA and accommodate the needs of Nestlé sister companies all across North America. Nestlé Business Services would operate as a separate business and contract with each company to deliver specific services at the lowest cost possible. Companies like Alcon, Nestlé Waters of North America, Nestlé Canada, Nestlé Mexico, Dreyer's Ice Cream, and even L'Oreal, in which Nestlé has a minority interest, all could take advantage of the shared service concept. But we understood that convincing independent companies to give up some control over certain functional areas might be difficult; therefore, we sought professional assistance in this area.

We interviewed a number of consultants who had extensive experience helping companies implement shared service concepts. We wanted to partner with a company that we felt had the best experience in this specific area and possessed the personality and talent that would work well with our people. Accenture fit the bill perfectly. We did not want a turnkey operation, but rather a shared service operation that would be developed by Nestlé executives with the assistance of our Accenture experts. At the end of the day, Nestlé associates would completely manage the final operation.

We established the Nestlé Business Service Steering Committee and identified the key Nestlé players who would serve on this task force. This group consisted of the CEOs of the major companies that would use the shared services, including the CEOs of Nestlé USA companies, Nestlé Canada, Nestlé Mexico, Nestlé Waters, and representation from Nestlé World Headquarters, so that our experience would not be lost from an international perspective. Although this required a high degree of commitment from these leaders, their input was vital to the success of the new structure.

The success of this process depended on the level of "ownership" and input we got from the "A" players of each company, which meant each company had to free up its best talent to participate. We established Nestlé Business Service Governance, which was similar to a board of directors. NBS governance was responsible for making the rules for NBS. The steering committee became a key ingredient to our successes because it helped each CEO feel personal equity in the project. It would also be important to have the ability to extrapolate our scale and our experience for a worldwide implementation.

The NBS leadership along with Accenture worked diligently to create a business case to support the shared service center concept, which included the benchmarking of all the functions we had identified for possible inclusion. The business case confirmed the key areas of scope for the project, which were purchasing (direct and indirect), transportation, human resources, finance, information services, and even some areas of sales. We then conducted a business case justification for each of these functions, and after a great deal of study, our gut instincts were confirmed—the potential savings of this model indeed justified a move forward.

Nestlé Business Services will take several years to be fully operational; however, we have already experienced initial success with purchasing. Previously, each of the five operating companies had their own purchasing teams. Under the new system, they were consolidated into one head of purchasing reporting directly to NBS. The result will be $200 million total annual purchasing savings in the long-term. This is a big win for us. However, we are still identifying best practices in the group and leveraging them across all of Nestlé USA. Importantly, we have learned that most of the savings realized thus far have come from implementing best practices across all the companies.

For the first time, a group of relatively unrelated businesses such as pet care, chocolate, frozen food, food services, ice cream, water, and Alcon products will be able to access common services more efficiently. In fact, we estimate that the aggregation of all these businesses will create the efficiency of a $20 to $25 billion company.

We are not quite there yet, however. Implementing the new business model is a strategic journey that we are still taking as a company. I am convinced, however, that once it is in place in early 2006, our planned business model and shared service center will generate significant benefits. Annual savings are estimated to be in the $300 million range. Nestlé USA will be positioned to improve from moderately above average operating profits to top quartile performance with a good possibility to be best in class in quality of earnings in the next three to five years.

There is no question that massive change like this will require leadership throughout the organization. That is why commitment to our vision and commitment to The Nestlé USA *Blueprint for Success* has never been more important for the company as it is today.

CHAPTER 6

The Vision Thing

Vision statements and mission statements have been around much longer than I've been in the business world. The vast majority of the ones I have seen over the years are very similar to one another, often making "motherhood and apple pie" statements about quality, employees, and shareholder value. Statements such as "People are our greatest asset" and "Our goal is to increase shareholder value" are typical of the corporate jargon found in almost all mission statements today. Usually, these documents promise and commit to a lot, especially people-related issues. Rarely, however, do they include an action plan on how to achieve the objectives they describe. I believe that is the reason that mission statements often wind up framed and hung on the CEO's office wall and tucked away neatly inside managers' desk drawers to be reviewed every twelve months or so.

Neither Carnation nor Nestlé had a formal written mission or vision statement, or anything that resembled one, over most of my thirty-seven years with the company. The prevailing wisdom within both of these organizations was much as just described. Nestlé and Carnation leaders did not believe in the usefulness of these types of statements in the day-to-day operations and deemed them as being mostly academic in nature. Additionally, my European colleagues at Nestlé considered these types of statements as uniquely American and not appropriate for a truly global company like Nestlé.

I had a different view, however. After returning from Australia, I believed in the value of having a united vision for the future—something the entire organization could rally around and work together to achieve. In his book *Leading Change,* John Kotter, professor of leadership at The Harvard Business School, explains that "Vision plays a key role in producing useful change by helping to direct, align, and inspire actions on the part of the large numbers of people."[1] My experience in Australia proved this to be true. We had been able to focus successfully the entire Australian organization behind a common set of objectives that had been developed by the Movers and Shakers. The results exceeded my expectations.

Creating a Vision

Once back in the United States, my thinking was that we needed a global, yet simple, vision upon which we could focus the attention of a very diversified organization. Keep in mind, the company at the time was made up of a collection of businesses we had acquired over the past several decades, and with the acquisition of every Stouffers, Carnation, Hills Brothers, and Libby, the company inherited another subculture unique to the acquiring organization. Therefore, after the wave of acquisitions in the 1970s and 1980s, the Nestlé USA culture was primarily a mix of some twelve or thirteen subcultures.

In developing a vision for Nestlé USA, the major challenge was to craft a vision that was general enough for these different subcultures to identify with, yet specific enough to describe what we wanted all of Nestlé USA to look like in the future. The overriding strategic question became, "What is Nestlé USA going to look like when it grows up?" We began exploring the answer to that question, which led to addressing the related question, "How can we create a 'living' vision (document) that can align all twenty-two thousand Nestlé USA employees behind a common set of objectives?"

The Nestlé USA Executive Leadership Team (ELT)—my direct reports—took a lot of the ideas from my Australia experience and improved upon them. First, we changed the name used to identify the key leaders of the company from the Movers and Shakers to the Leadership Forum, which we felt was more appropriate for the American group. Then the ELT group wrote, rewrote, and eventually honed the vision statement until we had a very tight expression of what we thought the company should be and what we felt the entire company, regardless of subculture, could unite behind. The vision statement consisted of eleven simple words: "To Be the Premier Diversified Food Company in the United States." This certainly represented an inspirational goal at the time because no one in our industry would have considered Nestlé USA a premier U.S. food company in the early 1990s.

In order to be an effective tool, we believed the vision document would have to be relatively short and easy to refer to and handle. Our goal, albeit a lofty one, would be to produce a single-page document that associates could review each day and understand what they had to do to make the company successful. We also realized that the document would have to resonate with everyone throughout the organization, regardless of title or level of responsibility, if we expected our associates to adopt it. It had to convey clear and specific direction to each associate, from the factory floor to the executive floor, and spell out their role in achieving overall company goals. Therefore, our next task was to identify five strategies that associates could employ to reach our overall goal and fulfill our mission.

We believed that in order for our employees to feel connected to the vision, they needed to feel connected to the company and understand what the company stood for in terms of values and principles. That is why we included in the document a description of our core values, which had not been identified formally until that point. They included people, quality, brands, customers and consumers, and performance. I felt that identifying these areas of importance for Nestlé USA also helped define the company's overall personality.

The team had worked for almost one year to capture on paper the true vision of the company, which we called Vision 2000, and appears in Appendix B. Now the challenge would be to take it to our employees and make it come to life throughout the organization. Only then could Vision 2000 empower our associates and motivate them to "get off the sidelines and into the game" to make the appropriate decisions and take the right actions that would collectively lead Nestlé USA *to be the premier diversified food company in the United States.*

We launched Vision 2000 at my first Leadership Forum meeting as CEO of Nestlé USA in May 1994. During this meeting, we distributed a one-page (back and front) document entitled "Vision 2000," which included our brief eleven-word vision statement, our five strategies, and our core values. Vision 2000 was well received by this group of the top two hundred executives across Nestlé USA. We knew this would ensure the success of Vision 2000 as we rolled it out to the entire organization in August.

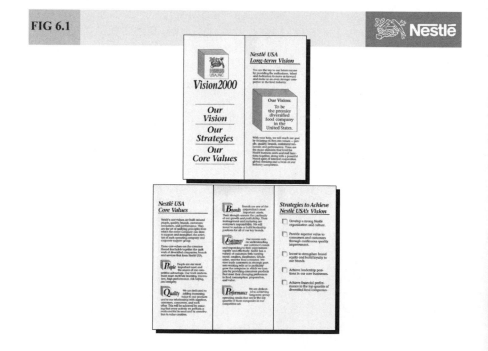

FIG 6.1

Taking the Vision to the People

In August of 1994, we took Vision 2000 to the entire twenty-two thousand employees of Nestlé USA with a series of five two-day meetings across the United States. It was clear that we not only had to get our associates to recognize the importance of a vision statement in general, but we had to get them to accept a specific vision that they had not directly helped create. I also had to build a case for why we needed one now and how it would help us achieve long-term success in the food industry.

To set the tone of each meeting, I congratulated each employee on the successful reorganization of Nestlé USA and formally thanked Timm Crull, former Nestlé USA CEO, for his leadership during this critical period of time. The good news was that the company had recognized excellent synergistic savings, and therefore was able to report both improved sales and profits from 1991 to 1993, while still investing heavily in new products. Had the restructuring not occurred during this period, we would have been in an almost impossible situation by 1994. The bad news, however, was that despite the great progress we had made during the prior three years, Nestlé USA still found itself posting a $300 million operating profit gap below the average of its competitive set of food companies in the United States.

So what was the solution? If good sales and profits still were not enough to keep us in line with our competitors' performance, what would it take to fill that $300 million operating gap? Our answer was to get all of our oars in the water and get everyone rowing in the same direction and toward the same destination. We had to abandon the idea that each company could go it alone and then just tally up the end results and hope that the mother ship had performed well. We had to unite our efforts and align our vision.

I confessed to our employees that we had done a rather poor job, up until that point, of describing to them the overall direction we wanted the company to go. I explained, however, that I hoped everyone would leave these meetings with a very clear understanding of Nestlé USA's long-term and short-term vision and the general strategies we expected would get us there by the year 2000.

I described to them how Vision 2000 had been developed over the course of the year, with the full participation of each member of the Executive Leadership Team. I also explained that we believed the vision was fully achievable, and if executed well, would result in a performance level that would give each employee the opportunities and the job security he or she deserved. Most of all, I wanted them to be excited about this defining moment in the company's history. I needed to be the teacher and leader that Coach Murray had been to his Duke football team, yet I also needed to create a little of the spirit that filled the Blue Devils stadium on game day.

One way we accomplished our goal of bringing the vision to life was to talk about our corporate values. It gave us a chance to talk about the personality of the company and let our associates relate to Nestlé USA in a new way. We discussed the importance of people, quality, brands, customers and consumers, and performance, as we knew these core values would drive our new united culture. This discussion also gave me a chance to introduce myself to the organization and let all twenty-two thousand associates get to know me as I talked openly about what each of these core values meant to me personally. By the end of the meetings, it was clear to every one of our Nestlé USA associates how they were expected to conduct themselves.

I concluded each of the five meetings with the following comments in an effort to bring the entire organization together.

"If we are to achieve our vision for the future, each of you must join with the entire Executive Leadership Team and be dedicated to our core values. As always some people will resist this change—they will not be able to shift to a true team management concept.

"I am sad to say that there are some people who like to gossip—they create disorder and dissention, and they play politics. These people simply will not survive in the new Nestlé USA 'Team' culture. You can no longer think of yourself as an employee of Stouffer, Carnation, Wine World, or Sunmark. You are first and foremost an employee of Nestlé. Nestlé USA is not Joe Weller or the corporate support staff in Glendale. Nestlé USA is each of you—and all of us collectively. If you remember nothing else over the next two days, please remember that.

"I like to compare this to our U.S. citizenship. I was born and grew up in Tennessee, a small southern state that was rich in tradition, culture, and history. Tennessee was the sixteenth state admitted to the union. Tennesseans played a major role in the development of the western United States. Andrew Jackson was one of the first senators from Tennessee—he lead a group of Tennessee volunteers who defeated the much larger British force at the battle of New Orleans in 1814. Andrew Jackson later became the seventh president of the United States and the first of three presidents to come from Tennessee. Sam Houston was one of the first governors of the state of Tennessee. He led a group of Texans to victory against the famous Mexican general Santa Ana, nicknamed the Napoleon of the West. That established the Republic of Texas prior to Texas statehood.

"I am proud of my Tennessee heritage, and I never want to forget where I came from, but when I travel internationally I do not travel on a Tennessee passport, I travel on a U.S. passport. The U.S. passport gives me access to resources around the world that I could never access with a Tennessee passport.

"Today many of you are traveling on Stouffer, Carnation, Hills Brothers, Sunmark, or Wine World passports. I challenge you to exchange them for Nestlé USA passports. With the Nestlé passport you have access to Nestlé's vast resources, unlimited career opportunities, and worldwide technologies.

"If we are to achieve our long-term goals, then each of you must begin to think of yourself as and feel that you are a part of the Nestlé USA team. This is a message that the entire organization must understand. Everyone must

FIG 6.2

Nestlé Passport

wear his or her Nestlé hat and make decisions that are in the best interest of the Nestlé Group first.

"I challenge each of you to join me, and your Executive Leadership Team, in realizing our Nestlé 'Vision' for the future. I invite you to measure your management team, yourself, and your own team by the core values we discussed. If we do not live up to the expectations of these values you have the right and the responsibility to challenge us. Likewise, we expect no less from you! I believe that when each of us looks back on our accomplishments five and ten years from now, we will be proud of what we have accomplished through this simple vision that we have now put into place."

I concluded my remarks by telling my associates that I was proud to be able to serve with each of them on the Nestlé USA team and that I was completely dedicated to Vision 2000. And I was. This speech was significant to me because not only did it close each of our momentous two-day meetings, it began my twelve-year stint as CEO of Nestlé USA.

Beyond Vision 2000

Vision 2000, coupled with our 13–30–6 financial objectives (ROS-ROIC-adjusted cash flow), served us well for the next four years as we made progress on sales, profits, and market share. It was also a time of significant organizational adjustment to the concepts of teamwork and alignment.

As for our then-famous 13–30–6 financial goals, great progress had been made since inception, and by 2000 Nestlé USA had achieved 11–53–8 on ROS, ROIC, and ACF—a far cry from the 1994 results of 8–18–2. We had over-achieved on two of our three targets (ROI and ACF), and elected to invest more in our brands, which kept us from achieving our 13 percent target on return on sales by the year 2000.

My Executive Leadership Team and I had learned a lot since the launch of Vision 2000 in 1994. So by 1998, we knew it was time to refresh our vision with the objective of taking it to the next level. We also needed to add some qualifying comments to our eleven-word vision statement so that associates could understand the essence of what the vision was all about.

As a result, Nestlé USA's *Blueprint for Success* was launched in February 1999, replacing Vision 2000. Now, it is updated on an annual basis. I believe it has become our most important leadership tool, and some of our global counterparts agree. For example, PetCare South America, Nestlé in Germany, Zone Americas, and various markets in South and Central America have now adopted Nestlé USA's *Blueprint for Success* format for themselves. This was particularly gratifying, knowing how strongly independent these markets are in a very decentralized Nestlé world. I am convinced that much of the performance success we have achieved for the past seven consecutive years (ending 2004) is a direct result of the fine execution of the principals of this document.

The Blueprint for Success

The Executive Leadership Team was given the responsibility of composing the *Blueprint for Success,* just as it had been in charge of developing Vision 2000. The process required many hours of discussion, debate, and teamwork by all of the members of the ELT. Over the course of several months, we isolated ourselves from the rest of the company at our Regional Training Center in Seattle for several days at a time. It was a rigorous process that often brought to light subtle and not-so-subtle differences in each of our philosophies and management styles. In the end, the process was very valuable, however. It gave everyone on the team equity in the vision and built trust between all of the team members, which proved invaluable once we began communicating the *Blueprint* to the entire organization.

When the process was complete, the entire ELT was proud of the new Nestlé USA *Blueprint for Success.* The vision statement had been updated and the supporting material had been designed to communicate how each associate could make a difference, each and every day, in taking Nestlé USA to the next level. Several of the characteristics of Vision 2000 were carried over to the new document. For example, we wanted the *Blueprint for Success* to be simple yet specific, adaptable to every division in the company, and understood by everyone within the organization. The first *Blueprint for Success* can be seen in Figure 6.3 and Appendix B.

The Nestlé USA *Blueprint for Success* is comprised of four basic elements:

- Vision—what we want to be in the future
- Strategies—how we intend to get there
- Measures—how we know when we are there
- Core Values—what we believe in

In addition to these four elements, each year we identify six to fourteen initiatives that support the four basic strategies. While the strategies have remained the same since the launch of the *Blueprint for Success* in 1999, the initiatives continue to

FIG 6.3

change based on market demands and circumstances. Also included in the document are the cultural drivers of the organization—teamwork, alignment, passion, and balance. These drivers are so vital to the successful execution of the *Blueprint* that they are discussed in detail in the next chapter.

The Vision

The ELT had worked diligently to craft the original vision: to be the premier diversified food company in the United States. The statement was succinct and broad enough that it could last over time, yet there was confusion over the words "premier" and "diversified" that required it to be rewritten.

A better company vision had been staring us in the face for decades; we just hadn't recognized it. The source of inspiration for our new vision was the famous Nestlé jingle that had appeared in television commercials almost fifty years earlier. Research shows that even after a hiatus of five decades, consumers can still identify Farfel, the hand-puppet dog singing the famous slogan, "N-E-S-T-L-E-S, Nestlé makes the very best . . . chocolate."

And there they were. Three simple words that would become the guiding words of our company—"The Very Best." For years we had possessed unbelievable brand equity in the words of that uncomplicated jingle, but we had never capitalized on it. Now was our chance. Our new vision statement became: "To be the very best food company in the United States." In fact, I have signed every letter that I have written and sent out over the past eight years below those three words—"The Very Best."

At eleven words, the vision statement was so simple and to the point that the team wrote a qualifying statement to frame the vision in context of the larger company. This effort was as time-consuming as the vision itself, and I believe it gave the entire team comfort that we were communicating a united sentiment that added value and enhanced the vision itself.

Vision—What we want to be
"To be the very best food company in the United States"

- We will not rest until our associates, our consumers, our customers, our suppliers, and our shareholders judge our companies to be the very best.

- All of us at Nestlé must strive each and every day to bring our consumers the very best food and beverages. We have a passion for food and the role it plays in the moments that bring people together—whether it's a weeknight dinner, holiday celebration, or nutritious food for the family pet.

- Nestlé USA makes delicious, convenient, and nutritious food and beverage products that enrich the very experience of life itself. That's what "Nestlé. Good Food, Good Life" is all about.

The Strategies

As we considered the strategies necessary to support the vision, we needed to take into consideration the direction of Nestlé S.A. to be certain that our strategies were consistent with the overall worldwide direction of the company. In 1997, newly appointed Nestlé S.A. CEO Peter Brabeck introduced to the worldwide company his four strategic pillars for international competitiveness in his first *Blueprint for the Future* document. They were:

- Low Cost/Highly Efficient Operations
- Renovation/Innovation
- Product Availability
- Consumer Communication

The ELT embraced Peter Brabeck's ideas on international competitiveness, and it became obvious to all of us that these strategies were as perfectly suited for the U.S. market as they were for the world at large. The one exception was that Nestlé USA would focus more on the renovation/innovation component rather than on lower costs and higher efficiency, since we really had those items under control because of our massive restructuring in the first half of the 1990s. These four strategies were adopted with enthusiasm and really made our Nestlé USA *Blueprint* a document that was fully supportive of our company's worldwide direction.

Our challenge would be to take these four global strategies and put them into context for the U.S. market so that they could be understood by our entire organization. This process generated many hours of discussion and caused a great deal of "word-smithing" by the ELT team. The final product, however, was well worth it. We created strategies that have stood the test of time and have remained constant since the first *Blueprint* was released.

Strategies—How we intend to get there

- **Renovation/Innovation:** Continuously revitalize our brands and products and, through portfolio management, prioritize and launch successful new products that drive consumer needs.

- **Product Availability—Whenever, Wherever, However:** Invest to ensure that our brands and products are in the widest distribution possible.

- **Consumer Communication:** Increase communication spending and effectiveness (especially advertising), communication integration, and co-marketing activities to drive demand and strengthen our brand loyalty.

- **Low Cost/Highly Efficient Operations:** Follow a disciplined continuous improvement process that optimizes our ability to fuel our growth initiatives by improving our delivered product costs and reducing overhead costs.

The Measures

A critically important part of the vision and the *Blueprint for Success* is the ability to monitor our progress toward achieving our objectives. We had to come up quantifiable terms to define "the very best" so that we could actually determine when we achieved this status. We chose three key metrics by which to measure our success and failure—growth, market share, and profits.

Growth, our first measure, was easy. Nestlé S.A. had a worldwide goal of achieving +4.0 percent real internal growth (RIG)—sales after pricing adjustments have been taken out. This is a very objective, straightforward, and easy-to-calculate measure of growth. A target of +4.0 percent RIG represents, on average, a growth factor above the food industry's average in the United States.

Market share is clearly one of the most important measures of the success of any brand, and consistent improvement in market share regardless of category growth is one of the key measures of success in the consumer marketplace. When you monitor market share, you always know where you stand versus your competitors in the eye of the consumer.

Profits are of course essential for the health of any business. Today we are measuring profits in terms of earnings before interest, taxes, and amortization (EBITA).

All of these measures have worked well over the years because they are easy to measure and monitor on a continual basis. They are also metrics that all employees can understand and to which they can relate. All employees can monitor how the company is performing by getting weekly updates on our Web site and during monthly team meetings. Finally, these measures gave us the opportunity to align our company goals specifically with our incentive programs for maximum impact.

Measures—How we know when we are there

- **Growth:** Achieve a minimum of 4% real internal growth every year.
- **Market Share:** Increase market share in our strategic categories and on our strategic brands, always striving for the number one position.
- **Profit:** Maintain annual percentage increases that exceed the increase in sales. Nestlé financial measures are individually important but collectively they should result in increasing economic profit.

Core Values

We were fortunate at Nestlé that most of our acquisitions over the years were of companies that had cultures similar to that of Nestlé S.A.'s culture. Granted, there existed many subcultures throughout Nestlé USA because of the wave of acquisitions in the 1970s and 1980s, but the overall values and guiding principles of these companies were not that divergent. One might even argue that had a company possessed values that were so in conflict with the overall principles of Nestlé, it would likely not have been brought into the Nestlé family.

Just as we had worked to create a vision statement, we also worked to define our culture and capture it in words. The result was a culture statement that accurately describes the corporate culture of Nestlé USA Our culture is described as fast and performance-driven, consumer- and customer-focused, competitive on the outside, and united and aligned on the inside. This description is so important to the company that it appears as part of the *Blueprint* document itself.

The selection of the six core values for Nestlé USA was a relatively easy process for the team. We agreed that the *Blueprint* core values would be exactly the same values we had agreed upon when we launched Vision 2000 in 1994. The more difficult realization was the fact that once formalized in an official *Blueprint* document, our organization would hold each one of us responsible for "walking the talk." It's one thing to talk about core values and a culture statement, but it's another to be held accountable to this set of values in every activity and every decision we make each day. The key is living the culture and understanding that it is either reinforced or contradicted every day depending on how members of the ELT and our associates throughout the organization conduct themselves.

People   Selecting people as our first core value was quite natural for all of us. We did this recognizing the awesome responsibility we all had to live this value every day and in every way. Diversity and risk-taking were the two major thoughts supporting people as our most important core value. Our focus on diversity follows in the footsteps of Nestlé S.A., which has a marvelous track record in that area, with most business meetings in Vevey resembling a gathering of the United Nations. While diversity is more of a traditional value, risk-taking was something that we wanted our employees to know that we recognize and value. Taking risks on the job is not always easy for employees because they often fear the consequences of taking a risk that doesn't pay off. We believe our associates need to feel safe in

---

Core Values—What we believe in
Our core values are consistent with and support
The Basic Nestlé Management and Leadership Principles

- **People:** People from all diverse backgrounds are our most important asset and the source of our competitive advantage. We operate in teams where we expect and reward responsible risk-taking.
- **Quality:** We are dedicated to continuous improvement in the food safety and quality of every product we make and in every activity we perform.
- **Brands:** Our strong brands ensure the continuity of our growth and profitability. Their support is every associate's responsibility.
- **Consumers:** Our reason for being is to understand, anticipate, and best fulfill our consumers' needs.
- **Customers:** We appreciate and support the critical role our customers play in getting our brands to the consumer while working closely together to achieve mutual value.
- **Performance:** We are all committed to achieving our financial and strategic objectives while adhering to our core values.

---

their jobs, knowing that taking a calculated risk, even if it fails, does not automatically put their jobs in jeopardy.

Quality The second core value we identified was quality. We all understood the critical need for quality as it relates to the safety and value of our brands, but we extended the concept to include every activity we perform in the organization, even how we answer our phones.

Brands Recognizing the vital role brands play in our ability to reach our goal of being the very best food company made it logical to include our focus on brands as one of our core values. Our brands are our vehicle for communicating to our consumers what we stand for in terms of quality, personality, and consumer benefit. All associates, whether they work in the factory making product or work in the warehouse shipping it to stores for on-time delivery, play a role in creating the brand image. We know that without strong brands there can be no growth or profitability.

Consumers and Customers   The order of these two core values would have been reversed in rank of importance fifteen years ago, but today there is no question that the consumer is the most important part of the equation. Meeting consumer needs has to be a top priority, and knowing who our most valuable consumers are through Nestlé's Consumer Relationship Marketing program must be a preoccupation of our entire organization. We now understand that knowing who our current customers are is even more important than knowing who our potential new users are because our current customers consume more Nestlé products per capita. That said, we also have to continue working hard to maintain strong relationships with our customers if we expect our brands to thrive.

Communicate, Communicate, Communicate

The topic of values was so important to the future of the company that I spent a lot of time talking to our associates about it. During the meetings in which I introduced the *Blueprint for Success,* I detailed all of the different sections of the document and covered the vision thoroughly. However, I focused heavily on our corporate culture. Without a strong moral and cultural foundation, the vision itself would likely never be accomplished.

In *Leading Change,* Kotter warns of the dangers of under-communicating the vision by a factor of ten, one hundred, or even one thousand and sacrificing its acceptance through the ranks of the company.[2] Therefore, I followed the philosophy that just as you think you've repeated your core message ad nauseam, the employees throughout the organization are just starting to "get it." To this day, I preach the *Blueprint* and expect my executives and managers to do the same. Figure 6.4 features some of the specific values-related topics I highlighted as I presented the *Blueprint* to our associates, when we first launched our core values in 1994.

Initiatives

The front page of the *Blueprint* focuses entirely on the future of the company and how to get the organization there in the most efficient manner. The back side of the one-page document, however, is about today and the present. It focuses on tactics, or short-term actions, that must be executed in support of the longer-term strategies this year. These are our initiatives. They represent the small step referred to in the ancient Chinese proverb that says, "A journey of a thousand miles begins with one small step." The *Blueprint* initiatives are made up of a number of small steps that collectively move the organization forward on the journey to reach its ultimate vision.

Since the inception of the *Blueprint* in 1998 and its launch in 1999, the vision, strategies, and values portions of the document have always remained the same. The one section of the *Blueprint* that changes each year is the initiatives that support our four major strategies. Each year individual company management teams and support groups meet to determine one to three initiatives they can implement to support each strategy. Each initiative is agreed to by consensus, which is important so that the entire team feels it is theirs and will support it accordingly.

Renovation/Innovation Strategy Several initiatives have been implemented to support our renovation/innovation strategy initiative, such as striving for a 60/40 percent (plus) consumer preference on leading brands. This entails consumer testing of our key brands against the leading competitive brand. If consumers do not prefer our brands 60 percent of the time or more, then a plan is initiated to improve the quality and/or appearance of the product in a short period of time. The "plus" is about adding a nutritional competitive advantage that competitors do not have to each brand. For example, Juicy Juice is 100 percent juice, whereas most competitive juice brands are 10

Figure 6.4
Describing Nestlé USA's Core Values to Our Associates
(My Personal Views)

People
- People are more important than systems. People, not systems, give us a competitive advantage.
- A factory doesn't make us successful! The people running the factory make us successful.
- We must support diversity because we live in a diverse society with diverse consumers. Diversity is good business pure and simple.
- People are the future of the company. Therefore, leadership must be involved in the selection of our future employees.
- We have a commitment to training and development.
- We want to empower people and we want to reduce layers—flatten the pyramid. Our bias is toward decentralization.
- We must promote high standards of integrity and honesty.

Quality
- Quality is everyone's responsibility—from the mailroom to the board room.
- We must eliminate activities that do not add value to the business enterprise.
- We must outsource an activity if it can be done more effectively on the outside.
- It means becoming low-cost producers in key core areas.
- Speed, innovation, and continuous improvement are required for us to achieve our goals.
- Sharing ideas leads to best practices, which lead to greater overall quality.
- We need to benchmark against our competition and industry leaders.
- Quality must become a way of life for all our associates.

Brands
- We must have a clear brand equity policy—how do we optimize brands by leveraging them across companies?
- Senior leaders must be personally involved in advertising development.

(continued)

Figure 6.4 (*continued*)

- Spend enough money on media to build a brand, but recognize that success in advertising depends much more on the quality of creative and the right choice of media than on the amount of money spent.
- Nestlé's image should be reflected in our advertising and our advertising should reflect our image.
- We do not want "sleazy" advertising or to appear on sleazy or violent programs. Nestlé is a family-oriented, wholesome company with wholesome, quality brands.
- We represent excellence in new product development and a commitment to nutritional superiority.

Consumers

- Understanding our Most Valuable Consumers (MVCs) is a must.
- Customer service must be a top priority.
- Adding real value to our products can create a meaningful difference between our competitors and us.
- We must focus on developing products that meet consumers' needs.
- We must develop products that create new consumer needs.
- We must be good corporate citizens by giving assistance to those communities in which we operate.

Customers

- We must understand our customers' needs and expectations.
- We must respond to them rapidly and effectively.
- Our trade customers need to be seen as our strategic partners.
- We need to work with our customers to grow profitably the categories in which we compete.
- We must leverage the Nestlé brand with our customers.
- Nestlé USA needs to mean more to our customers than just the sum of our operating company parts.
- We need to be a leader in ECR—efficient consumer response.
- We must manage our SKUs in a responsible way.

percent to 15 percent juice, and our Good Start infant formula contains unique "comfort proteins."

Other initiatives Nestlé USA has implemented to support this strategy include:

- Launching specific new products
- Accelerating new products prioritization and R&D relationships
- Implementing the Consumer Relationship Marketing program
- Achieving marketing superiority

Product Availability Specific initiatives designed to support our product availability strategy include:

- Investing more in increased channel visibility and penetration
- Leveraging the Nestlé portfolio to exceed the overall growth results of the ten leading retailers in the categories in which we compete
- Improving supply-chain performance such as customer service, forecast accuracy, and factory attainment levels

Additionally, product availability includes initiatives to increase retail distribution, and to increase food service channel penetration. For example, we created a specific program for the convenience store channel for Nesquik in plastic bottles, which has really increased our presence in "C-stores."

Consumer Communication The consumer communication strategy has been supported by initiatives such as:

- Increasing media advertising spending
- Exploring alternative communication opportunities
- Making trade spending more consumer-directed
- Optimizing multi-brand promotional programs

- Continuing commitment to community involvement, such as the adopt-a-school program
- Having all marketing plans embrace Consumer Relationship Marketing activities

The implementation of the "Good Food, Good Life" worldwide corporate sentiment was a major initiative of the 2002 *Blueprint for Success*. The phrase captures well what Nestlé stands for throughout the world. This expression or the sentiment is used whenever possible on all appropriate corporate communications.

Low-Cost, Highly Efficient Operations The low-cost, highly efficient operations strategy has been supported by a number of efficiency initiatives, including:

- Achieving overhead targets—selling, general, and administrative
- Delivering factory optimization targets
- Implementing BEST

The implementation of Business Excellence Through Systems Technology (BEST), which was designed to link many of our systems for better efficiency, was successfully completed in 2003.

As a result of improving factory operations, hundreds of millions of dollars have been saved and major improvements in factory safety have been realized over the past six years. Also, lost time accidents were reduced from double-digit levels to 3.6 or less per 200,000 man-hours worked and we reached "best in class" status. Additionally, in 2000, we launched an SG&A exercise, conducted by a committee of top executives to evaluate every function to determine exactly where cost reductions could be made. As a result, we have reduced overhead expenses by a significant amount in recent years.

Global Considerations for the *Blueprint for Success*

As CEO of Nestlé USA, it is my responsibility to make sure our goals are always in line with what Nestlé SA is doing. During Helmut

Maucher's tenure as CEO of Nestlé USA, his contribution was primarily to build Nestlé S.A. into the largest and most powerful food company in the world. Peter Brabeck's task was quite different. Peter's challenge was to make this huge company into the most efficient and the best marketing company in the worldwide food and beverage industry. Peter began by personally establishing a relationship with Wall Street and other important share markets. As CEO, Peter traveled with his team to New York, London, and Zurich each year to meet with analysts and answer their questions and concerns about Nestlé. Communication with the financial community had historically been handled by the CFO of Nestlé SA.

A major investment that was designed to help take full advantage of the company's size was Peter's launch of project GLOBE in 2001, which when fully implemented worldwide in 2007 and 2008 will give Nestlé management the ability from a systems point of view to slice and dice the business and to look at it any way it wants geographically, by business or by product type. GLOBE systems will be an enabler for Nestlé USA's new Nestlé Business Services Company, allowing this effort to reach its full savings and efficiency potential through common systems implementation.

Critical to Nestlé's future is Peter Brabeck's vision to transform Nestlé from an agriculture-based company to a "nutrition and wellness" company. With consumers living longer and desiring good quality of life in their older age, foods and beverages can play a major role in fulfilling this need by providing wholesome products with special nutrients. These concepts and more all get worked into our Nestlé USA *Blueprint.*

Executing the *Blueprint for Success*

The *Blueprint for Success* was a success in its own right. For the first time, Nestlé USA had put all of its goals and guiding principles into words and onto a formal document. But a plan, regardless of how excellent it may be, will be deemed useless unless it is executed well. That became our next challenge. Identifying and explaining our vision, our strategies, and our core values were not enough. All of these elements had to be executed and attended to throughout the organization. Our *Blueprint* was the catalyst for tremendous dialogue among our associates, and I found myself answering the question, "What does all of this mean to our organization?" Here are some of the things I said in response:

- It means that as an organization we have to be "lean."
- It means that we have to have a "sense of urgency" in everything we do.
- It means that we cannot be embarrassed to make a profit!
- It means that we have to eliminate internal politics and concentrate all of our energies on competition.
- It means that we have to be smart and hire smart people.
- It means that both sales and profits must be consistently above the industry average for long-term success.

The Nestlé *Blueprint for Success* has played a vital role in Nestlé USA's excellent performance results for almost a decade because it helped the leadership of the company focus all Nestlé associates on a small list of initiatives designed to support the major strategies, that in turn supported the vision to become "The Very Best Food Company in the United States." From 1998 to 2003, Nestlé had one *Blueprint* for the entire company, but in 2004, we took it one step further and had each operating company develop an individual *Blueprint* specific to their business. Of course, the vision, strategies, and values remained the same, but the specific initiatives varied from the overall company *Blueprint*. This made the *Blueprint* even more valued by employees. And in 2005, a Nestlé USA corporate *Blueprint* was established for the support groups and the company as a whole.

The exciting thing about a vehicle like the *Blueprint for Success* is to experience it in action—to watch it come to life. But bringing it to life required constant communication about the many elements of the *Blueprint* to everyone in the organization. The company leadership took to heart Professor Kotter's admonition to "communicate, communicate, and communicate the vision and then communicate it some more." And we are still-ing preaching it every chance we get to all of our associates.

The "Vision Thing" is an invaluable tool in the hands of an organization, if leadership can bring it to life through strong communications and execution. Each of today's more than twenty thousand associates has a copy of their own company or department's *Blueprint*, and you can find wall-size copies of the *Blueprint for Success* prominently displayed in factories, distribution centers, and sales offices all across the United States.

In short, this is the one document that employees can go to daily for direction. As a leader, you know you're on to something when associates have a miniature copy of the *Blueprint* in their wallets for handy reference. Or when associates use the *Blueprint* to set objectives and plan meetings. Or when they quote from the *Blueprint* and hold themselves and others accountable to its core values. In essence, the *Blueprint* has forced folks to "walk the talk" or lose credibility throughout the organization.

20/20 Vision

Looking back over ten years to the Vision 2000 meetings and the speech I gave in August 1994, I can say that I am proud of what the Nestlé USA leaders and associates have accomplished working as a team. In 1999, this team took the Vision to a whole new level with the launch of the *Blueprint for Success*—a document that improved the focus on the vision, the strategies, the core values, and added measures for sales, profits, and share, and initiatives to support each strategy.

Although it is always risky to declare victory prematurely, still a strong case could be made that Nestlé USA had indeed achieved a status of "premier" and could even be considered by many as "The Very Best Food Company in the United States" by 2004. Consider that when Nestlé USA was established in 1990, it had a return on sales ratio of a little over 8 percent, while the same statistic for the top ten companies in the U.S. food industry was 13 percent. At the end of 2004, on a U.S. GAAP adjusted basis, Nestlé USA operating profit was above the industry average at 16.9 percent (the industry average was 15.1%), as seen in Figure 6.5. For the seven-year period from 1998 to 2004, all of Nestlé USA, including the Purina acquisition, achieved organic growth of over 10 percent. Operating profits on the total business increased on average over 24 percent per annum, which was more than triple the average of our competitive set of food companies.

Separately in 1997, Nestlé USA was voted by *Fortune* magazine as the "Most Admired Food Company in America." *Fortune* did not even mention Nestlé USA in its top ten survey from 1990 to 1995, but that changed when it made the top ten for the first time in 1996, entering as fifth on the list of impressive companies. From 1997 to 2004, Nestlé would be voted by *Fortune* magazine as the number one "Most Admired Food Company" seven times, falling to second only once, to PepsiCo. In each of the past eight years, Nestlé USA has been ranked by *Fortune* as more

FIG 6.5

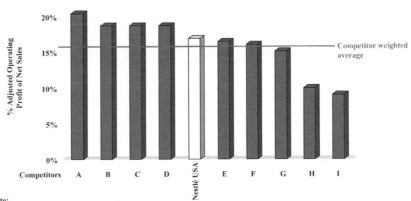

2004 GAAP Adj. Operating Profit as % Net Sales for Major U.S. Food Companies

Note:
Competitive margin estimates are from data in the public domain to compare trends in ongoing operations.

admired than great American companies like General Mills, Kellogg, Sara Lee, H.J. Heinz, Campbell Soup, and ConAgra.

The *Fortune* ranking doesn't pay the light bills, but it has been a good barometer of our progress in achieving our vision. It has also been invaluable in recruiting the brightest students on college campuses around the country and for keeping the morale of the organization strong and upbeat.

Yes, I think Nestlé USA associates can look back over the past ten years and be very proud of what they have accomplished. I believe that they are indeed living and breathing the Nestlé USA Blueprint for Success and have achieved the vision of becoming "The Very Best Food Company in the United States of America." Now the challenge is to keep the train rolling—full steam ahead!

FIG 6.6

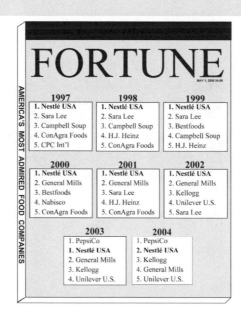

CHAPTER 7

Culture Drivers

How do we define corporate culture at Nestlé USA? I believe it is the manifestation by employees of the core values of an organization. A company culture is demonstrated by similar traits being exhibited by a majority of the employees a majority of the time. These distinctive culture traits are bred into the organization over time either naturally or in a strategically planned way. A strong company culture can give employees a certain comfort zone of predictability and identity in an uncertain world. A strong company culture takes years to build, but can be destroyed quickly through thoughtless acts by key people or groups within an organization that are in conflict with the company's established culture. In a sense, the culture of a company is its DNA or its personality.

Perhaps the most vivid example of living and breathing a strong corporate culture is Wal-Mart. And if there is one place to see it in action, it is at the Wal-Mart shareholder annual meeting. I attended one of these shareholder meetings several years ago. Over seventeen thousand Wal-Mart associates, shareholders, financial analysts, and members of the media gathered at the University of Arkansas' Bud Walton basketball arena in Fayetteville for this extravaganza. Wal-Mart told the audience about its activities in the United States and around the globe with presentations and video vignettes showing Wal-Mart associates doing what they do best—serving their customers.

139

The beauty of the meeting was how involved the audience became and how each person began to live the Wal-Mart culture. Every twenty minutes or so, prompted by the presenter, all seventeen thousand of us would cheer at the top of our lungs, "The Customer Always, Umph!" If you didn't know the difference you would have thought you were at a college basketball game rather than a Wal-Mart annual shareholder meeting.

While many companies now also declare that the customer is number one, Wal-Mart's focus on the consumer permeates everything it does. The company truly lives what it proclaims. Wal-Mart's relentless focus on the customer is demonstrated not only in the company's relentless cheer, but it drives how the company does business. For example, consumers really want a price/value relationship in the products they buy and consume. That is why Wal-Mart adopted its Every Day Low Price (EDLP) strategy. It is also why Wal-Mart sees itself as "the buying agent for the consumer." Wal-Mart has a consumer orientation that is obvious from the moment a Wal-Mart greeter meets you at one of its more than three thousand stores across the country.

Nestlé USA Corporate Culture Drivers

The challenge at Nestlé USA was to find the appropriate "culture drivers" to support our core values of People, Quality, Brands, Consumer, Customers, and Performance. Culture drivers are specific activities, actions, and attitudes of individuals or groups within the organization that reinforce the core values of the organization, thereby creating a certain culture. The goal was to get all of our associates to believe in the values that we, the Executive Leadership Team, believed in strongly.

We gave much thought to identifying the most appropriate culture drivers. While I talked to people both inside and outside of the company to solicit their opinions, I also relied on my instinct to identify a group of potential culture drivers. I finally settled on four culture drivers that seemed to fit today's business environment perfectly. They were also four culture drivers to which I could wholeheartedly commit. I often think of how much progress we could have made earlier had I figured out this combination years before.

The four culture drivers that we believe bring our core values to life are:

- Teamwork
- Alignment
- Passion
- Balance

These four culture drivers work together to create a culture that is fast and performance-driven, consumer and customer focused, competitive on the outside, and united and focused on the inside. That, in a nutshell, is the nature of Nestlé USA today.

Teamwork   *The Wisdom of Teams* states that "Teams outperform individuals acting alone or in larger organizational groupings, especially when performance requires multiple skills, judgments, and experiences."[1] We found this to be absolutely true. The principles found in *The Wisdom of Teams* became key tools in transforming Nestlé USA into a high-performance organization. The idea that teams always, always out-perform individuals became a rallying cry for those of us in leadership at Nestlé USA. But there was a clear distinction that now-retired Nestlé S.A. chairman Helmut Maucher always made, which was "Teams with leaders always out-perform individuals." These were wise words as well.

The value of teamwork came to me early in my career as a young first-line supervisor. I was responsible for the management of six sales people—a team in name only. I had been a sales rep myself only a few months earlier. My "go-to" sales representative was a star performer; he really could sell. Interestingly, however, we achieved little overall success. My star performer, as good as he was, could not carry the entire team. As trust was established between members of the group, each would commit to a certain share of the overall goal of the group. Some of the less experienced reps could only take five or ten percent of the group target, but others could take their fair share and more to help achieve the overall target. The reps shared success stories, assisted each other, and held each other accountable in order to achieve the team goals.

By working together, the team achieved results that could never have been achieved by six individuals working on their own. We often see this scenario played out in team sports. Good teams, often with average talented players, win against teams with star players that do not engage the power of their overall team.

I grew up in a company that was in many regards a one-man show—Carnation's chairman and CEO, H. E. Olson. Sure, teamwork could be found in some isolated pockets of the company, but the prevalent style was individualistic and internally competitive, exemplified by our leader at the time. A silo approach was often the result of internal competition that was fostered by a variety of company leaders. A great deal of competitive energy was expended internally between key individual executives and departments. For example, departments like sales and marketing were often pitted against each other. The tricky part was that the Carnation sales organization was more powerful than marketing, which meant that sales called the shots. Sales often claimed that they could not achieve higher levels of distribution unless marketing increased trade allowances. They argued that since advertising spend was far below industry norms, they were unable to force distribution with enough "pull power." In the end, the overriding problem was that too much energy was lost internally as opposed to being applied against the outside competition.

In the late 1980s, after Nestlé acquired Carnation, there was a changing of the guard, and Timm Crull replaced H. E. Olson, who retired. Timm was more team-oriented than Olson, but ran into team-building obstacles. When Nestlé USA was initially formed in 1990, Crull inherited a group of companies and CEOs who were very competitive and ambitious, thus making teamwork in the new organization difficult initially. After a number of key management changes in the early 1990s, teamwork at Nestlé began to evolve as vestiges of the old holding company business model, Nestlé Enterprises, transitioned into a new parent company, Nestlé USA. The new company now had a single financial target and operating plan to achieve. New incentive programs, such as a phantom stock option plan, also encouraged a certain amount of teamwork.

A significant further breakthrough on teamwork occurred in 1997 when Nestlé USA transitioned from a set of independent companies to four major companies that shared resources, such as a common retail sales organization and much of the distribution apparatus, as was discussed earlier.

While teamwork began to flourish in the ranks, it was still in its infancy in the Nestlé Executive Leadership Team. This is not unusual among corporate executive ranks, however. Katzenbach and Smith point out that "The complexities of long-term challenges, heavy demands on executive time, and ingrained individualism of senior people conspire against teams at the top."[2] This was true at Nestlé USA, where the top executives were so accustomed to performing as individuals that it was difficult for them to function as a true team, let alone as a high-performance team.

The team mentality began to take hold of our eighteen-member Executive Leadership Team in 1997 and 1998. We launched our annual *Blueprint for Success,* which set a group vision, company strategies, performance measures, and core values. The group began to share best practices in order to achieve the group targets, against which they were now evaluated. For example, rather than approach trade customers on an individual division or company basis, the sales organization united to approach each account on a team basis, avoiding a "divide and conquer" philosophy often used by the trade. Terms of sale were standardized, for example.

The ELT aligned behind the common *Blueprint* objective to achieve a minimum 4 percent real internal growth each year, which was above the industry average. To achieve this target required a high level of cooperation among the four companies. There were times during which one company leader would make an extra effort to surpass his target so the overall group could achieve its goal. What made this particularly gratifying was that this extra performance was voluntary—no additional bonus was paid for over achievement. It was done strictly for the good of the group. There developed a sense of mutual respect, accountability, trust, and commitment to a common purpose.

The Nestlé USA ELT began to excel as a high-performance team by 1999. Over the next seven years, we experienced a consecutive string of more than 4 percent real internal growth, tripled industry profit growth, and increased market share on the vast majority of our key brands. Achieving this level of superior performance year after year was critical in making teamwork a way of life at Nestlé USA.

As a leader, I realized that at the end of the day no one can legislate teamwork. Teamwork flourishes only when trusting relationships are built within a group over time through solid communication. Good communication leads to trust; trust leads to teamwork; and teamwork results in improved performance. Even so, high-performance teams at the top are difficult to build, as is so accurately described in *The Wisdom of Teams*.

Trust is an elusive phenomenon that requires value-added communication over a period of time. Trust comes from one's willingness to become vulnerable for a common good. If I understand that you have a certain talent or quality necessary for our team's success, and I have certain talents that also can help the team, then certain interdependency and trust grows as these qualities are nurtured and developed. Trust is the glue that holds teams together.

I believe that Nestlé USA's leadership team has earned the trust of most of our associates. This trust is measured against leadership's consistent modeling of the core values of the *Blueprint*. If we state that people are our most important asset, then leaders have to "walk the talk" and demonstrate that they really believe in people.

Alignment   Alignment occurs in an organization when individuals and teams ally themselves to fall in line behind a particular argument or cause to produce a certain desired outcome for the organization as a whole. Successful organizations find methods to encourage the majority of their employees to get off the sidelines and into the game. This ability to get organizational alignment behind a short list of critical activities is essential to focusing the organization on its vision.

At Nestlé USA, I credit our associate's alignment behind the various initiatives in the *Blueprint for Success* as the major factor in the record performance experienced in recent years. Our accomplishments are proof that once the organization understands the overall game plan, it's easier to line up the players for successful execution.

Clear communication is required for achieving alignment within an organization, but too many layers of management at the top can hinder this process. The most productive years at Nestlé USA occurred after I eliminated the COO layer from the company's structure upon the departure of our COO in 1999. I believe that when the top team members all report to the CEO, alignment is much easier to achieve because there is no intermediary through which information has to be filtered before it gets to the top. I also believe that the COO position in most companies is not only unnecessary but is an impediment to good communication and alignment. I have come to this conclusion through my own experience and also through observation. The one exception to this rule is when the CEO is close to retirement and his or her successor can be appointed COO for a defined short period of time to gain closer exposure to his or her future post.

The best CEOs surround themselves with strong leadership teams. In order to build these leadership teams, key executives such as the CFO and other functional heads must have the ability and the willingness to align behind the CEO's vision for the company. The new structure at Nestlé USA brought about full alignment of my direct reports—a critical success factor for the company. It was a good lesson, regardless of timing.

Alignment is certainly not exclusive to top management. True alignment includes everyone in the organization. The question becomes how to reach everyone with the same message and sense of urgency and motivate them to support a single plan. Many companies are able to generate critical alignment when they operate in a survival mode where employees realize that their company and their careers depend on each and every employee executing certain tasks to perfection. Performing out of this type of fear is inherently much easier for companies in trouble than it is for successful companies that must create a burning platform in order to raise performance levels.

At Nestlé USA another "dragon to slay" became the annual Nestlé worldwide target of 4 percent real internal growth, which was above the industry average. Nestlé is a very decentralized company by individual market, and here in the United States we like our independence. Our organization understands that our high performance allows us to maintain that independence. Anything less than 4 percent RIG and a minimum double-digit profit growth would be seen as a possible cause for international intervention that would likely lessen our independence in some way. It is often said in Nestlé circles that "Good performance brings independence, but poor performance brings help."

With our *Blueprint* in place and with a new leadership structure ready to go in 1999, all of the associates throughout the company had the opportunity to align themselves with the CEO and with each other. For the first time, everyone could stand united in one mission. All Nestlé USA associates know what Nestlé's strategic goals are and they are taken into consideration each day as the associates plan their activities. In essence, we have twenty-two thousand associates all across the United States off the sidelines and into the game, trying to accomplish the same thing.

That is both the beauty and the power of the *Blueprint for Success*. Creating the *Blueprint* and then implementing it have been far more than an academic exercise. As the CEO, I strongly believed that bringing the *Blueprint* to life in a meaningful way would both release and focus the energy of thousands of associates across the country and enable them to achieve great things.

Passion   Another characteristic that drives the culture at Nestlé USA is passion. I like to think of passion as a powerful emotion that shows itself in individuals with boundless energy and enthusiasm for a particular idea or thought. Passion is something that exudes from within people who are emotionally connected to a particular cause, idea, or thing. And when it is expressed to others, it can be "catching."

I have never met a truly successful person in any field of endeavor who did not have a passion for what they were doing. True success in life is never measured just in power or material possessions. Success is fulfillment realized when one makes a significant contribution to an effort and has the satisfaction of knowing that his or her contribution made a difference to the overall result. Therefore, it is logical that in order for employees to feel true success in their jobs, they have to feel some degree of passion in their work. That might be passion for the actual job and activities they perform, passion for the people with whom they work, or passion for the company and its overall mission. It might also be passion driven by personal motivations such as the satisfaction of performing well.

Personal passion among individuals is so important to a company's development and growth that it should be a prerequisite for employment. I believe that passion for life is often just as important to recognize when recruiting new employees as are aptitude and interpersonal skills. If an employee arrives on the job with a lot of passion but with fewer skills, I believe they will learn the skills they need to fulfill their passion for success. However, if a person arrives on the job with the required skills but does not have any passion for what he or she is doing, that employee is less likely to develop the level of passion that is required to impact the organization significantly. I believe it is easier to teach new employees the skills they need to perform a job than it is to teach the passion they need to really make a difference. It is the job of the organization, however, to do as much as it can to foster, stimulate, and maintain the passion of its employees. In fact, it is easy to measure passion by the enthusiasm and dedication that an individual gives to any task. At Nestlé we make every effort to place associates in activities that bring out and foster their passion to win. We are willing to relocate the best and the brightest to assignments that stimulate the passion that is necessary for success.

Each of my four brothers and one sister have had their individual successes, but I have often thought that Don, one of my younger brothers, was possibly the most successful of all of us based on the passion he has for his job. Don joined the Marine

Corps during his college days and did two tours of duty in Vietnam, eventually as a crew chief on a CH-46 twin rotary helicopter. This was the Marine Corps' smaller version of the Army's CH-47 helicopter used so extensively in Vietnam in the 1960s. This machine was susceptible to being shot down with small arms fire due to the exposed hydraulics and the risk of the pilot or a rotary blade being struck by rifle fire. Don was shot down twice, and has never discussed his wartime experiences in detail with any of us, but I always knew he had a passion for the Marine Corps. After Vietnam, Don became a police officer in our hometown of Chattanooga. His service as a policeman was exemplary and marked with displays of courage and professionalism. Don loves his work and has been recognized for heroic efforts beyond the call of duty. Today, he is retired in Chattanooga, but continues to work in the security industry.

I originally took a position with Carnation Company because of the passion for the company and business that was exhibited by those who interviewed me. It was clear to me that Bob Stevens, the college recruiter for Carnation, and later Timm Crull, both felt an excitement about and dedication to Carnation that I had not seen with other companies that visited the University of Tennessee campus. It was that passion that caused me to turn down seven other job offers with more lucrative compensation packages and ultimately choose to go to Carnation. Because everyone I met from Carnation, from the first interview to the last, demonstrated that same type of passion, I knew Carnation would be an enjoyable place to begin a career.

The passion exhibited at Carnation clearly left an impression on me, especially as I later saw it converted into an espirit de corps that I believe gave Carnation, and later Nestlé, a unique competitive advantage in the marketplace. I adopted a similar enthusiasm for excellence, which has spanned my career, from my very first job to my position today. I can honestly say that I am still excited to get out of bed every morning and arrive at the office shortly after six a.m. to see what challenges the day will bring.

It is always a thrill to be involved with individuals who have boundless enthusiasm for their career and for life in general. Just think how boring life would be without people who have a passion to win at whatever activities they undertake, whether professional or personal. When you surround yourself with the positive, passionate people, you'll find their energy to be both contagious and motivating. Thus, passion is a valuable asset to any team working toward a united goal.

The most important advice I could give to anyone entering the workforce is to search for a career in an area that you really enjoy. Never let yourself be overly attracted to the monetary rewards of a position; there are many other areas to consider. If you do not like the job and what it entails, no amount of money will make it fun in the long run, and life is too short to spend it doing something you don't like. On the other hand, when you find a job doing something you enjoy and are passionate about, the financial rewards will usually take care of themselves.

Balance   The first three culture drivers at Nestlé USA—teamwork, alignment, and passion—are very important to creating just the right work environment in which our associates can thrive. However, the culture of the company would not be complete were it not for the final culture driver—balance. Whereas the first three drivers are more common both in the workplace and in business literature, balance is foreign to most business enterprises, yet a vitally important element in the corporate culture equation.

What do I mean by balance? I describe it as a satisfying mix of life activities and relationships both in and away from the workplace.

The reality is that a balanced life is absolutely essential to having a healthy and highly productive career. Although it has been in vogue in the past to be labeled a workaholic, we instinctively understand that the workaholic is not only compulsive, but also psychologically unhealthy. Being a workaholic can jeopardize one's health and personal relationships, and it can limit an individual's perspective, which is a valuable tool for anyone in a leadership position. Paradoxically, a strong work ethic is one of the most admired traits for any businessperson to exhibit. If an employee has a satisfying personal and community life, all other things being equal, then chances are good that he or she will bring a positive and receptive attitude to work each day.

There are five basic aspects of a balanced life that I believe support this key culture driver, as seen in Figure 7.1, and I always talk about them in the order they appear.

Spiritual   While I think it is wrong to impose one's own spiritual beliefs on subordinates or peers, I believe it is essential for people to have some degree of spirituality as part of their life. As a Christian, my spiritual beliefs are an important part of every activity of my day. In terms of principles, it would be impossible for me to separate my spiritual life from my business life. It is critically important, however, that I perform my business responsibilities in a manner that support the values of the business from a secular point of view.

In the Bible it says that Christians are to give to Caesar what is Caesar's and give to God what is God's. As a Christian, I am bound to obey the law of the land and conduct the business in the best interest of the shareholder. While I would be willing to share my beliefs and my faith at the appropriate time and place with someone if he or she requests, the workplace is not the

FIG 7.1

Elements of Balance

Spiritual   Family & Friends   Career   Community   Hobbies

right place for religious activity. Individuals approach spirituality in their own personal way, and I believe this must be fully honored to protect the integrity of the corporate environment.

My personal spirituality evolved over the years as I began a spiritual journey in my early thirties, which culminated in my baptism at age thirty-eight. During this evolution, I came to appreciate that Christianity is not a highly structured religion or church denomination, but rather a personal relationship between man and God, via Jesus Christ. Because of this evolution, I understand and respect each individual's right to believe his or her own personal religious convictions, whatever they may be. Personally, I have found that a very simplistic and personal approach to spirituality and Christianity works best for me.

My spiritual foundation does give me comfort in my role as a leader. I feel an awesome responsibility for the decisions that I must make each day that affect the lives of our Nestlé associates and their families. Sometimes when you make the right decision for the company as a whole, it results in displacement and pain for some individuals, and this is always a bitter pill to swallow. But knowing that I am trying to do the right thing and praying for guidance when I have to make these difficult decisions is comforting to me.

Family and Friends Relationships with family and friends are essential for leading a balanced life. The positive benefits of healthy interactions with people we care about and people who care about us cannot be overemphasized. It is these relationships that provide the experience and develop the interpersonal skills that are so important in the workplace. Ongoing interaction with family and friends fosters personal growth and gives us confidence to stretch our wings. It is also these relationships that provide the support systems we rely upon during good times and bad.

I am never very impressed with bosses who are not flexible enough to allow their subordinates time off for family activities. As long as the requests are reasonable, I believe that this kind of flexibility pays off in the long run by creating loyalty among employees. My experience has always been that good associates always reward their employer with above-average effort when they are given reasonable latitude in areas of family and friends.

I have to admit, for most of my career I have struggled in this area, putting career ahead of family and friends. My children were certainly a high priority, but I did not spend the individual time with my lovely wife that was necessary to achieve the optimal degree of balance in my life. I am fortunate that Carol has had a lot of patience with me and has cut me much more slack than I ever deserved. Carol and I never took time for a vacation for just the two of us. We usually spent those rare vacations with our children in the United States, visiting relatives in Texas or Tennessee. And as far as siblings and friends go, I did not devote the time or effort needed to cultivate first class relationships with these groups either.

At one of my Work Out meetings with some of our junior people a few years ago, I began to understand that I was making real progress in this area. But one associate that I barely knew got right to the crux of the matter. She challenged me to walk the talk! She reminded me that I talk about balance a lot, but from her observation, she could not see it in my life. Everyone knows that I am usually in the office at least by six-thirty a.m. and that I rarely leave before five p.m. In recent months, I have tried to change my ways, making a pact with myself to spend no more than eight or nine hours in the office each day. My response to her was that I had always been a morning person, even during my middle management days, and therefore always went to the office early. It is my favorite time of the day. I also explained that I always took the time to attend my son's activities, like Little League baseball games, and my daughter's dance recitals. If I needed to leave the office at three p.m. to make those commitments, I did, even if it meant taking work home. I went on to explain that today I try to get home earlier so my wife and I can enjoy dinner together and have a few hours at the end of the day to enjoy each other and have meaningful talks about family and friends.

Spending time with your children is all about involvement. Sometimes I was able to involve them in what I was doing and sometimes I became involved in what they were doing. In my earlier management days, in the late 1970s, my daughter Robin, who was all of six or seven years old, would often accompany me to the office on Saturday mornings. She had fun pretending to be my secretary, busying herself with papers and even running small errands for me. These wonderful times resulted in a very strong bond between Robin and me that has lasted a lifetime. Maybe the hot fudge brownies with ice cream that we would share at Bob's Big Boy across the street had something to do with it too. When my son Jeff was ten or eleven years old, we spent hours throwing the baseball and going to coaching and batting practice. He played first base and also pitched. If he had an afternoon game when I was in town, I tried to attend to give him moral support. As with Robin, these were great bonding years for us that paid great dividends later in life.

Today both Robin and Jeff have children of their own and being grandparents is a joy that one cannot imagine until that day arrives. Spending time with our grandchildren is becoming a pleasure that Carol and I look forward to and enjoy as often as possible.

Whenever I *have* invested time and effort into relationships, they have been rewarding. I was fortunate, on several occasions, to work for bosses that became friends. One such man was Carlos Represas, who became a good friend over the ten years that we worked together. Carlos' three children, Leticia, Luciana, and Carlos, Jr. are wonderful individuals and reflect well on their parents. Carol and I were very honored to attend the weddings of both Leticia and Luciana in Mexico City and Carol and I were pleased to host Carlos and Leticia at our son Jeff's wedding in Los Angeles.

Overall, I'm not proud of my shortcomings in this area of my life, and I certainly cannot make any excuses for how I handled relationships with family and friends. But at the time, there always seemed to be a good reason for the choices I made and for how I spent my time. Does that sound familiar? If it does, take a step back and look down the road of life. Then ask yourself this question: In the end, what will I remember the most? Another late evening at the office or watching my child in the school play or taking my wife out for a romantic dinner? That is where balance comes in—knowing when to prioritize work over family and friends in order to complete an assignment versus knowing when to prioritize family and friends over work in order to have complete relationships.

While today I feel I am much better in developing and nurturing relationships than I was even ten years ago, I still struggle to put in enough time and effort that lasting, meaningful relationships require. However, renewing several relationships in the past few years has been very rewarding and is encouraging me to expand this area of my life.

Career   Although career should never be the most important aspect of life, I believe it should not be lower than number three on your scorecard. Unfortunately, when career is exclusively the most important aspect of your life, it is difficult to experience fully the other important aspects of life—spirituality, family and friends, hobbies, and community involvement. Ironically, these four areas, which workaholics often neglect, greatly impact an individual's personal growth and career development on a long-term basis.

At first, ranking your career third in order of importance might seem counterintuitive to being professionally successful, but in actuality, it is likely to make your career flourish. The reality is that a healthy spiritual life and a healthy relationship with family and friends, coupled with hobbies and community involvement, make you a more interesting and a more knowledgeable person. A more well-rounded person is better able to interact with associates, thereby enhancing job performance and creating greater job satisfaction. Conversely, trouble in personal relationships and low levels of social involvement outside the workplace inhibit personal growth and can lead to stress that typically drains a person's energy and creativity.

For most of my business career I have instructed my subordinates to work hard above all else. Years ago one of my favorite sayings was, "You get paid based on what you do from eight to five, and you get promoted on what you do from five to eight." If there is one thing I've learned over the past ten years, however, it is that the most important thing is what you accomplish and not the amount of effort put forth. You might have heard others phrase it as working smarter rather than working harder. At the end of the day, it is results that count.

Having said all that, however, do not lose sight of the fact that good results seldom come from mediocre efforts. An important part of personal and professional growth is finding the right balance between the number of hours spent working and the quality of performance and results achieved. Passion for our careers plays a vital role in how we approach our jobs, how much satisfaction we derive from them, and the degree to which we attain that elusive balance we all need to be happy and successful.

Community   At Nestlé USA we donate time, money, and support to the communities in which we work and live. Working on the behalf of the community is an American tradition that goes back to the Judeo-Christian foundation of our country. The American approach to philanthropy has today become part of the fiber of American business. Nestlé USA's major community involvement is the Very Best Volunteer Adopt-a-School program, which is closely associated with Reading Is Fundamental (RIF). Nestlé associates volunteer their time at a school in the company's local area. Usually these schools are disadvantaged and are in need of extra financial support and assistance with primary and secondary education programs. Nestlé USA volunteers serve as mentors, teacher's helpers, and tutors. They conduct field trips and book fairs, and even become pen pals. In the early years of this program, Carol and I were both very personally involved as volunteers. We would visit fifth and sixth grade classrooms to talk to students about civics or health and hygiene. In the past few years, we have been replaced by thousands of Nestlé volunteers all across America. Our associates volunteer each month for a maximum of twenty-four hours per year with paid time off at one of Nestlé's forty-eight adopted schools in communities all across the United States.

The Nestlé Very Best Volunteer Adopt-a-School program has been a successful and rewarding venture for our associates and for our adopted schools. When we designed this program, our thinking was that even though the United States has some of the finest universities in the world, many of our own students cannot qualify to attend them. The graduation rate at inner-city schools was dropping, thereby creating a dearth of students qualified to go on to college. Our goal was to provide local schools with volunteers and some financial aid in order to help these children stay in school and graduate. Everyone involved in our associate volunteer program—the volunteers, the teachers, and the students—are winners. In the beginning, teachers were a little skeptical about the long-term viability of the program; they were concerned that Nestlé would lose interest after a year or two of involvement. But after ten years, Nestlé USA is more committed today to the Nestlé Very Best Volunteer Adopt-a-School program than ever, and we continue to add volunteers and schools to our program each year. We are proud to say that the teachers and principals of our adopted schools give the program and our volunteers rave reviews.

Nestlé is a strong proponent of education. As such, it was awarded the United Negro College Fund's most prestigious award in 1998. On behalf of all my associates at Nestlé USA, I was honored to receive the Frederick D. Patterson Award from UNCF's president and my good friend, Bill Gray III. Nestlé was recognized for its work in primary and secondary education and its commitment to UNCF, where we were a charter member through Carnation Company. Nestlé and UNCF continue to believe that indeed, "A mind is a terrible thing to waste." It was a privilege to be recognized with the Patterson Award alongside two outstanding actors, Sidney Poitier and Samuel L. Jackson. I learned that evening that Samuel Jackson and I grew up in the same hometown, Chattanooga, Tennessee. Out of our partnership with UNCF we have a commitment to UNCF scholarships for high school graduates from any of our forty-eight adopted schools across the country.

A number of Nestlé executives give to their communities by staying involved in education at the university level, participating in programs sponsored by their alma maters. Since 1996, the

Executive-in-Residence Program at the University of Tennessee has been my favorite place to teach and encourage talented students looking to enter the workforce and begin their careers. Many of these students go on to become loyal Nestlé consumers and some even become Nestlé employees. In 2001, I was honored to receive the University of Tennessee College of Business' Distinguished Alumnus of the Year Award for Nestlé's work at the University of Tennessee and in education in general. I accepted it on behalf of all of my Nestlé associates.

Community involvement can also extend beyond the programs sponsored by your employer to include opportunities in which your family can become involved. My wife Carol shares my passion for giving back to the community, and I am very proud of the contributions she has made. Carol has raised over four hundred thousand dollars for an inner-city private school in Pasadena, California, primarily through celebrity basketball games held during the past several years. This particular school was part of Nestlé's volunteer Adopt-a-School program, but she took it one step further and identified another way to help. Additionally, she helped to design the school's classrooms and learning center.

In 2001 and 2002, Carol co-chaired L. A. Alive!, the largest charity event in the city of Los Angeles, which benefits the L.A. Philharmonic. This event helps support the Fund for the Performing Arts, which gives school children the opportunity to participate in the arts. The L. A. Alive! event is so large that it is held every two years. In 2001 and 2002, the auction and dinner raised a record $1.6 million for a 23 percent increase over the previous event.

Carol has also been a board member of the Los Angeles YMCA and has supported the National Kidney Foundation and the Second Harvest Food Bank of Orange County. She is also a member of the Los Angeles Costume Council and a Daughter of the American Revolution. Carol received a commendation from the County of Los Angeles for her work in the community. In 1998, she also received a proclamation from the U.S. House of Representatives in recognition of excellence, achievement, and commitment to the community.

Carol and I feel blessed and grateful to have the time, talent, and resources to contribute, and we try to be good stewards of what we have. Charitable activities in the community and at church help create balance by making us aware of the needs of others. By focusing on the needs of others, we gain purpose, connectedness, and we also serve God.

Hobbies Having hobbies that are both physically and mentally stimulating can help you balance your career responsibilities and keep you fresh. Sports activities, photography, fishing, games, and numerous other activities can be a great way to recharge your batteries and refresh the body and soul. This allows you to take on business issues with a renewed vigor.

I am not impressed with workaholics who never take more than a few days of vacation time away from the office during a given year. I believe it is important to take all the vacation time you are allotted, and if possible, take at least two consecutive weeks away one time each year for travel and other hobbies. This is a lesson I learned the hard way over the years.

One of the hobbies that I have enjoyed greatly over the years is photography. Because I worked as a young boy in a pharmacy, I had access to cameras and film at discount prices. My family and friends enjoy flipping through the twenty-five photo albums I have filled with pictures dating back to 1947. Through the years, I have recorded the most important events in our lives, and I find it fun to go back and relive some of those events. I have found that although your family changes quickly over the years, you can freeze those treasured moments forever through the lens of a camera.

Several years ago I organized a photo album to recognize Carol's life. I embarked on this project to express visually my gratitude for her many accomplishments and creative talents. I wanted to do this so Carol would have something tangible that reflects the respect and admiration I have for her many talents. This project was to be a surprise for our thirty-first anniversary on September 26, 2001, and I worked on it over several months, whenever I found an hour or two of alone time. I must say that going through hundreds of photos spanning the past fifty years was an emotionally uplifting journey for me. I realized that Carol was an even more remarkable person than I had understood before I started the project.

Needless to say, Carol was thrilled with the final product, which included photos with my added comments from early childhood to recent times. The album included shots of Carol as an actress, artist, clothing designer, seamstress, real estate agent, restaurateur, movie producer, educator, poet, board member, fundraiser, grandmother, mother, and most importantly a wonderful wife. And she still believes she has not done enough in life!

Putting together this album and developing my favorite hobby in a new direction encouraged me to create similar "This Is Your Life" photo albums for Robin's thirtieth birthday and Jeff's twenty-fifth birthday. I wanted each of my children to know that I had recognized their talents and was proud of them. It also helped me relive each moment and each epoch of their lives. I am just pleased that my hobby of photography over the years had such a wonderful payback for me.

Culture Drivers—Putting It All Together

The four Nestlé USA culture drivers of teamwork, alignment, passion, and balance have been instrumental in establishing Nestlé's core values over the past eight years. The core values of people, quality, brands, consumers, customers, and performance have been literally brought to life at Nestlé through the company leaders and their dedication and attention to emphasizing the four culture drivers at every opportunity. Nothing has more impact on associates than seeing senior leaders carrying out the core values and culture drivers through their words, actions, and behaviors.

Perhaps one of the greatest compliments and indications that our Nestlé USA team got it right when we made people our number-one core value was when Nestlé SA chairman Helmut Maucher and CEO Peter Brabeck asked for my input as they were drafting Nestlé S.A.'s very first Basic Nestlé Management and Leadership Principles. First published in 1997, the document lists people as Nestlé's greatest asset, incorporating suggestions I made based on the values of Nestlé USA and making them worldwide policy.

Recognition of people as the company's most important asset was a major statement for a European company to make—especially one that was built on its expertise in technology and brands over a one hundred and thirty year period. Bottom line, this philosophy is more American in expression than it is European, which became apparent at many of our international workouts. Whenever we had a mixed group of Americans and Internationals I would ask the question, "What is our most important asset?" Invariably the Internationals would answer, "Our brands!" The Americans would answer, "Our people!" Eventually, I was able to point proudly to page 8 of the Basic Nestlé Management and Leadership Principles, where they could see for themselves the value that Nestlé worldwide places on its people. I like to leave these meetings letting them ponder the thought that "Over the years people have invented brands, but when was the last time a brand invented a person?"

Chapter 8

Corporate Leadership

I have had the great privilege of working for and being exposed to many different leaders, including Pete Haynes, H. E. Olson, Henry Arnest, Timm Crull, Helmut Maucher, Rudi Tschan, Peter Brabeck, Carlos Represas, Paul Bulcke, and many others. Each of them helped shape me as a leader and influenced my leadership style. Some were great motivators, communicators, and delegators, while others were great listeners, agents of change, and decision makers. Some were outgoing and charming in their delivery, while others were more quiet and subtle. But the one ingredient that they all possessed was the ability to create loyalty and dedication to their visions among their employees. They were each masters at building a bond of trust with their subordinates, and I consider myself fortunate to have forged a bond with each of them.

Leadership is not a science, although enough has been written about it that one might think it is. And leadership is not an art form, although the amount of creativity involved in being an effective leader at times can be surprising. I think leadership is a combination of skills (from communication and marketing to finance and operations) and intuition. Most people will not end their careers holding the title of CEO, but they will at different times and at different levels have to lead others, as project leaders, division leaders, or even as leaders in the community. That is one reason why we can't seem to get enough information on the topic of leadership. But there is no magic formula for becoming a strong, effective leader—only guidelines and case studies based on what has worked for others in the past. Many great leaders do share some common characteristics; however, each leader is different, which makes what great leaders say about the topic valuable, interesting, and applicable to most people's careers and lives.

The Difference Between Managers and Leaders

Even with a flood of books, seminars, and classes about leadership, most companies, ironically, still do not foster a true leadership environment. I believe this is due to the common notion that there is a fine line between leadership and management. In my opinion, nothing could be further from the truth. True leaders demonstrate behaviors that are much different from managers, even if the managers are good at what they do.

There are several variables that distinguish management from leadership. According to John Kotter, management is "a set of processes that can keep a complicated system of people and technology running smoothly."[1] These processes include functions from planning and budgeting to staffing and problem solving. Leadership, on the other hand, "is a set of processes that creates organizations in the first place or adapts them to significantly changing circumstances."[2] In short, managers are consumed with the processes required to achieve something, while leaders are much more interested in achieving the results than the specific processes that will get them there.

From my experience, leaders have a vision for the future and an understanding of what intellectual and capital resources are necessary to direct an organization and get them there. Leaders may not precisely understand the most efficient process to achieve the vision, but they understand the human talents that are required to develop the strategies and the initiatives that are necessary to achieve the vision. In other words, they know how to put the right team together that can develop a plan or a blueprint for a successful realization of the vision.

In contrast, a good manager focuses on the processes needed to control an organization. He or she understands how to recruit and hire, budget, plan, and do the typical problem solving that is necessary to smoothly run an organization. Managers can be very good at managing an ongoing operation that is not in crisis mode, but often fall short when out of the box creative solutions are required to shift to a new business model.

According to Kotter, "Leadership defines what the future should look like, aligns people with that vision, and inspires them to make it happen despite the obstacles."[3] Similarly, I like to characterize great leaders as being both strategic and visionary, two attributes that would likely fall on any list of required leadership qualities. A leader must determine what he or she wants the organization to stand for in the long-term, and then set the strategies in place that will achieve that vision, which is exactly what we did when we created Vision 2000 and then the *Blueprint for Success.*

In addition to being visionary and strategic, effective leaders can also be very tactical. When Nestlé S.A. acquired Carnation Company in 1985, I was very impressed with Nestlé's strategic orientation. Nestlé had a detailed long-term plan that highlighted the goals, direction, and even some of the tasks of the company for the next three to four years. Personnel reassignments were sometimes made a year or more in advance, allowing for smooth transition periods. It was also not uncommon to schedule meetings over one year in advance. Some years ago I remember attempting to schedule a meeting for a key Nestlé S.A. executive with Wal-Mart's top management at its world headquarters in Bentonville, Arkansas. The appointment date we were trying to secure was over ten months in the future. The folks in Bentonville thought we had lost our minds; they couldn't believe we were planning visits one year out. At Wal-Mart they were still working on the next week's and the next month's schedules. Although this is just one small example, it does show the difference between a long-term, European, strategic orientation versus a short-term, tactical, American way of thinking. It also shows how various tactics can be executed in a long-term strategic manner.

Leadership has evolved over the years. In fact, if you had worked for me thirty-five years ago you would likely have described me as an autocratic manager. My early role models, like Carnation's H. E. Olson and ITT's Harold Geneen, were successful leaders in their times, but they were "command and control" autocrats. This style of management worked in the 1950s and 1960s, when the generational impact of the Great Depression still had a substantial effect on workers' general lack of security. Companies could depend on workers' loyalty throughout their lives, and a cradle-to-grave job experience was the norm across most businesses in the United States. As the Great Depression influence waned and as opportunity in the United States expanded in new industries, people became better educated and more mobile. Autocratic management styles became less successful. In the 1980s and 1990s, successful companies were more likely to be headed by enlightened Leader CEOs rather than Manager CEOs, like Jack Welch and his successor Jeffrey Immelt. These were leaders who were able to influence workers through good communication, delegation, and empowerment that built trust and encouraged teamwork.

Leadership Throughout the Organization

One of my personal goals at Nestlé USA, when assuming full responsibility as CEO in 1994, was to create and lead an organization that blended the best of Nestlé's European long-term strategic thinking and planning with Carnation's more American short-term tactical execution orientation. We spent the early 1990s consolidating the company by rationalizing our factories and businesses. We divested or closed half of our seventy factories over a fourteen-year period. We divested seventeen businesses over this same period. Helped by these efforts, we began to realize significant improvements in performance results from the back half of the 1990s. We achieved real internal growth and EBITA (earnings before interest, taxes, and amortization) growth significantly above the industry average each year.

Joe Weller

During this process, Nestlé USA not only achieved great performance results, but we began to experience true leadership throughout the organization. The presidents of the various operating companies, Brad Alford of Nestlé Brands, Pat McGinnis of Nestlé Purina Pet Care, and Stephen Cunlitte of Nestlé Prepared Foods Company, executed their responsibilities in an exemplary manner, as did their direct reports. In fact, the outstanding performance results of the past seven consecutive years can be, in large measure, attributed to the outstanding group of Nestlé USA leaders in Glendale, Denver, St. Louis, and Solon. It goes without saying that a separate book could be written on the individual leadership accomplishments of Brad, Pat, and Stephen. These three CEOs made my job easier, more interesting, and very satisfying. Working with each of them has been a wonderful experience and I will always feel indebted to them for their contributions.

But it wasn't only individuals who began leading the company more effectively—our high-performance teams kicked in, as reflected by key performance indicators. For example, our finance and M&A leaders guided, advised, and led their teams to a superb performance during this period of rationalization and reorganization. Additionally, leaders of other Nestlé USA support teams in finance, legal, information technology, and others also achieved best-in-class results to support the strategic areas of our business. Overall, our marketing and sales, manufacturing, and human resource leaders began to excel in ways that not only set a new standard for excellence within the company but also pushed the envelope of success in the industry.

Sales and Marketing Leadership   The sales and marketing teams had performed as separate units at Nestlé USA, until key executives recognized the importance of focusing on consumers and meeting their needs, and moved to create collaboration between the two functions. Until that time, marketing had most often taken a back seat to sales.

It was during a Work Out (described in detail later in this chapter) that a number of our middle-level marketing associates told us that they were only spending 25 percent of their time on

165

true marketing activities—the rest of their time was spent chasing figures or doing paperwork. I was shocked when I heard this. Other Work Out groups later concurred, and we made the decision to reverse this so that our marketers would spend 75 percent of their time on marketing. Although we did not want to become less of a sales and manufacturing company, we realized that our future success would depend on our ability to recognize and meet consumer needs. Marketing would have to be our key focus to be competitive in the new economy.

As a result, we began hosting Annual Marketing Summits in the spring of 2000, which were designed to bring all of our marketing people from our various companies together each year to talk about marketing issues with a focus on the consumer. In addition to discussing issues and hearing from outside speakers and ad agency representatives, these meetings facilitated face-to-face contact with consumers, enabling our marketers to learn firsthand what concerns are on consumers' minds and their thoughts about our products and brands. Through marketing excellence, the goal of the summit is to encourage our marketing teams to be champions of the consumer and to focus on the future. Ed Marra, Brad Alford, and Al Stefl have served as corporate sponsors of the Market Summits from their inception. Their leadership was the catalyst that made these gatherings so productive for our marketing associates.

It was at one of these summits that Nestlé USA formalized its focus on marketing by deciding to invest $10 million in consumer relationship marketing (CRM). We wanted to understand better who our most valuable and loyal customers are. With our new Nestlé Consumer Relationship Marketing program, we are constantly learning about the most effective way to engage our most valued consumer (MVC). All of these activities have not only created a dramatic shift in attitude toward marketing within the company, but they have also affected our overall sales effectiveness.

Nestlé USA has also shown leadership in the area of branding. Although Nestlé owns many well-known brands, some of which are featured in Figure 8.1, our ultimate marketing strength lies in the superior *collection* of brands under the Nestlé umbrella. Brands are something that we don't take lightly. We have seen how the consumer marketplace in Europe has changed in the past decade, as the traditional national brands have given way to the private brands of retailers like Tesco and Aldi. In the U.S., however, consumers value national brands; they look to them to deliver quality. In fact, they often measure the quality of a product by the brand on the label. For us, our brands act as shorthand for what our products stand for—great taste, great quality, and consistency. When a consumer buys a Stouffers, Lean Cuisine, or Nestlé product, she is putting her trust in us to deliver the quality she has come to expect from our food. By emphasizing the strategy of innovation, we help ensure that our brands will remain important and valued in the market. That is a primary reason for our focus on innovation.

Sales and marketing have performed at an exceptional level over the past seven years. I continue to be singularly impressed with the quality of sales leadership and execution by the Nestlé USA sales organizations and their food broker partners year after year.

Nestlé Business Services The business case for a shared service center concept was launched in late 2003 and provided Nestlé USA top management with convincing financial evidence to justify a Nestlé North American shared service center. The details of Nestle Business Services' evolution are outlined in Chapter 5.

As of June 2005, the NBS team, led by its president Dan Stroud, has completed the design phase for all four in-scope functions—purchasing, retail sales execution, transactional finance and control, and human resources. NBS's ultimate goal is to provide the right services to Nestlé operating companies at best-in-class costs.

The NBS effort is taking a phased approach and is proceeding right on schedule. One success story is that the team, as of this writing, had already contracted over $100 million in savings, which is the result of the Strategic Sourcing initiative to

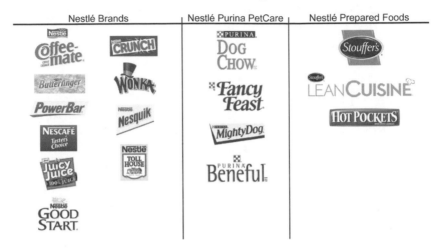

FIG 8.1

Nestlé USA – Key Brands

Nestlé Brands	Nestlé Purina PetCare	Nestlé Prepared Foods

leverage our size and share best practices when buying goods and services. Under Dan's leadership, NBS will be fully operational by Q1, 2006.

Consumer Communication Leadership   Our senior VP of communication, Al Stefl, brought Nestlé USA's entire consumer communications effort into the twenty-first century under his watch over the past twelve years. In fact, he has set the standard for communication VPs for Nestlé globally with his initiatives. In 1994, Nestlé USA established four new policies that would serve Nestlé very well for over a decade.

1. *Wholesomeness Policy.* This policy focuses on our attitude against violence and indecency in our communication with customers and consumers. The Nestlé image is family-oriented, wholesome, and responsible. It is imperative that all communication, including advertising, promotions, product placement, packaging decisions, and so on,

reflect this viewpoint and avoid situations that we deem inappropriate. Content to avoid includes:

- Excessive violence or unusual brutality
- Highly controversial subjects, extreme bias, bad taste, or questionable moral tone
- Any issues contrary to prevailing and accepted social mores
- Situations that appear to take an editorial position
- Story lines that reflect negatively on pets: mistreatment, medical uses, or violent or destructive animals

2. *Agency Management.* Advertising agencies are a U.S. resource. Agency management—the authority to hire, fire, assign, and compensate—resides with the Nestlé USA vice president of communications, who reports to me and works closely with the operating companies and Nestlé SA.

Strategic, creative, and media direction for the advertising are the responsibility of the operating companies, which also determine agency bonuses. Under Al's supervision, we reduced our advertising agencies from sixteen to five, which eventually, via acquisitions, increased to eight mainline agencies and two Hispanic-focused agencies. Since Al took his position in 1993, advertising spending has increased by $100 million per year in our core businesses alone.

3. *Advertising Involvement and Information Guidelines.* For routine matters, as soon as possible prior to airing or publication, all finished commercials and print ads must be forwarded to the U.S. vice president of communications for his information and review. It is his responsibility to ensure that I am aware of all routine advertising on a monthly basis.

I must be informed of all exceptions to the routine early enough to permit intervention. Examples of these exceptions are:

- Modification to brand positioning
- Change in advertising strategy

- A new campaign
- New product launches
- Use of personalities/celebrities
- Reference to competitors by name
- Price points
- Negative claims
- When the compelling, focal point is not the brand
- Any situation the operating company president/general manager feels merits early involvement

4. *Package Design and Other Visual Properties.* I must also be informed of all packaging and other design changes affecting branding early enough to permit involvement. It is the responsibility of the operating company president to keep me informed on a timely basis, with the assistance of the U.S. vice president of communication and the U.S. director of visual properties.

During the past ten years, Nestlé USA's advertising creative and effectiveness has improved significantly. Because of heavy submission requirements, we do not value or encourage awards, but still agencies will make the effort on their best commercials.

The Effie award is the most significant award in the advertising industry because it honors the one truly significant achievement in advertising—results. Nestlé's recent Effie awards include a 2003 and 2004 Effie for Coffee-Mate, a 2004 Effie for Nestlé Crunch, a 2005 Effie for Nestlé Good Start Infant Formula, and a 2005 Effie for Purina Cat Chow. I believe these awards are indicative of the discipline that Nestlé USA has put in place in recent years on advertising effectiveness.

Manufacturing Leadership   Manufacturing has continued to be an area of strength for Nestlé worldwide for over a hundred years, and Nestlé USA has really stepped up to the plate to become a leader in this area, generating cumulative savings of over $500 million over the past seven years. Some of these savings were importantly reinvested back in the business to drive overall quality and growth of the company. Safety teams in the factories improved OSHA recordable accidents from 18 accidents per 200,000 man-hours worked in the early 1990s to 3.6 per 200,000 man-hours in 2004. (The food industry average is currently 9.3 per 200,000 man-hours.) Even more impressive are our figures for lost time accidents. Nestlé USA's rate currently is 0.53 lost time accidents per 200,000 hours versus the food industry average of 2.2 per 200,000 hours. If this does not represent best-in-class, it is safe to say that Nestlé USA is today operating in the top quartile of food companies in the United States in factory safety. Additionally, out of the top nine food manufacturers in 2004, Nestlé USA had the lowest workers compensation costs, reflecting our best-in-class safety record.

In addition to these tremendous results, first-time quality on the production lines went from 95 percent to 99.8 percent with no major product recalls in the past three years, and our purchasing teams reduced the cost of goods to 43.3 percent, or almost seven percentage points in seven years, which was significant. Martin Holford, executive VP of technical and manufacturing, played an important role in these achievements.

Business Excellence Through Systems Technology (BEST)   BEST was launched in 1999 and was successfully implemented in 2003, with Kim Lund, who is now Nestlé USA's CIO, as one of the key leaders. The purpose of the BEST program was to achieve operational excellence through organizational structure, common business processes, and information technology for Nestlé USA. The program included purchasing, finance, customer service, transportation, sales, co-manufacturing, and information systems for Nestlé Brands and Prepared Foods. We estimated that the project would take over four years.

Overall, the BEST program removed complexity and simplified our operations in many areas of the company. Specifically:

- General ledgers were reduced from 9 to 1
- Information systems were reduced from 300 to 65
- Accounts payable sites were reduced from over 40 sites to 2 sites

- Points of order entry were reduced from 31 to 4
- Financial close process went from 25 days to 3 days
- Forecast accuracy went from 40 percent to 70 percent
- Customer service level increased to 98.6 percent from 97.3 percent
- Outstanding deductions were reduced
- Product returns were reduced
- Weeks of inventory were reduced
- Spoils rates were reduced

In summary, if Nestlé USA had not implemented BEST, significant benefit opportunities would not have been captured between 1998 and 2003, and the transition to GLOBE would have been more difficult due to the magnitude of change at one time. The BEST business case benefits of over $300 million were achieved by the end of 2003, which more than covered the cost of the program. Clearly, we have learned a great deal from the BEST project that is applicable to GLOBE.

Human Resources Leadership   One of the most dramatic improvements in a support function over the past ten years has been in the area of human resources. Executive Vice President Cam Starrett, who was recruited to Nestlé in 1990 with an HR background at Federated Department Stores, Avon Products, and Maxwell MacMillian publishing in New York, was the catalyst for this change. Under her leadership, we developed a first class human resources group, replacing a personnel department that had been born in the 1960s. Although the old system kept accurate employment records and completed the payroll function correctly, it had not been designed and therefore was not able to support the most important of Nestlé USA's new core values—people.

The goal of the new human resource function was to facilitate the business agenda every day, while keeping the focus on people. This demanded a new and much closer day-to-day collaboration between HR and the CEO. The HR group took on a true leadership position when it developed compensation and incentive programs that enabled Nestlé USA to compete far

172

more effectively and retain longer the best talent in the industry. It also developed programs that enable associates to use a standardized menu approach to selecting the benefits that best suit their individual and family needs.

We also involved HR more intimately in the succession planning process. To begin this process, annual discussions are held to identify leaders, with high priority placed on diversity because of the increasing number of women and minorities in the workplace and in the marketplace. The focus on people as a core value has impacted how we promote, support, and even celebrate diversity within our company. Each year, we celebrate Black History Month with a series of events culminating in an outside speaker series. The celebration of Black History Month has attracted some of the top African American leaders in the United States to the Nestlé USA campus for lectures. Black leaders such as Andrew Young, Julian Bond, Rosa Parks, and Robert Johnson—among others—have spoken at this event.

In short, HR responded to the new direction of the company by helping drive alignment, building leaders not managers, and dramatically supporting the business culture of personal accountability and performance.

Nestlé University   One of the great shining stars of the HR group's accomplishments is Nestlé University, headed up by Claudia Horty, vice president of training and development. Nestlé University provides training courses for all managers including, importantly, leadership development training for high-potential executives. In order to take our existing training program to the next level, Claudia and her team focused on the components that would differentiate Nestlé University from other training and education centers.

We considered several options and decided to examine closely one of the true leaders in the area of corporate training and education—GE's famed Crotonville. After studying GE's model, we realized that with the right focus and dedication we could build upon the Nestlé Regional Training Center and create our own Crotonville. Today, Nestlé University's home campus is located adjacent to The Nestlé Regional Training Center

(NRTC), just outside Seattle, Washington. This one thousand–acre campus consists of housing, classrooms, and dining facilities to accommodate concurrent training and team building sessions. NRTC offers a wide variety of opportunities to our associates. In addition to management, legal, and information systems (IS) training, we also offer functional training. For example, we train first- and second-year marketing employees on how various products and brands are marketed at Nestlé. The component that was missing, however, was leadership training.

To develop this type of leadership program, we turned to Richard Vincent, who became director of executive development for Nestlé USA. Rich received his BS in psychology from Brigham Young University and his MS in management from Chapman University. He was a U.S. Air Force captain for seven years, specializing in leadership training, before entering the corporate world where he became a manager of training at Zurn/NEPCO in Redmond, Washington for three years. He joined Nestlé in 1996 specifically to help the company develop a leadership curriculum. This has been his focus for the past eight years.

The initial challenge we faced in developing Nestlé USA's leadership training was to determine the appropriate curriculum. We wanted a pragmatic, rather than an academic, series of courses, so we began by talking to accomplished leaders. We interviewed about two dozen successful leaders at Nestlé USA, and from those conversations, we created a list of the core competencies to include in our program. In the process, we also captured the "golden nuggets" and stories we would use later in internal case studies. We also interviewed leaders who had been less successful and identified competencies that would have enhanced their success or, at the least, averted setbacks.

From the master list of competencies we generated, we pared down the entries and organized them into clusters. These groupings became our Leadership Development (LD) classes. We ended up with ten classes organized into five units, and under each class heading we had a healthy list of concrete competencies to be reviewed and learned. By illustrating the relationship between the competencies, we were able to produce a universal model and framework for leadership development, as seen in Figure 8.2.

Next, we benchmarked against some best-in-class leader programs to determine how America's most prestigious institutions were teaching the material we wanted to offer. We sent Rich Vincent to Harvard, Wharton, Stanford, and other equally distinguished schools.

In developing these courses, we integrated the unique cultural aspects of Nestlé with the various learning styles of discussion-based learning and action learning approaches. Key leaders and a business steering committee reviewed the material, which produced buy-in throughout the company. Finally, we rolled out the courses with a senior executive sponsor for each course. I launched many course sessions myself.

Today, Nestlé University offers a variety of management and leadership programs, including:

- General Business Development
- Management Development
- Leadership Development
- Operations Management (supply chain maps)
- Marketing
- E-Learning
- Sales

Nestlé University has been a great success and will play a key role in determining the future of the company.

Community Leadership When I came back from Australia in 1992, we had a philanthropy department that was staffed with several people. We evaluated thousands of requests each year for contributions, from the YMCA to the Boy Scouts to numerous charities and Good Will projects. After review, we decided to eliminate the philanthropy department because we felt we needed to have a clearer strategy toward giving. A new community involvement strategy changed the way we approached corporate giving. We decided to focus on a narrowed list of programs and organizations that our employees felt good about and organizations that were congruent with the overall values of our

Figure 8.2
Nestlé's Leadership Frameword

Leading People
Leading people is the ability to unite individuals, make them believe in themselves and in what they are doing, so they push their limits and are encouraged to outperform. It implies actively demonstrating the behaviors which are consistent with Nestle Management and Leadership Principles.

Developing People
Developing people means helping individuals identify their short and long-term development needs, encouraging their individual learning by providing them with appropriate support.

Practice what You Preach
Practice what you preach means acting consistently with and embodying the Nestle Principles and Values, including "Walking the talk" even when it is difficult to do so.

Results Focus
The drive to meet or exceed stretching performance objectives and quality standards, deliver business results and continually find sustainable improvements to methods and processes.

Initiative
Initiative makes people act in a proactive way by doing things and not simply thinking about future actions. People with initiative not only react to situations but also anticipate future opportunities or problems, and act upon them well in advance.

Innovation/Renovation
People exhibiting this behavior challenge the status quo in a drive for improvement, and come up with new ideas to operate more efficiently. At a highly developed level, they act as "change catalysts" for the whole organization.

(continued)

Figure 8.2 (*continued*)

Proactive Cooperation

Proactive cooperation implies working collaboratively with others, demonstrating commitment to achieve group objectives, understanding the needs and goals of others and adapting one's own views and behavior when appropriate. It may involve the sacrifice of individual with a view to achieving the group objectives.

Impact/Convincing Others

Convincing others, either directly or using appropriate third parties, in order to get their commitment to ideas, projects or actions that are in the Company's interest.

Know Yourself

Knowing yourself is the ability to accurately identify and understand one's own strengths and improvement areas, understand their implications on one's effectiveness in the organization and take them into account to optimize performance.

Insight

Insight is the capacity to identify links between facts, ideas and situations which have no obvious connection with one another and to assemble them into a useful explanation. At a highly developed level, insight manifests itself by the creation of new ideas or the development of a long-term vision.

Service Orientation

Service Orientation is the desire to help and serve one's customers in a way that best meets their actual needs. It is shown in the efforts a person will make to understand the customer's expectations and needs, to provide them with high quality service for a long-lasting and mutually profitable relationship. "Customer" can be any person or organization the service is intended for (internal client, colleagues at all levels, distributor, consumer etc...).

(continued)

Figure 8.2 (*continued*)

Curiosity

Curiosity means people are open minded to learn more about environment things and people, by asking probing questions, or doing ad hoc research to get a better understanding of the context.

Courage

Courage is linked to people's confidence in their capabilities and judgment. It allows them to take decisions, or make choices while ascertaining the risks and being conscious of their responsibilities.

In support of Nestlé on the Move, effective with the Planning Phase for 2004, Nestlé in the United States transitioned our Performance Management approach to match the Nestlé global process—the Progress and Development Guide.

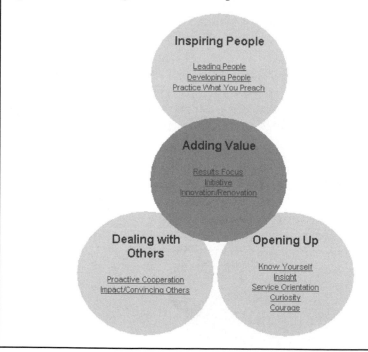

company. Not only were we were able to eliminate controversial programs from our giving list, but we were able to make larger contributions to the programs we supported, which in turn gave us a greater presence with our philanthropic partners.

Community involvement at Nestlé USA is now a major activity, as thousands of associates volunteer at one of Nestlé's forty-eight adopted schools in communities all across the country. Associates throughout the company have supported this program wholeheartedly. Once they get involved and begin volunteering, they feel good about themselves and about Nestlé. Community involvement through our Adopt-a-School program has been a great way to give a large organization a personal touch.

Nestlé USA as a Leader

The ultimate measure of leadership is how the company performs in the marketplace and against its competitors and how it is progressing toward its vision. On a worldwide basis, Nestlé S.A. has been cited for her leadership in the industry by being named *Fortune* magazine's "Most Admired Global Food Company" several years running. Our vision of becoming the best food company in the United States was validated when Nestlé USA was voted by *Fortune* magazine as "The Most Admired Food Company in America" in 1997, as described in Chapter 6. With that ranking, Nestlé USA was proclaimed "a leader," making our company the one to which others would be compared.

The *Fortune* survey is a good independent indicator of how the company is generally perceived because it registers the opinions of competitors, analysts, and business insiders who have good knowledge of their industries. The ranking is comprised of eight attributes that are voted on by customers, competitors, and the financial community. The eight attributes are innovation, employee talent, use of corporate assets, social responsibility, quality of management, financial soundness, long-term investment value, and quality of products and services. In the 2002 *Fortune* ranking, Nestlé USA was voted number one for the first time in all of the eight attributes measured.

Nestlé USA's consistent record of performance, as reflected in its consecutive superior rankings in *Fortune* and its superb operating results, is never the result of any individual. Rather it is always the result of many high-performance teams with strong leaders across all functional areas of the company aligning behind the Nestlé USA *Blueprint for Success.* In order for a company to become a leader in and of itself, it needs to exhibit leadership in the various functions throughout the organization. Nestlé USA has evolved as a leader in the industry in areas such as manufacturing and sales and marketing. A great CEO can't produce best-of-breed results if he or she doesn't have quality leadership throughout the organization.

CHAPTER 9

Leadership Qualities

As I mentioned earlier, not everyone will be able to become the CEO of his or her company—there just aren't that many CEO titles to pass out. But everyone at one time or in one aspect of life is likely to find himself or herself in a leadership position. This makes understanding the common qualities of great leaders valuable to all of us, especially those who are aspiring to be the leaders of the future.

When thinking about the excellent leaders I have had the honor of knowing over the past fifty years of work experience, I realize that they were all exceptional in the areas of vision and strategy. In addition, I have identified ten commonalities among the host of great leaders I have met along my career's journey. These ten leadership qualities separate managers from true leaders, as well as distinguish between good leaders and bad leaders.

1. Leaders Have Good Character

Clearly, the most important quality that a true leader must have is good character. Good character includes moral and ethical strength, integrity, and a good reputation. Honesty and trust are critical ingredients for successful interaction with a leaders' constituency. Character is so important that just a few years ago, it would have been a given on almost any list of leadership characteristics. But the Enron, WorldCom, Tyco, and Parmalat corporate scandals of late have sensitized us to the fact that we cannot assume that good character is a given. We must, however, expect and demand that our leaders have strong character because without character and integrity, all the other qualities of a good leader are compromised.

Leaders come in many different shapes and sizes; they can be autocratic, democratic, or something in between. Good leaders, however, are always trustworthy. They have the best interest of their followers at heart, and therefore, they work hard to make each of their associates successful. A solid, moral foundation (knowing the difference between right and wrong) reflects a leader's character, which in turn affects the degree to which others want to follow him. A strong conviction and a sense of fairness, on the other hand, go a long way in determining how forgiving people are likely to be should a leader make a mistake. Leaders always try to do the right thing. Even if they don't achieve the desired results or even if their decisions are deemed wrong in hindsight, people tend to be more understanding when they know a leader's decisions were based on the intent to do the right thing.

When considering character, I am reminded of President Clinton, who would likely have gone down in history as one of our better presidents, were it not for a serious flaw in his character, which led him to make several poor decisions. It is unfortunate for him and for our nation that these events, rather than the good works he did, are likely to become his greatest footnotes in history books. A person's good name and reputation are priceless; there is no amount of money great enough to repair a tarnished reputation. At the end of the day, it is the example that we set by our life that is the most powerful aspect of a person's ability to lead others.

2. Leaders Are Good Communicators

It is difficult to be an effective leader without being an effective communicator. A CEO has to do much more than be a visionary and work to create a long-term plan for the company. He or she must be able to communicate that vision—along with a host of other important messages—to the associates who must work to carry out the vision. As such, a CEO must be flexible in how he or she communicates. Sometimes a corporate leader has to relay information to employees, which requires him or her to explain strategies or technical information in a way that can be understood by employees in a variety of positions and from varied educational backgrounds. Sometimes a leader has to rally the troops, which requires knowing how to inspire employees and evoke emotion from them. And sometimes CEOs have to deal with the financial community and with the media, both requiring the ability to communicate serious matters with confidence and authority.

Good leaders can communicate effectively in all of these situations, altering their delivery depending on the audience. One day they may teach and inform their employees, much like professors do. (Jack Welch was a master at this.) And at other times they may motivate them, like Lou Holtz, Woody Hayes, and other great coaches of our time. Regardless of the situation, good leaders communicate the same message to everyone through all channels available to them. And when they speak, they speak with clarity, conviction, and authority. There is no doubt in the minds of the listeners as to the content or veracity of the message or the messenger.

One of the key elements in communicating effectively is repetition. I first learned about the role of repetition when I was a first-line supervisor in Houston, Texas back in the late 1960s. My small team of seven people never seemed to get the message on a particular strategy or policy until I had talked about it so much that I was sick of hearing myself discuss it. I finally realized that the team had so much information overload that repetition was the only way to break through the clutter. It wasn't that they didn't care, but they finally understood how important a particular issue was by the attention I gave it over time.

I was reminded of this experience as we began to communicate the *Blueprint for Success* throughout Nestlé USA. We found that in order for the vision to be adopted by the company, all associates had to understand the concept, and that took repetition,

repetition, repetition. Just as I was getting tired of hearing myself talk about the vision, our associates were just beginning to get it. Repetition of a message is key to the retention of its content.

Nestlé USA has taken major strides in the area of communication. We devised a comprehensive communication strategy that uses multiple tools and delivery platforms to reach our associates, thereby building and maintaining trust throughout the company. Executing our communication strategy helped to squash the grapevine that exists in many companies due to the lack of clear and timely communication. Once this strategy was in place, associates came to expect to hear directly from my direct reports and me. Some of our best communication efforts are discussed in the following sections.

Town Hall Meetings   During these regularly scheduled meetings, one of our other business leaders or I would face several hundred associates at a time for a very candid discussion of performance, problems, opportunities, and suggestions. No subject was off limits at these sessions—our associates could ask questions about anything. We talked about issues from strategy and vision to employee concerns and company values.

One key to the success of these meetings was the ability to establish an open and friendly environment early on. I broke the ice with a five to ten minute update on performance results against bonus targets and a few comments about current events. Then we would move into the real topics and issues on people's minds. My support staff always did a wonderful job of sensitizing and preparing me to handle some of the controversial issues that might come up, which saved me a few embarrassing moments over the years. Some Town Halls were better than others, of course, but I always felt that every associate had the opportunity to make a point or ask a question. Whether they decided to exercise that option or not was up to them. But the message was clear—we wanted and fostered an environment of open communication.

The *Blueprint for Success*   Another method that has been quite effective in giving direction to and building trust among our associates is the annual publication and distribution of the *Blueprint for Success,* as described in detail in Chapters 6 and 7 of this book. By giving associates their own copy of this one page document, they know exactly where Nestlé's leadership wants them to spend their time and effort. This has become a very empowering tool.

State of the Company Meetings   Nestlé USA had its very first annual State of the Company (SOC) meeting on March 3, 1995. This ninety-minute to two-hour meeting has now been held for eleven consecutive years at the beautiful eighty-year-old Alex Theater in Glendale, California, a short walk from Nestlé USA's U.S. headquarters. The theater is always packed with some fifteen hundred local associates, with a satellite hook-up to the other two major campuses of Nestlé USA's largest operations in Solon, Ohio and St. Louis. A video of the entire meeting is sent to all 110 U.S. facilities several days after the SOC meetings.

At the SOC meeting I review the accomplishments of the past year for major companies, divisions, and major product groups. The associates hear directly from me and other top leaders about every important aspect of the past year's performance and about future expectations. Each year I like to focus my comments on a topic I believe is important to the future of the company. This year (2005), I focused my comments on balance—one of our culture drivers. I opened up to our associates about some of my own personal beliefs about balance. Of course a leader can't dictate to employees how they spend their time, but I offered myself as an example of the importance of this culture driver.

Nestlé Times   Our company newspaper, published regularly since 1994, reports the accomplishments of associates, marketing, promotions, and business events over the previous six to eight week period. One of the features of this newspaper is "A Word from Joe," a column in which I talk about things that are on my mind. Through this column, I am able to send personal messages to all of our associates about interesting issues of the day, ranging from everything from Nestlé community involvement to the economic environment. This vehicle is so important in my ability to communicate to all of our Nestlé USA associates that I devote a lot of the final chapter of this book to it. I've also presented a few of my favorite columns in Appendix C.

What's In–What's Out The What's In–What's Out list became a very effective vehicle for communicating broad cultural message points to the organization through memorable sound bites. These sound bites were communicated in print in the *Nestlé Times,* electronically through our intranet, and orally through various other vehicles such as the annual State of the Company meetings. These lists defined what was acceptable and encouraged that behavior, and discouraged behavior no longer acceptable. For example, on the 2001 list, sharing information, time to think, and risk taking were "in," while keeping information to yourself, Friday meetings after ten a.m., and waiting for permission were "out." (See Figure 9.1.) The impli-

FIG 9.1   🐦 Nestlé

What's In	What's Out
100% Alignment with Blueprint	Sitting on the sidelines
Teamwork	Silos
Trust	Hidden agendas
Passion	Apathy
Balance	All work and no play
One-page briefing sheets	Thick decks
Straight talk and diverse opinions	Not speaking your mind or afraid to disagree
Sharing Information	Keeping information to yourself
Leveraging the global knowledge of Nestlé	Thinking we have all the answers
Leveling with employees about their performance — Performance Ranking	Not knowing where you stand
Personal accountability	"It's not my job"
Time to think creatively	Friday meetings after 10 a.m.
Quality work anytime, anywhere in or outside the office	"Face Time," staying late to impress the boss
Risk taking	Waiting for permission
Speed	Missed opportunities
Being a leader	Micro-managing, not letting go
The consumer!	Internal focus

cation was that if you were not adding value to the organization, you were falling behind. I had fun working with my communication team on the What's In–What's Out lists. We had several versions over the years that we revised according to what we wanted to communicate.

The Leadership Forum   This meeting was held twice per year to inform the top two hundred leaders of the company of our progress against our annual targets. My direct reports and I carefully selected high-potential leaders and always contributed to and participated in the agenda. We confronted tough issues, conducted workshops with external experts, and celebrated successes for two and a half days each summer, with a half day update meeting each winter.

The Internet   The Internet has also been very effective in communicating information to the entire organization quickly via the Nestlé USA Web site. Current sales results are posted on this site along with key information on products and current programs. Additionally, policy changes are posted in real time, so that employees can monitor company changes at all times and always feel connected.

In the end, no matter how sophisticated communication programs are, without consistent and solid communication from the leader of an organization, positive change is difficult, as the hearts and minds of the associates are never captured. Trust is the building block of respect, but it cannot be legislated. It must be earned over time. Leaders who have the courage to expose their human vulnerabilities in their communication platforms are usually rewarded with trust and loyalty from their employees.

3. Leaders Are Good Listeners

In addition to being great communicators, effective leaders need to be great listeners. If a leader really wants to know what is happening in the company, or if a leader wants to unleash the talent and creativity necessary to keep an organization competitive, he or she needs to have good listening skills. Perhaps King Solomon, from approximately 700 B.C., said it best. Solomon wrote, "He who gives an answer before he hears it is folly, and shame to him." He was considered to be the wisest person in the world during his time.

There are times that it is more important for a leader to listen than to speak. One of my most talented executives, who was extremely insightful and energetic, would constantly answer every question and address every problem or issue that would arise at our monthly Executive Leadership Team meetings. Eventually, some of the team members became somewhat frustrated and even hesitant to give their candid opinions for fear that they would be challenged by this bright executive.

One day, I took the executive aside after one of our meetings. I told him that while I respected his intellect and found his conclusions to be right a majority of the time, I wanted to keep an environment of open discussion and full participation. I wanted to hear everyone's response to each question raised and have the benefit of a number of different perspectives on the key issues facing the company. I asked him to hold his comments to the end of the discussion of each issue to allow everyone to participate and to allow me to get the entire team's input. Otherwise, I suggested, just he and I could have the meetings without the other team members. He got the message. After that, the meetings became more productive for everyone.

One way we foster an environment of participation and listening in Nestlé USA is with our Work Out sessions, which are held six or seven times each year at the Nestlé Regional Training Center located outside of Seattle. Our Work Outs, modeled after the sessions Jack Welch devised while leading General Electric, are designed to provide the CEO and other senior leaders the opportunity to listen to what a small group of about twelve to twenty middle-level executives have to say without their immediate bosses present. The primary topic of discussion is how to improve the company. The CEO's or assigned executive leader's job is to arrive during the middle of the exercise to listen to the team's recommendations and make a decision on the spot about the team's proposal, if possible.

Many positive changes have been made in the company as a direct result of listening to input from these bright mid-level managers and leaders in the making. As mentioned earlier, one of the most significant changes was shifting the company emphasis from a sales and manufacturing orientation to a marketing and consumer orientation.

Nestlé USA's monthly operations meetings have also become an invaluable listening tool to drive the business. Sales, marketing, and supply chain leaders identify current gaps between the high-performance targets and current estimates, and they approve actions to close those gaps. Each month the new current gap is identified and remedial action is taken to close it. This process has eliminated the need for typical revision of operating plans that used to occur each November and December.

Listening to Nestlé associates is not unique to Nestlé USA. Peter Brabeck holds his Nestlé Key Markets Conferences twice a year to listen to and gain input on a variety of strategic issues from his top nineteen market heads from around the world. While he gains valuable insights, these meetings afford Nestlé's key leaders the chance to influence policies and operating decisions on a regular basis. Attending these meetings is invaluable for the market heads to help them set the local market direction when they return to their respective markets around the world.

Henry Arnest, who affected almost every function and operation of the Carnation Company during his tenure as executive vice president, used to say it this way, "Sometimes the hardest thing to do is nothing." Since Henry was a very action-oriented, hands-on leader, I can only imagine how difficult it was for him to keep quiet on any subject, but he often did because he knew he would learn from listening to what others had to say. In turn, I learned this valuable lesson by listening to Henry.

4. Leaders Empower

A lot of lip service has been paid to the practice of empowerment in recent years, but companies often struggle with its implementation. I think of empowerment as delegating responsibilities and giving permission to individuals or teams carry them out. Sometimes empowerment can come from something as simple as recognition. H. E. Olson, with all his toughness, was a man who appreciated exceptional performance. I will always remember a note I received from him in 1984, which exemplified his approach to empowerment. Olson wrote:

> Dear Joe,
> The estimate of your sales managers, district managers, etc. for March of 9,000,000 cases is very good news and will give us a 10% increase for the first quarter, which is by far the largest increase we have had for quite some time. As I have previously mentioned to you, the way you and your fellows can call these numbers and their accuracy is phenomenal.
> H.E.O

Call it encouragement, or call it motivation. I remember feeling a complete sense of empowerment from these words of praise from the leader of my company over twenty years ago.

In order for empowerment to be an effective strategy, however, employees have to be given the tools and skills to have a good chance of succeeding. They also have to know that they won't be fired if they take a calculated risk and it doesn't pan out. Without the appropriate strategies and vision in place, empowerment itself can be risky. But when a company adopts a sound plan and appropriate strategies, empowerment can be life-changing for the organization. In essence, empowerment is the antithesis of micro-management!

Leaders empower subordinates by delegating authority to make the decisions necessary to move the business forward. They instinctively realize that they cannot themselves perform every important task necessary to drive a successful business, however tempting it might be. They learn early on to multiply themselves through others by delegating responsibility, thereby empowering their subordinates to make the decisions necessary to operate the enterprise successfully. The CEO should never confuse this delegation of power as an abdication of responsibility or accountability. The CEO still has full accountability for total enterprise performance.

In 1997, I empowered a committee of three senior leaders to interview heads of every support group and operating group in the company to determine areas to improve efficiency and performance of Nestlé USA. This high-performance team performed the task much better than I could have because the members were closer to the issues and solutions than I was. After this successful SG&A exercise, each member of the team returned to his or her respective operations and support groups to run the day-to-day business. Sometimes empowerment can be permanent or, as in this case, it can be bestowed for a specific project or period of time.

It is obvious that I cite the *Blueprint for Success* and its enthusiastic acceptance by my management team as one of the key factors in the many performance successes that followed. In the end, the *Blueprint* has empowered associates throughout Nestlé USA. By relaying the specific strategies and initiatives required to reach our goals, all associates have a clear understanding of what they have to do to be successful. This is liberating. With the *Blueprint* in hand, our associates have the authority to take calculated risks without having to ask anyone in the organization for permission to do so. I believe this is true empowerment!

5. Leaders Earn Respect

My entire business career I have heard it said that as a leader, it is more important to be respected than to be liked. In principle I agree with this philosophy, but in today's world I would submit that it's not good enough for a leader just to be respected. Surveys show that most people leave their careers today because they do not like their boss, so it's much better if, as a leader, you are both respected and liked. Still, I would agree that respect is the most critical element, all things being equal.

I learned early in my career from one of my early mentors, Pete Haynes, not to mistake compassion for weakness in leaders. You may recall a scene in the movie *Patton* where the great general visits a field hospital during the Sicily campaign. He is moved to tears as he kneels to pin a purple heart on the pillow of a critically wounded soldier. No one in the Seventh Army would think of Patton's act of compassion as a sign of weakness. When leading in battle, Patton was known as Blood & Guts Patton for his aggressive approach to pushing his troops, which is portrayed in the next scene in which he strikes a soldier he considers to be a coward. Patton actually lost a lot of respect from people back home for the slapping incident and it almost cost him his military career. Fortunately, he was later able to redeem himself as a strong leader, and he was awarded the command of the Third Army after the D-Day invasion at Normandy. Not only did Patton have to earn the respect of his soldiers, he had to regain it once it was lost, which is even more difficult than earning it the first time.

Leaders earn respect in many different ways. I believe that one of the most genuine ways is to give credit for success to the people who deserve it. When leaders credit their subordinates for their overall success and performance, it resonates within people throughout the company. To do this requires a great deal of self-confidence and confidence in one's own abilities. I have been blessed at Nestlé to have a number of leaders who have shared publicly with their teams the accolades and credit that follow good performance and success. John Harris, president of the Friskies Pet Care Company prior to the Purina acquisition, was particularly adept at this aspect of leadership. John was never afraid to give others credit for his ideas. I have been present on many occasions when John would give credit to a subordinate for a successful idea that I knew was his. At this writing I am proud to say that his ability to lead and therefore rise through the corporate ranks has led John to the helm of all European pet care operations for Nestlé S.A.

H. E. Olson had a bronze plaque in his office with these words embossed on it: "Never Be Afraid to Let Someone Else Take Credit for Your Idea." Many leaders have earned the respect of their organizations by being true to this idea. I was so taken by this saying that I had it printed and framed, taking it with me to Australia in 1989 and back to Nestlé USA in 1992. These words are displayed in my office to this day, reflecting what I believe is the essence of good teamwork.

6. Leaders Are Change Agents

One thing is for certain—change is a constant in today's world. Business experts have bombarded us with the message that we should embrace change, and while that is a good sentiment, it isn't always easy. Leaders need to understand the fear that many employees feel when confronted with change, especially change at today's accelerated rate.

The bottom line is that in today's evolving marketplace, an organization must change if it wants to avoid falling behind the competition. Therefore, it is the responsibility of organizational leaders to create a climate of change in order to ensure growth and market viability for the company and its people. Without change, as painful and as scary as it sometimes is for employees, there is no possibility for growth.

Consider the change forced on many industries, including the food industry, in the United States due to the phenomenal growth of Wal-Mart over the past thirty years. Today Wal-Mart is the largest retailer in the world and the largest grocery retailer in the United States, growing from minimal food sales in 1990 to over 15 percent of all grocery sales in the United States by 2004. Not only are other retailers competing with the giant for the mighty consumer dollar affected, but so too are the vendors trying to supply the giant and grow with it. As power changes in the distribution channel, all companies throughout the supply chain are affected.

Our relationship with Wal-Mart has brought about changes in our organization in terms of supply chain efficiency, value innovation, and technology such as radio frequency identification (RFID). In the past, new products often began as loss-leaders, but working with Wal-Mart has forced us to approach new products differently. We have to add real value to new products and establish the price for the long-run. At the famed Wal-Mart Saturday morning meetings in Bentonville, management can review actual sales by store, category, and country, even when registers close on the Friday night before. Not only does this send the signal of a sense of urgency, but it also frames any discussions about change in real time and with up-to-date data.

Nestlé's U.S. operations have evolved over the past one hundred years into a number of different structures responding to the changing retail landscape. The company moved from a functional business model to a holding company model and then to a divisional structure. Now we are moving to a network or matrix business model to improve our efficiency in a market increasingly dominated by Wal-Mart. But what makes the transitions to new operating models even more challenging is the ever-accelerating rate at which these changes have to be made. For example, the functional business model lasted for seventy years, from 1900 to 1970, while the holding company structure lasted twenty years, and the divisional model about thirteen years. At this rate of change, we could anticipate that the new network business model might be ready to be revamped in as little as five years. This significant rate of change is challenging for leaders who must react to it. And therein lies a real test for a leader—the ability to anticipate changes before they are forced upon an unprepared organization.

Leaders can also bring about change in the policies and philosophies of an organization, which in turn affect the performance of the company. Peter Brabeck made the decision early in his tenure as CEO of Nestlé SA to open a dialogue with the stock market, which was a significant change from his predecessors' practice of avoiding the scrutiny of the investor community. This new relationship, which included regular meetings with the share market, has resulted in putting healthy internal pressure on Nestlé to become more efficient and monitor the numbers. A focus on efficiency and EBITA margin improvement has been a hallmark of Peter Brabeck's tenure. Nestlé's worldwide margins, which were below food industry averages, are now moving toward that average. Nestlé USA, at 18 percent of group sales, is helping to lead the way with major margin improvement in the past ten years. (Nestlé USA's margins were above the competitive average in the U.S. food industry for the first time in 2003, and moved even higher after 2004, after being significantly below the industry average in 1990.) Brabeck's launch of project GLOBE and Nestlé USA's launch of a shared service center, which will both come fully online in the 2006 to 2007 period, will have a significant impact on further improving the efficiency of Nestlé in future years.

Sometimes simple changes made by the CEO of an organization can have a profound symbolic impact throughout the company. Two changes that fall under this category resulted from our Work Out sessions. The first change started as an observation and suggestion. The group felt that the top executives, who resided in the mahogany paneled twenty-first floor (the top floor) of the building had become elitist and distant from the rest of the associates. They further commented that top management talked a lot about teamwork, but were not located with their teams. Shortly after this particular Work Out session, I announced to my direct reports that I wanted each of them to relocate from the twenty-first floor to the floor where their teams resided. I also relocated the office of the chairman and the CEO down to the eighth floor, where we had some unused space. This made the twenty-first floor available so all associates could use the video-conference rooms, telephone conference rooms, and meeting rooms of different sizes and shapes. Everyone's new digs, including mine, were much smaller, but were still more than adequate.

After about a month of grumbling, everyone settled in with his or her teams and it has been very smooth since. Big executive offices and the trappings of power were commonplace by the 1970s and 1980s in corporate America, but times have changed. This was the right thing to do at the right time in the history of the company. Word about the decision spread like wildfire and created a very positive attitude within the company. Particularly pleased were the Work Out group members who had suggested the changes.

Another popular change that resulted from the Work Outs was the decision not to have meetings on Fridays. A number of bosses were consistently having Friday meetings, with some running late in the day. This was a situation that was in conflict with one of our four culture drivers—balance. I felt strongly that our associates should be spending Fridays wrapping up the current week's activities and planning the next week's work, so that they could spend the full weekend with their families. On many Fridays after this new policy was announced, I walked the floors of our Glendale offices throwing people out of meeting rooms. I must say that for a few months, I was more popular with the associates than I was with management. The word quickly got out that we really believed in balance, and that we expected people to be organized enough to have all their meetings conducted between Monday and Thursday. Our associates arrived back at work on Mondays refreshed and ready to aggressively tackle their assignments.

When a leader acts as a true change agent, he or she can bring about changes with something as ground-shaking as a new business model or as subtle as moving an office. Sometimes the changes that seem "token," such as moving an office or changing Friday meeting policies, can be extremely significant because they send a meaningful message throughout the organization about culture and leadership. Because others either don't have the authority or they don't want to upset the apple cart, sometimes leaders need to take the lead on things such as these in order to get them implemented throughout the organization.

7. Leaders Are Servants

The notion of servant leadership is relatively new, but I believe the idea resonates strongly with today's associates. The principle basically states that anyone wanting to be a leader must first be a servant. The idea is that leadership authority and influence come as much from service to others as they do from the traditional authority that automatically comes with a position of leadership.

In his book *The Servant,* Jim Hunter describes this idea as the Law of the Harvest.[1] The more the leader serves associates, the more he has the right to be considered a leader. This brings up an interesting paradox—the greatest leader is the one who serves the most. Hunter describes leadership as a simple four-word job description, "Identify and meet needs." Although I find this rather simplistic, the servant leadership model is very attractive in today's competitive and demanding economy, where employees generally have less loyalty to companies than at any time in my career. When leaders identify and meet the needs of their associates, attitude and morale surge and good things begin to happen.

Four individuals that I have had the privilege of meeting over the years could be servant leader role models. They are the late Frank Wells of Disney; Roger Staubach, former Dallas Cowboys quarterback; Mike Huckabee, the governor of Arkansas; and Jack Brown, chairman and CEO of Stater Bros. Markets, headquartered in Colton, California. These four leaders are constantly identifying and meeting the needs of their associates. Their stories are so compelling that I want to highlight them here.

Frank Wells

I got to know Frank Wells because of a ten-year contract that we signed with Disney in the early 1990s to use Disney characters on Carnation and Nestlé products, with joint promotions and signage at the Disney theme parks. We had numerous problems and opportunities with the Disney contract from its inception, but over and over again, Frank Wells assumed the role of the knight in shinning armor coming to the rescue and saving the day. He was the ultimate servant leader, often using self-depreciating humor to get things back on a positive track. When we hit an impasse on a decision that had to be made, Frank would ask if he could come to our offices to discuss the problem. Disney was located in Burbank, just five minutes down the freeway from Nestlé's Glendale offices, but Frank, the star problem-solver, never wanted to inconvenience me, so he almost always came to Nestlé, even though he was a high-ranking executive about ten years my senior. I never saw ego in Frank's leadership style; his focus was on identifying and meeting my needs.

Over the years, I have seen few CEOs with a right-hand man as talented as Frank Wells. I always wondered if Michael Eisner ever really knew what a gem he had in Frank. Clearly, Disney hasn't been the same since Frank's untimely death in 1994 from a tragic helicopter skiing accident. Frank was one of those leaders who could have been the CEO of almost any company he wanted.

He could have even switched arenas to be governor of California. But I believe Frank would much rather have served than assume any role where displaying his ego would be paramount.

Frank left me two things that I will always remember—one much more profound than the other. For some reason Frank always admired my neckties. As a token of our friendship, he sent me a beautiful *101 Dalmatians* necktie that I will always treasure, especially because of the sentiment behind it. Frank also left me with a kernel of wisdom that I reflect upon often and one that I will always remember. A few months before he died, Frank said to me, "Joe, what I have learned about life is that life's final victory is humility." Yes, Frank was a true servant leader. Solomon said it well when he said, "Humility comes before honor."

Roger Staubach

Most football fans would agree that Roger Staubach is one of the greatest men ever to play the game. My first exposure to Roger was in 1963 at the Duke-Navy football game held in the Wallace Wade Stadium in Durham, North Carolina. As a junior, Roger was the star Navy quarterback, and I was a freshman football player at Duke. I watched him almost single-handedly defeat Duke (38–25) with a series of unbelievable touchdown passes. From that day on, I always thought of him as a quality athlete and a quality person. You find out a lot about a person through athletic competition. Even then, Roger had the respect of all the players in the game, regardless of which side of the line of scrimmage they stood.

Fast-forward forty years, to a small gathering of executives that I attended at a popular Beverly Hills restaurant. Present that evening was Roger Staubach, who would go on to entertain us with great football stories and to teach us lessons about leadership based on his experiences on the field. I remember one story in particular that confirmed Roger's role as servant leader. In Super Bowl XIII, held in 1979, the Dallas Cowboys lost to the Pittsburgh Steelers 35–31. There was a key play that turned the game for Pittsburgh. Pittsburgh was ahead 21–14 late in the third quarter with the Cowboys threatening to score. On third down and seven from the eleven-yard line, Coach Landry called a play-action pass. Pittsburgh took the bait, just as the play was designed. Jackie Smith, the Cowboy's tight end, trying to sell a run, had stunned the Pittsburgh linebackers and then released into the open area in the end zone. A wide-open Jackie Smith dropped Staubach's sure touchdown pass. That changed the momentum of the entire game.

When asked if he was angry at Jackie for the mistake, Roger said that the dropped pass was really his fault, as he had thrown the ball too soft and the receiver was used to receiving this pass with a much firmer throw. Dallas had to settle for a field goal and Pittsburgh came back to score a touchdown at 28–17. Dallas made a valiant comeback in the last minutes of the game but lost the game by four points.

Roger's attempt to protect Jackie Smith from scrutiny and unnecessary blame by taking responsibility for something that according to most people's accounts really wasn't his fault, shows a first-class approach to leadership. As a leader of a company, I've tried to remember this lesson. I recognize that whatever happens on my watch, even if the poor result cannot be attributed directly to me, is my responsibility. Today, Roger Staubach is the head of one of the largest commercial real estate companies in the United States, which bears his name. He has applied to the business arena his outstanding approach to leadership that led him to so many victories on the field. Today, he continues to be focused on other people's needs, with his ego fully in check.

Mike Huckabee

Nestlé's grand opening of its Jonesboro, Arkansas frozen food factory in the fall of 2003 gave me an opportunity to meet Arkansas governor Mike Huckabee. This was my first meeting with the governor, and I was favorably impressed with his approach to people and politics.

Mike Huckabee was born in the little town of Hope, Arkansas, the birthplace of another Arkansas governor, who later became president. Mike was born into a blue-collar family of modest means. He went on to attend Southwestern Baptist Theological

Seminary in Forth Worth and spent twelve years as a Baptist pastor before going into politics—a most unusual background for the first Republican governor of Arkansas since Reconstruction.

In his book, *Character Is the Issue,*[2] Governor Huckabee says, "A big part of dealing with people is to treat others as you would have them treat you. If you don't want people yelling at you, don't yell at people. If you don't want to be betrayed by people, don't betray others. If you don't like being laughed at, don't laugh at others. I believe in servant leadership. And servant leadership is not cracking the whip."

Servant leadership is the highest form of leadership. It's not the same as what Governor Huckabee calls doormat leadership. To see your role as servant leader is the ultimate biblical model of leadership. Governor Huckabee goes on to say, "I expect our employees to treat others like they want to be treated, that they understand their job is not to be served but to serve, that they are never to be rude." What is interesting to me is that on one hand Mike Huckabee seems to represent a *new* type of public leader—one that leads by serving and meeting the needs of his fellow Arkansans. Yet on the other hand, he exemplifies the traditional definition of public service, which is supposed to focus on leading by serving and identifying needs of constituents and representing them in the political arena. I believe that after several decades, which can be characterized by politicians doing things for their own promotion and re-election, the best leaders are helping swing the pendulum back toward embodying what public service is all about.

Jack Brown

Jack Brown, chairman and CEO of Stater Bros. Markets in southern California, is one of the true servant leaders in the U.S. food industry. In his twenty-four years as Stater's CEO, Jack has grown his company from 79 supermarkets and 3,300 employees generating $475 million in sales to 164 stores with over 16,000 employees reporting $3.7 billion in sales in 2004. Additionally, Jack took Stater Bros. private along the way and today owns the company. This is a remarkable achievement in and of itself, but there is more to the story.

Jack's mother was an orphan and near death from tuberculosis when she gave birth to her only child. Jack's father died when he was only eight years old and his single mother, raised son Jack alone. Jack began his career in the food industry over fifty years ago as a bagger in an independent grocery store in his hometown of San Bernardino, California. Today, Jack is a generous and caring supermarket owner who knows how to get the maximum loyalty and output from his employees by constantly looking for ways to reward them and meet their needs. In a recent period when Stater Bros. profits benefited from a Los Angeles grocery labor strike, Jack took $7 million of profit and shared it with all of his employees, from courtesy clerk to executive.

I have known Jack Brown for over thirty years. He is what people often refer to as the "real deal," living his life as a natural leader, constantly in search of ways to encourage and support those around him. In his commitment to the community, Jack founded the Children's Fund of San Bernardino and the Boy's and Girl's Club of San Bernardino. Jack is also a champion of education and provides scholarships to deserving students at California State University, San Bernardino where he is a major supporter. Stater Bros., under Jack's leadership, is the largest contributor to the Inland Empire Food Banks. Stater Bros. is also a major supporter of the Food for All Anti-Hunger Program, to which Stater Bros. employees and customers have contributed over $2 million since 1987.

In 1992, Jack Brown was one of ten distinguished Americans to receive the Horatio Alger Award and is a current member of the Horatio Alger Association of Distinguished Americans. In 2005, Jack received the coveted Sidney R. Rabb Award for a lifetime of exceptional service to his community, to his customers, and to the supermarket industry. And wouldn't you know, this great American was born on Flag Day, June 14.

8. Leaders Act Decisively

Being decisive is critical to good leadership, but it is not inconsistent with taking the time to make sure you are making the best decision possible. At twenty-five years old and only two years out of college I was faced with the decision to terminate my first employee. He was fifteen years older than I was and was married with a family. I did not sleep much the night before that termination, thinking about the following day. Even though I believed the termination was justified based on failure to complete sales calls—and my superiors agreed—it was an unpleasant experience and more difficult than I had ever imagined. It was something that no college course could prepare me for. After the termination, I had to drive this salesman to his home so I could retrieve his company car. His wife and small daughter were waiting for him. Even after all these years, the look on his wife's face as I was driving away is still frozen in my memory. I felt tremendous compassion for the family, and I vowed that in the future I would do everything in my power to avoid such a terribly difficult experience.

I quickly learned, however, that making this decision, regardless of how difficult it was, had a very positive impact on the activities and attitudes of the remaining six members of my team. The sales group was actually expecting the termination of this individual and would have lost respect for me, as their supervisor, had I tolerated such incompetence from one salesperson and expected the rest of the team to make up the overall sales shortfall.

I also learned, however, never to terminate an associate until every effort has been made on your part, as the leader, to help that individual overcome his or her shortcomings. Although individuals should always be given a chance to redeem themselves, never hesitate to terminate associates quickly for dishonesty. After all is said and done, as a leader you have to look at yourself in the mirror each day and be happy with what you see staring back at you.

Over the years, I've taken many cues on leadership from Professor John Kotter and his book *Leading Change*. It has become an important tool for our Executive Leadership Team and throughout the organization, especially in terms of driving culture change at Nestlé USA. I consider it a must-read for all leaders. One piece of advice that Kotter uses that I have repeated often is: "Act now. Don't, don't, don't delay!" I can't think of anything that drives home the importance of decisiveness in leadership better than this simple and poignant piece of advice.

The opposite of decisiveness is indecisiveness. I believe the worst decision is to not make a decision, which occurs more often than you might think. The culprit often is information—either having too much of it or not enough of it. When information is lacking, many people don't have the confidence to make a decision and rely on their intuition, gut, knowledge, and experience. When there is too much information available, the paralysis of analysis can set in, delaying a decision at the expense of valuable time. As a leader, you have to know your own comfort zone in terms of quantity of information and quality of the source. Is 80 percent enough information to make a sound decision, or is 60 percent enough? How much faith do I have in the people giving me advice? Personally, I rely heavily on my team to give me accurate information and advice—they are the subject-matter experts, not me. I take their input, evaluate it based on its overall merit, compare it to other input, weigh the time and risk factors, and make the decision. I know that if I make a mistake, I can correct it, but not making a decision is not acceptable.

As we were launching our second annual *Blueprint for Success,* I invited Dr. John Kotter, the newly-named Konosuke Matsushita Professor of Leadership at The Harvard Business School, to speak with our top young leaders and to work directly with the ELT. I was struggling with getting everyone on the team fully committed to the vision I had for and the direction in which I wanted to take the company. Professor Kotter asked me three questions that had a profound impact on my view of our team's dynamics.

- What percentage of your team do you feel is fully supportive of the vision and has the same passion as you do toward the vision?
- What percentage support the vision but have not yet reached the level of passion and commitment you want?
- What percentage do not yet buy into the vision?

Without hesitation I answered one third, one third, and one third. He advised me to give the last third a reasonable amount of time to get on board, but if their support was not forthcoming I should make some changes in that group. His advice was right on target.

9. Leaders Create a Sense of Urgency

In my opinion, complacency is the biggest obstacle to consistent performance results. When I returned to Nestlé USA in 1992, sales and profits were improving each year but the actual profit margin was extremely low. The issue had become an elephant in the room that no one talked about. To get the entire organization focused on the $300 million competitive profit gap problem, we had to create a sense of urgency. We named our *dragon to slay*. A sense of urgency is what often moves people along the continuum of change from the realization of a problem to actually doing something about it. It is only after people understand the necessity of taking action that they actually act because maintaining the status quo is so much easier than change.

The first step in identifying our dragon was determining its size and scope. As such we benchmarked our competitive set of approximately ten similar food companies. We found that in 1993 they collectively averaged 13 percent return on sales and 30 percent return on invested capital. Even when we consolidated Carnation's above-industry performance results into the overall Nestlé results, we only realized 8 percent ROS, 18 percent ROIC, and 2 percent ACF (adjusted cash flow).

The next step was to define the goal in a way that everyone could understand, or else it would be difficult to get everyone to rally around it. As discussed in Chapter 4, our dragon to slay became known as 13–30–6, which stood for 13 percent ROS, 30 percent ROIC, and 6 percent ACF.

Getting everyone to agree to a new platform or a unified goal is not always enough to bring about the required change. It is often necessary for a leader to create a sense of urgency to motivate the organization to abandon a business as usual mentality and bring about change. Taking the initiative in these situations is an important part of a true leader's job. The consequences of not taking action can include putting the company into survival or crisis mode, which is often too much for a company to overcome.

10. Leaders Develop Leaders

I am always very suspicious of CEOs who retire, resign, or are terminated and have not cultivated at least one qualified replacement within the organization. More times than not, these successors are not developed because the CEO is a micro-manager and wants to be involved in the details of most decisions, thereby robbing his subordinates of the opportunity to learn and grow. Some CEOs may also feel threatened by the thought that if they really develop someone else's leadership skills, this new leader might be more effective than they are. And if someone else can do their job, the current CEO may no longer be invaluable to the company. Future CEOs cannot be developed when there is no delegation of responsibility or empowerment that affords an opportunity for personal growth. The development of a qualified successor is one of the CEO's most important assignments. It is important for the long-term stability of the company.

True leaders have a strong desire to see their efforts continued and realize that successful organizations cannot thrive long when a micro-management orientation exists at the top. True leaders understand from their own experience that learning and growth come from natural failures that are by-products of delegation and empowerment. At Nestlé USA I made a conscious effort to delegate some of the most important projects to the brightest people in the organization. Not only did I realize they were closer to the issues than I was and had the aptitude and specific expertise required to make the best decisions, I knew they needed these experiences to develop their leadership skills. I delegated, but didn't abdicate my responsibilities; I remained a resource and guide for their efforts. In every case where I put my brightest and best high potentials into position, the results were extraordinary and above anything I could have accomplished myself.

I believe that one of the most important responsibilities of a leader is to select a replacement with the talent to take the organization into the future. Often this means selecting a person with more talent than the leader himself or herself has. This calls for a great deal of self-confidence and a high sense of responsibility to the company. But nurturing and developing an outstanding successor does not happen by mere chance or through osmosis. It can only occur if the leader takes the risk of empowering top talent in the organization to make decisions and accepts a few mistakes along the way. A good example of this sense of responsibility can be seen in how Helmut Maucher, former CEO of Nestlé SA, developed Peter Brabeck to succeed him as CEO in 1998.

As a leader, I understand that my performance will only be as strong as the performance of weakest link in my Executive Leadership Team. When a spot on that team opens up, it is a unique opportunity to replace the departing executive with someone who is better prepared to address the marketplace's current dynamics and the company's market opportunities. A true leader strives to improve the talent in the organization every chance he or she gets, because that is in the best interest of the company in the long-term.

In the end, a CEO's responsibility is creating stability for the company today and tomorrow. Therefore, a leader's true performance is not judged only by how the company performs under his or her watch. It is ultimately judged by how the company performs during the tenure of the current CEO's successor.

CHAPTER 10

A Final Word from Joe

The introduction to this book is titled "A Word from Joe," named after my column that appears in each issue of the *Nestlé Times* newspaper. Therefore, I thought it only fitting that I close this book with "A Final Word from Joe." Over the years, I have used my column to speak to our associates about all kinds of subjects, from succession planning and our company performance to the *Blueprint for Success* and our culture drivers. In keeping with this platform, I wanted to use this last chapter to discuss a few things that are on my mind.

Out of Adversity Comes Greatness

In times of tragedy, people look to leaders to give them direction and hope, be honest with them, and relieve some of the fears and pressures they are feeling. They need leaders to tell them that it is OK to be scared and even to weep. Leaders need to be strong, so that others can grieve and deal with their feelings. But the need for strength and conviction does not imply that a leader should not show compassion during difficult moments. Compassion does not mean weakness. In fact, compassion often builds trust, which can fortify both individuals and teams with newfound strength and resolve.

I have had experience in the area of leadership during times of national crisis and natural disasters. During my time as CEO

A WORD FROM JOE

As we look forward to continuous change I think it is important to protect and to nurture the Nestlé culture that we have developed over the last 15 years in the U.S.

I believe a "Corporate Culture" is the manifestation by associates of the core values of an organization. A company's culture is demonstrated by similar traits being exhibited by the majority of associates the majority of time.

In 1998 the challenge at Nestlé USA was to find the appropriate "culture drivers" to support our new Nestlé USA *Blueprint for Success*. We finally settled on four that seemed perfect for today's business. They were also culture drivers that I personally could wholeheartedly commit to: Teamwork, Alignment, Passion and Balance.

After eight years, the top three culture drivers — Teamwork, Alignment and Passion — have been woven into the fabric of the organization. Balance, however, is challenging in a time of constant change.

Balance as a company culture driver is foreign to most business enterprises. Yet a balanced life is absolutely essential to a healthy and highly productive career. We instinctively understand that "workaholism" is unhealthy. Paradoxically a strong work ethic is one of the most admired traits for any business person. If an associate has a satisfying personal and community life, all other things being equal, then chances are good that he or she will bring a positive and receptive attitude to work each day.

Balance is not an associate benefit. It is about setting priorities in life to give us flexibility. In other words, achieving balance is up to each of you.

I believe there are five aspects of a balanced life:

Spiritual
While it is wrong to impose one's own spiritual values on others, I believe it is essential for people to have some spirituality as part of their life. Individuals approach spirituality in their own personal way and this must be fully honored and respected in the corporate environment.

Family and Friends
Relationships with family and friends are essential if one is to have a balanced life. It is these relationships that provide the experience and develop the interpersonal skills that are so beneficial to promoting personal growth and enhancing career performance.

Career
While career should never be the most important aspect of life, certainly it should not be lower than number three on your scorecard. Unfortunately, if career is the most important aspect of one's life then it is difficult to experience other aspects that add so much to one's growth as well as benefit career development.

Community
All of us have a responsibility to give back to the communities where we work and live. Nestlé USA's major involvement in our communities is our Very Best Volunteer Adopt-A-School Program. This program is closely associated with Reading is Fundamental (RIF). Several thousand Nestlé associates all across the country volunteer their time each year to this program.

Hobbies
Having hobbies that are both physically and mentally stimulating helps you balance your career responsibilities and keeps you fresh. This allows you to take on business issues with a renewed vigor.

I believe that each of us must continue to strive for that elusive balance in our lives that is so important to our success in business. I believe balance at Nestlé USA must be more than aspirational.

Joe Weller
Chairman & CEO

of Nestlé USA, not only did our country suffer the effects of terrorism with the 9/11 attacks, but we watched in helpless horror as Malaysia, Thailand, and Indonesia were ravaged by a series of storms and tsunamis. These events forever changed me as a person, and they forever changed me as a leader.

The events that occurred in New York City; Washington, D.C.; and the fields of Pennsylvania on September 11, 2001 had a profound impact on me and every citizen of the United States, changing us all in ways we could not have predicted. The only event in modern history to compare to 9/11 was the Japanese attack on Pearl Harbor on December 7, 1942, which also devastated the country. The difference was that Pearl Harbor, while on U.S. soil, took place off the mainland. It also occurred prior to CNN and today's twenty-four-hour, live television and media coverage, which seems to transport viewers instantly to the scene of the disaster being covered. I understood that as a society, we would never feel truly safe within our borders again. And while the 9/11 attacks were perpetrated against the financial and political heart of America, they reached the soul of each American, changing how my family, friends, associates, colleagues, and customers would think, act, and behave.

Already in my office when I learned of the World Trade Center attacks, my first thought on that fatal morning in September was to pray for the victims and their families in New York, Washington, and Pennsylvania. My second thought was to speak to my wife and family and to make sure they were safe. My third thought was to comfort and communicate everything we knew to our Nestlé associates in Glendale and across the United States. As a leader, I understood that one of my greatest roles during this time would be to project a sense of security throughout my organization. So, for the first time in my career, I personally went on our building's public address system to give our employees an update on what we knew about the events back east. I instructed all Nestlé associates to return home if they felt they needed to be with their children and families. I told them that we would continue with updates throughout the day for those who felt they wanted to stay at work. We checked to make sure we did not have associates at the World Trade Center, the Pentagon, or on the airplane in Pennsylvania. Thankfully we did not!

Once we had done everything we could do to let everyone know what was going on, I remember feeling an almost overwhelming sense of love and patriotism for this great country and for the many freedoms that we enjoy. The Nestlé USA headquarters was over three thousand miles from Ground Zero, but the impact on our people was profound and immediate. Within a matter of hours and days, the Nestlé USA associates responded with a level of kindness and patriotism that would make me very proud. By September 14, three days following the attacks, Nestlé USA associates had accomplished so much, including the following:

- Donated $100,000 to the American Red Cross
- Donated 50,000 Powerbars to relief workers
- Sent supplies of Taster's Choice Coffee, Juicy Juice, Carnation Hot Cocoa, Coffee-Mate, and Nestlé Water to rescue workers and to the Red Cross
- Sent pet food products to animal shelters for displaced animals
- Donated saline solution, antibiotics, and artificial tears from Alcon to area hospitals and triage centers
- Set up on-location feeding facilities for rescue workers through Nestlé Food Services Company
- Opened its cafeteria to soldiers at the Army reserve station across from that facility (Nestlé's Freehold, New Jersey coffee factory)
- Sent several hundred pairs of heavy-duty leather gloves and dust masks from Nestlé factories to New York rescue workers

It was inspiring to see how all twenty-two thousand Nestlé USA employees united in response to the tragedy. We sent out a note to everyone in the company, including our new Purina associates, thanking them for their contributions. We also let them know that the best thing we could do for our country and the economy was to get back to work. We wanted everyone to focus on our vision of making Nestlé USA the Very Best Food Company in the United States, which would be a way to prove the strength of our country and our commitment to our way of life. We had to prove that we would not allow a handful of terrorists to paralyze this great nation.

At the end of my note to our associates, I added, "Always remember—out of adversity comes greatness! God Bless America! In spite of 9/11, the future is bright for America and for our Nestlé Associates. I believe that both America and Nestlé's best days are ahead of us." As a follow-up to this letter, we later sent every employee in the United States an American flag lapel pin that many associates still wear today.

Our Nestlé USA associates would once again come through as a team as they responded to the tsunami disaster in the Indian Ocean in late 2004. Within a few weeks, our associates donated over $188,000 in cash to help the countless victims, which Nestlé USA matched dollar-for-dollar for a combined contribution to the American Red Cross of $375,000.

Nestlé S.A. was even quicker to the rescue, providing water, food, and many other types of support to those affected in Malaysia, Sri Lanka, India, Thailand, and Indonesia, almost immediately following that event. Nestlé trucks distributed free bottled water throughout the area, and vehicles normally used to hand out Nestlé product samples delivered hot meals to victims instead. Nestlé USA associates were proud of the quick local action of our parent company and its compassion for those impacted by this unthinkable disaster.

Instilling Values and Strong Work Ethic in Our Children

I have bright expectations for the future. We live in a country—and my associates and I work for a company—where regardless of your pedigree or whether you are born rich or poor, you can have a rewarding and a fulfilling life. Everyone can make a difference if they participate in the many interesting experiences that come their way, learn from these experiences, and make the appropriate mid-point corrections along their life journeys. The key is to start this process at a young age. When we come into this world it is important to understand that we are not automatically entitled to health, wealth, or happiness. Rather, we are blessed by what we do with these gifts if we are so fortunate as to have one or more of these in this life.

When we are blessed with the freedoms we have been given just by virtue of living in this country, one of our greatest responsibilities becomes providing a solid foundation for the next generation to thrive. This is a responsibility I bear as a leader of a company, but also as a parent. Growing up poor forced me to work and learn throughout my childhood and early adult years. I had no choice. Looking back today, I wouldn't change a thing—all those early experiences have made me who I am today. The challenge for many of us today is how to expose our children to the same foundational lessons and experiences we had while raising them in an affluent society and in well-to-do homes. This has been a topic in several of my *A Word from Joe* columns.

In our home, Carol and I insisted that our children, Robin and Jeff, have useful entrepreneurial experiences as young children, even though they were obviously raised with more material things than Carol or I had as children. Robin and Jeff had the normal neighborhood lemonade stand and Robin sold Girl Scout cookies. But one of the best experiences was helping Robin, then age eight, and Jeff, age five, sell refreshments at our local high school's annual Junior/Senior Rivalry Day. Each year on a cool January day, teams of students would compete against each other in a variety of sports activities. Needless to say, both the students and on-lookers were in need of refreshments throughout the day. Our whole family would make homemade doughnuts out of canned biscuits and containers of Carnation Hot Cocoa, which we would place in Jeff's red wagon and pull, with his little tractor, the one block to the school's activity field. Robin and Jeff would then sell their doughnuts and drinks to the students. The first year they netted six dollars, and the following year their profits doubled to twelve dollars. By the third year, Robin and Jeff made over fifteen dollars. The lessons they learned in the process were priceless. They learned how to make products, mark them up for a profit, take price increases, sell, make change, and have a great time doing it.

There definitely is no substitute for the positive impact on the psyche of young children that comes from successful experiences in early real-life activities. Seemingly small events like selling Girl Scout cookies or lemonade in the neighborhood can affect children's self-confidence and also help parents teach their children basic life skills, such as the importance of finishing what they begin. After-school jobs like washing cars, mowing grass, baby-sitting, or working at McDonald's are experiences that build confidence that lasts a lifetime.

I believe strongly in the value of work, even when children don't have to work from financial need. The money they make from early jobs is secondary to the lessons they learn about discipline, work ethic, responsibilities, communication skills, time-management skills, and appreciation for the almighty dollar. I also consider organized sports activities and competitive sports to be a form of work. They teach kids team-building skills, discipline, goal-setting skills, and valuable lessons about winning and losing that are very important later in life.

What it takes to succeed in today's world has evolved over the years. Today higher education includes more than just classroom work to reflect these enhanced requirements. Recruiters no longer just look for the students with the best grades, although good grades always fall into the plus category. They look for young people with well-developed interpersonal skills, life experiences, and leadership qualities. I likely overstated this point when I told my son as he was leaving for college that in the real world, "C" students often manage "A" students. I was trying to emphasize the value of developing his interpersonal skills during this time in his life. (Looking back, if I had it to do over again, I would change my example from a "C" student to a "B" student.) Companies today like to hire students who have taken advantage of the opportunities provided to them at school, namely student organizations, sports, fraternities and sororities, debate teams, and clubs. All of these activities help develop the personalities, character, and communication skills that, along with aptitude and creativeness, are necessary to become successful leaders.

The Future Belongs to . . .

At this stage in my career, I reflect often on the many years of wonderful work and life experiences I have had. I recall the many moments of trial, tribulation, turbulence, and ultimately triumph. One of the wonderful things that I am afforded at this point is the ability to review the past, look beyond the present, and think about the future. When I do, I think about the individuals and organizations to which I think the future will belong.

The future belongs to those who accept change. Personal success depends to a large degree on a person's ability to accept and even thrive on change. Change, whether in personal or business life, is often a painful experience, in part because it requires you to give up something known and try something new. Change requires openness to new ideas, new skills, or new relationships. Some people thrive on change, while others are paralyzed by it. The most successful executives that I have known have not only had the ability to change with the times, they have thrived on such change. And while they may have experienced some level of stress regarding potential changes, they were never paralyzed by change.

The future belongs to the companies with the best people, from factory workers and sales associates to junior executives and leaders. The key is identifying talented employees throughout the organization and placing them into positions in which they can blossom. Junior executives who are team players, who attract mentors, and who have passion for their careers will find themselves in a much more positive position within the company than those who don't understand collaborative thinking or are unhappy in the workplace. We have found that promoting a balanced life (spirituality, family and friends, career, hobbies, and community involvement) often results in better employees who exhibit more passion in all areas of life, including in their jobs and careers.

The future belongs to the companies with senior leaders who delegate, empower, and develop other leaders. I believe servant leadership is a philosophy by which to live. Those who focus first on serving others will be more effective leaders and therefore be greater assets to the companies they lead. In the long run, the stability and future of a company depends on how well future leaders are developed throughout the organization. It is worth repeating that one of the most significant responsibilities of a CEO is to identify and nurture the next generation of executives and potential CEOs.

The future belongs to the companies with long-term, market-driven vision. Some truly global companies, like Nestlé, have been able to respond to global competition *and* local market needs to get the desired performance outcome. As a result, some of these companies have grown their businesses and brands, but at the expense of higher short-term profits. Many American and regional companies, however, have failed to grow in order to deliver a higher short-term profit target. The reality is that successful companies must grow both sales and profits at an above average rate.

The future belongs to the companies that fully understand and cater to their Most Valued Consumers (MVCs). We define our MVCs as current heavy users of our brands, and understand that they are critical to building a strong brand franchise. In the past, most packaged food companies invested more on attracting new customers than retaining current ones. Today, Nestlé USA and other winning companies focus on increasing purchase and consumption of their brand among their Most Valued Consumers. We have found that encouraging our fans to use more of our brands is more cost-effective than trying to create trial among current non-users.

The future belongs to the companies that market effectively to the forty million Hispanic consumers that live in the United States. The Latino population will account for more than 45 percent of the U.S. total population growth from 2004 to 2010. By 2020, the Latino population is likely to double from its current size. Companies will have to focus on analyzing the demographic and psychographic traits of this market segment in order to tailor products, packaging, marketing, and advertising to this customer group. In general, while the Latino population continues to grow rapidly (both because of immigration and because of high birth rates), these consumer trends tend to be heavily concentrated in specific cities and states, which makes target marketing very cost efficient. I believe that researching ethnic tastes and food trends can be very effective in driving new product offerings to meet those taste profiles.

The future belongs to companies that invest in employee training. A formal university education is very important in providing students with general information and knowledge about a variety of business subjects. Most importantly, these courses often provide sound frameworks for analyzing information, which can be used once graduates begin their jobs. But a university education is only the beginning point in knowledge development. It can never take the place of continuous on-the-job training that is specific to a particular brand, company, and industry.

Training is the lifeblood of the most successful organizations, and its role will only become even more vital in the evolving global economy. The most important education for a Nestlé associate begins after he or she joins the company. Nestlé University provides a very significant continuing education system that will benefit the individual throughout his or her career.

The future belongs to the companies that renovate their products and make them more relevant for today's consumers and invest in product innovation. Nestlé's Coffee-Mate non-dairy creamer, for example, is a brand that epitomizes this thinking. Although originally launched in 1961, Coffee-Mate is more relevant and successful today than when it was first introduced. The brand has morphed into new forms, flavors, and packaging never dreamed of by the original inventors. Coffee-Mate has been totally renovated to meet today's consumer needs for convenience in a liquid variety with a state-of-the-art, non-drip dispenser. Additionally, the need for better nutrition brought about the development of a low-fat, cholesterol-free, and lactose-free product.

At Nestlé USA, we are committed to developing new products and services that meet the ever-changing requirements of modern consumers. I believe that will be one of our most important success strategies as we move forward.

The future belongs to the companies that have the courage to change their corporate cultures to reflect and respond to the realities of a changing marketplace. Peter Brabeck made a bold statement by changing Nestlé's culture from what was historically a manufacturing-driven culture to one that emphasizes nutrition, health, and wellness. His action clearly positions Nestlé to take advantage of a specific, long-term worldwide trend toward enhanced nutrition. Nestlé is well equipped to accept this industry leadership position in the area of nutrition because it has the largest private nutrition science research facility in the world (located in Lausanne, Switzerland). In 2004, the Nestlé Research Center published over two hundred papers in medical and scientific journals and received seventeen patents. Although consumers think of Nestlé as a chocolate company, in reality Nestlé is much more of a nutrition company.

In February 2004, an article in *Forbes* magazine began with the following headline: "Fight Cancer! Reduce Heart Disease! Live Longer!" The article posed the question: "What's the elixir that does all this? Red wine? Green Tea? No, hot chocolate."[1] The article went on to say:

> A recent comparative study conducted by Cornell University researchers and published in the *Journal of Agricultural & Food Chemistry* found that a hot cup of cocoa contains the highest concentration of antioxidants, the chemicals that help fight cancer, heart disease and aging. The race wasn't even close: Cocoa's antioxidants were almost two times stronger than those found in red wine and up to five times stronger than those in black tea.[2]

This nutritional fact about chocolate is a great side benefit for chocolate lovers. We maintain that the primary benefit of chocolate is the pleasure derived from eating it. Chocolate tastes good and is an acceptable indulgence that is part of a healthy, happy lifestyle. It is a reward of sorts. We would never confuse our customers by having our advertising stress nutrition as a major benefit.

Sometimes product innovations come from new discoveries and advances in science. For example, we found that infant formula products can be fortified with nutrients that enhance brain development and comfort proteins that aid infant digestion, which caused us to renovate our products accordingly. We believe that nutrition and well-being are long-term consumer wants that will only grow in intensity, and therefore we envision products to meet the personal nutritional requirements of consumers.

The future belongs to companies that effectively address consumers' desires for ubiquitous distribution of the company's products. The fact is that today's consumers want the convenience of buying and consuming their favorite food and beverage products wherever and whenever they want. They want products that meet their on-the-go lifestyles. To address these consumer desires, we reformulated Nesquik and enhanced its distribution. Whereas five years ago Nesquik could only be found in powder form on the shelves of supermarkets, today the single-serve chilled bottles of Nesquik fly out of convenience stores and vending machines around the county.

Product availability will be critical in the new economy as new channels offer consumers ever-increasing opportunities to purchase their favorite products anywhere a cash register or credit card reader is available. Profits await those companies that organize themselves to develop, sell, and distribute products to these new sales venues.

The future belongs to the companies that can effectively cut costs and continue to add increasing value to their brands. Wal-Mart's Every Day Low Prices strategy has influenced consumer expectations regarding prices. They expect long-term low prices on all products at all times. In 2003, Wal-Mart actually lowered the prices of its total mix of products, which forced manufacturers to find new ways to cut unnecessary costs out of their supply chains. Hot Pockets has been a very popular and successful product for many years. There has not been a price increase for this product in over twenty years, but there has been constant attention to new ways to reduce costs and improve quality simultaneously. Not surprisingly, this business has one of the lowest overheads as a percentage of sales in the food industry.

The future belongs to companies that are lean and efficient and operate cost effectively. To compete effectively in today's global marketplace, companies need to become more efficient across the board. At Nestlé USA, we have been able improve our manufacturing productivity dramatically since 1990, as we slashed the number of factories by more than half, yet produced more total output. But increasing efficiency and cutting manufacturing costs is relatively old news in the corporate arena. Similarly, looking to outsourcing to solve the problem of high manufacturing costs is also not a new concept. But looking to outsourcing of transactional functions (white collar jobs) is still a relatively new concept that many corporations are now implementing.

The fact of the matter is that companies can no longer afford to perform every activity internally and maintain the level of efficiency and cost effectiveness that is required to be competitive in the long run. The ability to move much of the transactional activities to shared service centers, centers of excellence, or to on-shore or off-shore outsourcing will have the added benefit of improving the quality of the work done in the strategic areas.

The outsourcing of routine transactional activities from America to countries that can perform them for less cost should result in more higher-paying jobs here in the United States. The real opportunity for the American worker does not lie in reducing outsourcing, which would lessen our competitiveness; it lies in increasing the opportunity for upward mobility of American workers. When this happens, retraining workers who are displaced by outsourcing allows them to be able to fill more value-added jobs. High-level skills that are taught in our universities and by many companies will always be in demand. The goal in the United States should be to have a larger percentage of our workforce trained to have these world-class skills.

The future belongs to companies that learn to harness technology. The information technology age has made incredible amounts of data availability to organizations. The ability to use this information effectively for decision-making, however, still falls short for most companies. Learning to use technology in areas like consumer effectiveness will open up many new opportunities for companies to grow their businesses. At Nestlé, the investments in BEST and GLOBE will not only enable Nestlé Business Services to make Nestlé more efficient by reducing complexity, but will free up scarce resources, allowing the business operations to have greater focus on the consumer.

The future belongs to people and businesses that can compete globally. At the end of the day, the entire U.S. economy, companies, and individuals will benefit from the ultimate result of globalization, as new jobs and new industries will be created from the capital made available by lower unit costs incurred from outsourcing opportunities. Real job security in the new economy will be based on the increasing value that the individual adds to the organization and to the team.

I believe that a global economy is rapidly replacing America's economic dominance in the world. India, Korea, China, the European Common Market, NAFTA, and other trading blocks are becoming economic powerhouses and are beginning to compete effectively in the world economy. Consider the potential of India. This country boasts approximately one billion people, with over one hundred fifty million of them highly educated and speaking English as their main language.

The United States will still have a bright future, but it will have to share the stage with other countries. I believe that this is a good development for the world overall, and therefore, must be a positive for America as well. When it comes to the job market, the United States still has the lowest long-term unemployment rate in the West. And while labor is expensive in the United States, it is still cheaper than in Europe. U.S. workers are much more flexible geographically as well. When it comes to productivity, consider that manufacturing production in the United States. has doubled in the past ten years, while the number of people employed in factories has gone down. I believe similar productivity gains will maintain the United States' leadership position in the new world economy.

The future belongs to those with the ingenuity and spirit to access the vast opportunities that America offers. In what other country in the world could Arnold Schwarzenegger arrive from Austria with no money and poor command of the language and go on to become one of the most successful movie stars in Hollywood? And to top that, go on to become a successful businessman and governor of California—the fifth largest economy of the world? Only in America!

The future belongs to individuals who understand how to be successful. In early 2004, I was invited by Gene Kummell, chairman emeritus of McCann Erickson Advertising Agency and a dear longtime friend, to give a Gordon Grand Fellowship Lecture at Yale University. During the luncheon, I shared many aspects of my personal life, career, and success with the students and faculty. Because Gene had given one year's notice, I had plenty of time to think about what I would say to the students preparing to enter the workforce when I spoke to them in January 2005.

I decided to share with them what I believe are the basic requirements for keeping a job once you get it. These "givens" are primarily common sense, but I have found that new graduates often disregard them as they accept and begin their first jobs. I told them how important it is to always be on time, work hard, move fast, have a positive attitude, be trustworthy, and treat people the way you would like to be treated. These are definitely the minimum requirements to keep a job with almost any organization today. I also talked to them about seven principles that I thought would boost their success in the marketplace.

1. Never make your career the most important thing in your life. Having a balanced life is critical to a successful career.
2. Do not allow compensation to be the deciding factor in your career selection; go for the job opportunity that inspires the most "passion" in you.
3. Be a team player! Teams always outperform individuals.
4. Never be afraid to let someone else take credit for your idea. This is the essence of teamwork and a sign of confidence and humility that true leaders possess.
5. Be a good listener! You will learn a lot and you will look smart!

6. Develop leadership skills like delegation and empower-ment, as opposed to just managerial skills, such as control and micro-management.

7. Remember that in the real world the "B" student often manages the "A" student! It is just as important to de-velop your interpersonal skills as your intellectual skills in college.

If I could pass on a few more tidbits of knowledge to these students, I would tell them that I believe the future will be ex-citing for those who take action now and do not delay and for those who make the most out of every opportunity presented to them, no matter how seemingly insignificant at the time. I would tell them to be a role model for their families and busi-ness associates, find individuals they can mentor, give to others what they have received, and make their lives a celebration of giving. I am more convinced than ever that one person can make just as much difference tomorrow, as they did yesterday or today.

Tomorrow's Leaders

As with every generation before ours, the leaders of tomorrow are being developed today. Whether they make their mark in business, education, the sciences, theology, politics, or other areas, they will be influenced by our diverse, open, free, and cap-italistic society that provides for numerous experiences and at a relatively young age. Our future leaders are being taught as chil-dren and teenagers that they can make a difference in this great country regardless of their socio-economic background. These young people believe that if they persevere and never shirk their responsibilities they can become teachers, doctors, lawyers, en-gineers, and even president of the United States. I believe The American Dream is alive and well! And it is our responsibility to work to keep it alive.

The American Dream is more likely to come true for those who embody pluck—a hardworking and tenacious can-do spirit that drives someone to never give up. To quote the philosophy that helped E. A. Stuart build Carnation Company, "Pluck always wins!" Pluck is the key ingredient in executing any company's strategic plan or blueprint for success, and any country's vision. I believe that it is the greatest hope for America's future.

As I prepare to ride off into the sunset, I am thrilled with how many young leaders there are in every walk of life in this country. It's going to be fun watching them take their companies, their communities, and even our country to the next level with their own versions of the *Blueprint for Success!*

A Last Thought

At the end of the day, when you know it is time to take on life's next journey, you can't help but look back and try to figure out what it has all meant. I am at that turning point now in my life and find myself reflecting on the most wonderful experiences of my life. I remember my early jobs—selling ice cream with my brother and working at Pryor's Pharmacy. I remember my heyday as a local football hero, the embarrassment of failing out of Duke, and the determination to save enough money to go to the University of Tennessee. It was after that that my life really changed. After I took my first job with Carnation Company, I never looked back—my career seemed to take a fast-paced, natural progression toward my ultimate position as CEO of Nestlé USA, and I cannot imagine any company that would have been better to spend my career with than Nestlé. Even more importantly, along the way, I met and married Carol, became an evangelical Christian, had and raised Robin and Jeff, and most recently took on the role of grandfather.

I was reminded of this at my sixtieth birthday party. Carol invited all of the people who had been important in my life; I have never felt so successful, but not in the way you might think. That evening, I listened to my grown children tell my family, friends, and associates how much they appreciated me being there for them as they were growing up, how their values were shaped by mine and Carol's, and how I had inspired them. And Jeff added how proud he would be if someday people said that he was like me. Their words of respect and love were much more important to me than any recognition or promotion I had received in my thirty-seven-year business career.

And that's when I knew what real success was. In the end, I had developed the right balance in my life and my personal blueprint for success in life had been achieved. I have indeed been blessed beyond what I could have ever imagined!

Nestlé Timeline

1867

Henri Nestlé develops the first infant food in Vevey, Switzerland. Condensed milk production follows in 1878.

1899

CARNATION® evaporated milk is introduced by CARNATION Company founder E.A. Stuart in Kent, Washington.

1900

Nestlé opens its first facility in the United States.

1929

Nestlé purchases PETER'S CHOCOLATE, a European company specializing in chocolate for chefs and bakers. Its founder, Daniel Peter, produced the world's first milk chocolate, using Henri Nestlé's condensed milk.

1934

FRISKIES® dry dog food is introduced.

1938

NESTLÉ® CRUNCH® candy bar is introduced. Today, NESTLÉ CRUNCH is consistently among the most popular candy bars in the United States.

1939

Nestlé introduces the world's first instant coffee — NESCAFÉ®. Today, NESCAFÉ is one of the company's top-selling products worldwide.

1939

NESTLÉ® TOLL HOUSE® morsels are introduced, becoming an American baking tradition.

1947

Nestlé acquires Maggi, a European company specializing in food seasonings. MAGGI® bouillon cubes remain a worldwide favorite.

1948

NESTEA® instant tea is launched. NESTEA is soon reformulated to be cold-water soluble, making Nestlé the "iced tea expert."

1948

NESTLÉ® QUIK® chocolate powder is introduced. It soon become the top-selling chocolate flavoring for milk in the U.S., with popular television advertising featuring Farfel the dog, a singing puppet, who exclaims: "N-E-S-T-L-E-S, Nestlé's make the very best ... **chocolate**."

1958

FRISKIES® introduces the first dry cat food.

1959

Nestlé establishes FIDCO, a flavoring and ingredient company, to meet the food industry's demand for more sophisticated flavorings.

1960

Nestlé acquires CROSSE & BLACKWELL, a British company specializing in gourmet foods such as condiments, sauces, chutney, orange marmalade and holiday desserts.

1961

Carnation introduces CARNATION® COFFEE-MATE®, the first powdered non-dairy coffee creamer. Within two years it becomes the top-selling brand in its category.

1965

CARNATION® INSTANT BREAKFAST® is introduced nationwide, establishing a new category of consumer products.

1968

Nestlé acquires a minority interest in Vittel, a French mineral water company.

1971

Carnation launches CARNATION® hot cocoa mix nationwide.

1973

FRISKIES® MIGHTY DOG® is introduced. It is the first canned dog food in a convenient single-serving can.

1973

Nestlé acquires STOUFFER'S®.

1981

STOUFFER'S® LEAN CUISINE® is introduced, setting the taste standard for calorie-controlled entrées.

1982

FANCY FEAST® gourmet canned cat food is launched in 3 oz. cans.

1983

Nestlé acquires the popular confections brands CHUNKY®, BIT-O-HONEY®, RAISINETS®, OH HENRY!®, GOOBERS® and SNO-CAPS® from Ward-Johnson.

1984

Nestlé acquires Kathryn Beich which provides chocolate confections for fund-raising efforts.

1985

Nestlé acquires Carnation Company which includes CARNATION® milk and ice cream products, COFFEE-MATE® non-dairy creamer, CARNATION® Hot Cocoa Mix, CARNATION® INSTANT BREAKFAST®, BUITONI® pastas and sauces, LIBBY'S® Pumpkin and FRISKIES® pet food products.

1985

Nestlé acquires HILLS BROTHERS Coffee, Inc. which includes MJB® and CHASE & SANBORN® brands.

1985

Nestlé launches LIBBY'S® JUICY JUICE® nationwide.

1986

Nestlé acquires The L.J. Minor Corp., Inc. which manufactures food bases, sauces and gravies for the food service industry.

1988

Nestlé USA enters the infant nutrition category with the launch of CARNATION® Infant Formulas.

1988

Nestlé acquires Rowntree Confections (TURTLES® candy and AFTER EIGHT® Biscuits and Mints and QUALITY STREET® candy).

1988

Nestlé acquires Sunmark, maker of popular sugar confections such as WILLY WONKA® candy, SWEETARTS®, NERDS.

1988

Nestlé acquires the Buitoni-Perugina Pasta Company based in Italy.

1990

Nestlé USA is formed, bringing together some of the nation's most popular brands

1990

Nestlé acquires BABY RUTH®, BUTTERFINGER® and PEARSON NIPS® confections from Planters Lifesavers Company.

1991

Nestlé acquires The Drumstick Company. The original DRUMSTICK® ice cream cone was created by I.C. Parker in 1928.

1992

Nestlé acquires Perrier bottled water. Brands include PERRIER®, ARROWHEAD®, CALISTOGA®, DEER PARK®, POLAND SPRINGS®, VITTEL® and ZEPHYRHILLS®.

1994

FIDCO and L.J. Minor merge to become FIS (Food Ingredient Specialties, Inc.), a provider of flavor systems to food manufacturers.

1995

Nestlé acquires ALPO® pet foods.

1995

Nestlé acquires ORTEGA® Mexican foods. Ortega was founded in 1897 by Emilio Ortega.

1995

Nestlé sells World Wine Estates.

1997

Nestlé sells Contadina.

1998

STOUFFER'S® skillet meals is introduced — easily prepared, complete meals in a bag.

1999

NESTLÉ® QUIK® gets a new name, NESTLÉ® NESQUIK®, and an innovative new package.

1999

Nestlé USA and Pillsbury form a joint venture — Ice Cream Partners USA — that combines the ice cream business of Nestlé with Häagen-Dazs.

1999

Nestlé USA's *Blueprint for Success* is implemented.

1999

Nestlé sells HILLS BROTHES®, CHASE & SANBORN® and MJB®.

2000

Nestlé celebrates 100 years in the U.S.

2000

Nestlé acquires PowerBar.

2001

Nestlé acquires Ralston Purina pet foods. Founded in 1894 by William H. Danforth of St. Louis, Mo.

2003

Nestlé divests Flipz to Lincoln Snacks Company.

2002

Nestlé acquires Chef America.

PETER'S CHOCOLATE

2002

Nestlé divests PETER'S® Chocolate brands to Wilbur Chocolate Company, a subsidiary of Cargill, Inc.

Kathryn Beich

2002

Nestlé divests Kathryn Beich to Lincolnshire Equity Fund II, L.P.

2003

Nestlé divests ORTEGA® Mexican foods to B&G Foods, Inc.

2003

Nestlé divests FLIPZ™ to Lincoln Snacks Company.

2004

Nestlé divests WONDERBALL to Frankford Candy & Chocolate Co., Inc.

2004

Nestlé divests CROSSE & BLACKWELL® brands to J.M. Smucker Company.

2004

Nestlé divests LIBBY'S® KERNS® nectars juice business in the USA and Mexico to Stremicks Heritage Foods.

Nestlé USA
Vision and Blueprint

Vision2000

Our
Vision

Our
Strategies

Our
Core Values

Nestlé USA
Long-term Vision

You are the key to our future success by providing the enthusiasm, talent and dedication to move us forward and make us an even stronger competitor in the food industry.

Our Vision:
To be
the premier
diversified
food company
in the
United States.

With your help, we will reach our goal by focusing on five core values — people, quality, brands, customers/consumers and performance. These are the main elements that hold the Nestlé business units and staff functions together, along with a powerful Nestlé spirit of internal cooperation, global thinking and a focus on our industry competitors.

Nestlé USA
Core Values

Nestlé's core values are built around people, quality, brands, customers/consumers, and performance. They are the set of unifying principles from which the entire company can draw to support and strengthen the activities of each operating company and corporate support group.

These core values are the common thread that holds together the quilt work of diversified companies, brands and services that form Nestlé USA.

People People are our most important asset and the source of our competitive advantage. Our work environment must motivate learning, innovation, high performance, risk taking, and integrity.

Quality We are dedicated to adding increasing value to our products and to our relationship with suppliers, customers, consumers, and each other. This will be achieved by ensuring that every activity we perform is evaluated for its need and its contribution to value creation.

Brands Brands are one of the corporation's most important assets. Their strength ensures the continuity of our growth and profitability. Their management and nurturing are everyone's responsibility. We will invest to sustain or build leadership positions for all of our key brands.

Customers/Consumers Our success rests on understanding our customer's needs and responding to their expectations rapidly and effectively. Nestlé has a variety of customers with varying needs: retailers, distributors, wholesalers, and the final consumer. We view trade customers as strategic partners working with us to profitably grow the categories in which we compete by providing consumers products that meet their changing preferences in food consumption, preparation, and value.

Performance We are dedicated to achieving long-term group operating results that are in the top quartile of those companies in our competitive set.

Strategies to Achieve
Nestlé USA's Vision

☐ Develop a strong Nestlé organization and culture.

☐ Provide superior value to consumers and customers through continuous quality improvement.

☐ Invest to strengthen brand equity and build loyalty to our brands.

☐ Achieve leadership positions in our core businesses.

☐ Achieve financial performance in the top quartile of diversified food companies.

Joe Weller

USA BLUEPRINT FOR SUCCESS

Vision – What we want to be

"To be the Very Best Food Company in the United States"

Nestlé is the world food company dedicated to providing people and their pets with the best food and beverages throughout their lives. We will not rest until our employees, our consumers, our customers, our suppliers and our shareholders judge our company to be the very best. Our commitment to achieving our vision is the source of Nestlé pride.

Strategies – How we intend to get there

- **Renovation/Innovation:** *Continuously revitalize our brands and products and, through portfolio management, prioritize and launch successful new products that drive consumer needs.*
- **Product Availability – Whenever, Wherever, However:** *Invest to ensure that our brands and products are in the widest distribution possible.*
- **Consumer Communications:** *Increase communications spending and effectiveness (especially advertising), communications integration and co-marketing activities to drive demand and strengthen our brand loyalty.*
- **Low Cost – Highly Efficient Operations:** *Follow a disciplined continuous improvement process that optimizes our ability to fuel our growth initiatives by improving our delivered product costs and reducing overhead costs.*

Measures – How we know when we are there

- **Growth:** *Achieve a minimum of 4% Real Internal Growth every year.*
- **Market Share:** *Increase market share in our strategic categories and on our strategic brands, always striving for the number one position.*
- **Profit:** *Maintain annual percentage increases that exceed the increase in sales. Nestlé financial measures are individually important but collectively they should result in increasing economic profit.*

Core Values – What we believe in

Our core values are consistent with and support The Basic Nestlé Management and Leadership Principles.

- **People:** *People from all diverse backgrounds are our most important asset and the source of our competitive advantage. We operate in teams where we expect and reward responsible risk taking.*
- **Quality:** *We are dedicated to continuous improvement in the food safety and quality of every product we make and in every activity we perform.*
- **Brands:** *Our strong brands ensure the continuity of our growth and profitability. Their support is every employee's responsibility.*
- **Consumers:** *Our reason for being is to understand, anticipate and best fulfill our consumers' needs.*
- **Customers:** *We appreciate and support the critical role our customers play in getting our brands to the consumer while working closely together to achieve mutual value.*
- **Performance:** *We are all committed to achieving our financial and strategic objectives while adhering to our core values.*

Nestlé. Good Food, Good Life

APPENDIX C

A Word from Joe (Select Columns)

WHAT'S ON MY MIND — A Word from Joe

Many of you have asked for clarification of our key goals and strategies for the U.S. You've also asked me how our goals fit in with *The Basic Nestlé Management and Leadership Principles*, published by Messrs. Maucher and Brabeck, and Mr. Brabeck's *Blueprint for the Future*, which includes the four pillars — renovation/innovation; product availability; consumer communications; and low cost, highly efficient operations. Just as these pillars support Nestlé worldwide, they also are the strategies behind our effort to become the Very Best food company in the U.S.

Our Nestlé USA *Blueprint for Success* pulls all these ideas together and shows how our goals relate to Nestlé S.A.'s and vice-versa. There is not enough space on this page to write about all the details of our *Blueprint for Success*...that's why it's the theme of our state-of-the-company and Leadership Forum meetings next month. Your management also will be discussing this with you in more detail. I ask that you read it carefully and use it to guide your decisions on the job. That's how essential it is that every Nestlé employee supports our Nestlé USA *Blueprint for Success*. A copy of the Blueprint will be included in next month's issue of *Nestlé 2000*.

Our vision remains unchanged: To be the Very Best food company in the United States. Mr. Brabeck's four pillars are our strategies to achieve that vision. If we are successful in these four areas, we absolutely will be the Very Best food company in the U.S. Our Blueprint also includes three measures of our progress: growth, market share and profit.

And, like our vision, our core values don't change. They are the principles that we want to characterize the Nestlé USA culture.

The Nestlé USA *Blueprint for Success* is a "call-to-action" for all Nestlé employees to jump into the middle of this very competitive "game" we call the food business and to make a difference.

None of our 19,000 employees can stay on the sidelines if we hope to achieve our vision to be the best.

We now have our *Blueprint for Success* and it's up to each one of us to execute, execute, execute!

The Very Best,

Joe

Joe Weller
Chairman and CEO

WHAT'S ON MY MIND A Word from Joe

I hope that every Nestlé USA employee values diversity in our workforce as much as I do.

We're not focusing on diversity because it's politically correct. Developing and maintaining a diverse organization is good for our business: it gives us a competitive advantage because it helps us reflect our customers and consumers and their needs; it shows we value people; and it is a prerequisite to recruiting and retaining top talent. Diversity also fuels innovation. It is an ongoing process that must be incorporated throughout our corporate culture and considered in all internal and external operations.

But what is diversity? Diversity must be viewed broadly — it's about race, gender, ethnicity, family situation and needs, disabilities, lifestyle, work style and personality, age and even amount of time in the workforce — perhaps you're just entering or perhaps you're nearing retirement. As you can see, "diversity" encompasses basically any criterion that characterizes uniqueness.

People are a core value, and are truly our greatest resource. Without diverse people, there is no way that we can understand, anticipate and best fulfill the needs of our consumers — one of our other core values. And we are part of a global food company, Nestlé S.A., which exemplifies diversity and must be linked to local social and eating habits. Nestlé's management philosophy to "think globally, act locally" reinforces just how important it is to recognize and respond to the diverse people, cultures and traditions of the countries in which Nestlé operates.

I want diversity to touch every part of our organization — every plant, every division and every functional area. We all need to participate as individuals to work on behalf of Nestlé and our *Blueprint for Success* — bringing not only our various skills and knowledge to the game, but our unique perspectives that stem from our diverse backgrounds and life experiences. Uniformity is not going to get us to be the Very Best food company in the U.S.

Diversity must be integrated into the way we do business by valuing, having respect and benefiting from each of our unique backgrounds within our overall business goals and objectives. Perhaps *The Basic Nestlé Management & Leadership Principles* says it best: "Nestlé is not a faceless company marketing to faceless consumers. It is a human company providing a response to individual human needs the world over."

The Very Best,

Joe

Joe Weller
Chairman and CEO

WHAT'S ON MY MIND A Word from Joe

When you define the importance of manufacturing to a company like Nestlé, it comes down to the basics: If our factories don't make it, then we can't sell it!

Even more importantly, our products represent Nestlé to consumers. If the finished products coming out of our factories aren't of the highest quality, our consumers won't see Nestlé as a company that provides the "very best" products for their families.

Our factories — and the people who work in them — symbolize Nestlé in many communities across the country. Nearly 67% of all Nestlé USA employees work in manufacturing. We make a significant investment in manufacturing because it is a primary source of our competitive advantage. For every dollar we spend as a company, 80% is on manufacturing.

Our factories in the U.S. also help provide Nestlé products worldwide. For example, we make **Stouffer's** and **Stouffer's Lean Cuisine** frozen entrees for Canadian consumers and **Friskies** pet food for consumers in the balance of Zone Americas and in Japan. This is one way to achieve our 1999 operating plan goal of factory optimization.

You all know that one of the key strategies of our Nestlé USA *Blueprint for Success* is low-cost, highly efficient operations. As part of this effort, we've worked hard to become more efficient in the manufacturing area. Since 1997, we've taken $61 million out of the cost of manufacturing our products by improving our systems and processes.

Manufacturing is also playing an integral part in making the BEST initiative a success. Many of the process changes driven by BEST impact the plants, including purchase card, production planning, and e-procurement.

Our goal is not just to make the very best products, but to have the safest factories in the food industry. We've reduced the number of accidents in the plants and rank among the top food companies in this area. We will continue to focus on safety — our goal is zero accidents.

The real edge in the future goes to companies that recognize manufacturing as part of a strategic team that includes sales, marketing, and supply chain. Throughout the Nestlé world, we are seen as leaders in this area. And, of course, manufacturing is a core competency for us — we cannot achieve our goal of being the Very Best food company in the U.S. without a solid and strategic manufacturing effort.

The Very Best,

Joe

Joe Weller
Chairman and CEO

At a recent plant tour in Gaffney (pictured from left to right): Martin Holford, executive VP, Technical & Manufacturing; Elizabeth Fincher, line operator; Joe Weller; and Plant Manager Pat Emrich.

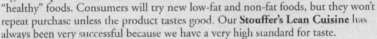

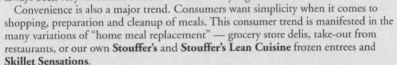

Consumers are one of our core values for one very important reason: our entire reason for being as a company is to understand, anticipate and best fulfill our consumers' needs. One way we do that is by learning what's most important on their minds.

The key consumer trends that continue to be strong are taste, convenience, and value.

Consumers want good-tasting food — taste is still king. It's that simple. They are unwilling to compromise on taste when it comes to "healthy" foods. Consumers will try new low-fat and non-fat foods, but they won't repeat purchase unless the product tastes good. Our **Stouffer's Lean Cuisine** has always been very successful because we have a very high standard for taste.

Convenience is also a major trend. Consumers want simplicity when it comes to shopping, preparation and cleanup of meals. This consumer trend is manifested in the many variations of "home meal replacement" — grocery store delis, take-out from restaurants, or our own **Stouffer's** and **Stouffer's Lean Cuisine** frozen entrees and **Skillet Sensations.**

Our product line-up is very convenience-oriented. In fact, 92% of our product portfolio (based on sales) offers some level of convenience, whether it's ready to eat/drink or ready to heat, cook or mix. The remaining 8% of our products are ingredients used in scratch cooking or baking.

One reason why so many people want easy meal preparation is that there is a continuing deterioration of cooking skills among consumers. Our Stouffer's Skillet Sensations hits the mark in providing easy and delicious meal solutions to consumers as well as helping them feel like they're creating a home-cooked meal.

The third key consumer trend is value — people are willing to pay a higher price for a product if they perceive it to have higher value. None of this comes as a surprise to any of us, since we are all consumers ourselves.

Consumer needs are always changing and evolving — and keeping on top of these trends is crucial to our success now and in the future.

The Very Best,

Joe Weller
Chairman and CEO

What's On My Mind
A Word from Joe

Many of you have asked me how you can get off the sidelines and into the game. Well, John Hubbell, head of our Sales Division, has a great idea that every single employee can do to get in the game and make a difference in achieving our 2001 goals.

It's called Adopt-A-Store, and it's as simple as introducing yourself as a Nestlé employee to the manager at the store where you regularly shop. It can be a grocery store, club store, convenience store, etc. The goal is to build a positive relationship with your store manager — both as a valued customer of the store AND as a Nestlé employee. For example, when the store manager has a choice between Nestlé and a competitive product for an end-aisle display, he or she is more likely to choose Nestlé because you've helped personalize the company.

John is rolling out the Adopt-A-Store program to all employees this month, so check the *Nestlé Very Best Web* or your local bulletin board for more information on how to participate. It's easy to do and I believe you'll be glad you did!

Each of us CAN make a difference. You can have a direct and positive impact on our Blueprint goal of Product Availability through the Adopt-A-Store program. This is strictly a volunteer program, but I strongly encourage all employees to participate. It's a great way to show your Nestlé Pride!

The Very Best,

Joe Weller
Chairman and CEO

244

Joe Weller

What's On My Mind
A Word from Joe

As you can see in the photo, I'm getting ready to celebrate the holidays with plenty of **Nestlé Toll House** cookies. They are one of my family's favorites. This year, particularly after the tragic events of September 11, it's especially important that we take time over the holidays to be with family and friends. I urge each of you to relax and re-charge, wherever you celebrate the holidays.

I know it's a challenge to find time to relax when November and December are two of our busiest — and most important — months. By the time you read this, we will be in the final few weeks of the year, and I know that each of you are doing everything you can to help us make, sell or deliver our products to consumers.

At the end of December, we'll measure our success in terms of Real Internal Growth (RIG) and operating profit. Our 150% stretch goal of 4.0% RIG and our original 100% goal of 3.6% RIG are probably out of reach at this point, but I'm still hoping we can make a run at achieving a RIG of close to 3.5%. Anything over 3.2% would still be ahead of our competitors as the economy and the events of September 11 have taken a toll on the food industry.

In addition to our year-end push for results, we also are focused on our intended acquisition of Ralston Purina. As this issue of the *Nestlé Very Best Times* goes to press, we are still awaiting U.S. government approval, but we are still on track to close the deal by the end of this year. Once we receive approval, we will merge our Friskies PetCare Division with Purina and form Nestlé Purina PetCare Company. The U.S. and Canadian headquarters for this new company will be in St. Louis, Missouri.

And, in preparation for the start of the new year, the 2002 Nestlé USA *Blueprint for Success* is enclosed in this issue of the *Nestlé Very Best Times*.

The Blueprint is one of the most important tools we have to make sure each of us is united and aligned behind shared, common goals. I encourage you to get a head start in December and January and develop your individual goals based on the clear direction in the Blueprint.

Wishing each of you a safe and happy holiday season.

Joe

Joe Weller
Chairman & CEO

245

What's On My Mind
A Word from Joe

I've just finished reviewing the succession plans for our whole organization plus Nestlé Ice Cream Company — three full days of meetings. The goal of succession planning is to continually develop leadership talent to be ready to meet Nestlé's business needs in the U.S. and internationally.

I work with the Executive Leadership Team and our Human Resources team to identify top-performing employees at the manager, director and vice president levels who are candidates for leadership roles in the future.

Once we identify these high-potential employees, we commit to having a clear understanding of their career aspirations. Our goal is to retain these top-performers to ensure continuity of management and high productivity levels in the future.

These succession planning meetings also help us identify areas in our organization where we have a gap in senior-level talent.

Why spend time on succession planning when we're in the middle of a major restructuring? As you know, the organizational changes we're making will impact every employee in one way or another. Unfortunately, some jobs will be eliminated. Even though I do spend a lot of my time working on the restructure, it's also my responsibility to look ahead and focus on leading the organization into the future. That's where succession planning comes in — I think of it as making sure we have strong players on the bench that are ready to take a leadership role when the opportunity comes up.

I'm very proud of Nestlé's longstanding overall commitment to providing training and development opportunities for employees at all levels. Nestlé Succession Planning is just one piece of this commitment, and our commitment will not change — in fact it becomes even more important as we go through the many changes of the restructure and beyond.

Joe
Joe Weller
Chairman & CEO

246

Joe Weller

What's On My Mind
A Word from Joe

The big news as we go to press is that *Fortune* magazine ranked Nestlé USA as the #1 food company for the sixth consecutive year! Congrat-ulations to each of you on this achievement.

We held our ninth annual State-of-the-Company meeting this month in Glendale, with satellite broadcasts to Solon and our new "sister company" colleagues at Nestlé Purina PetCare in St. Louis. A videotape of the meeting was sent to all Nestlé USA locations.

The most exciting news at the State-of-the-Company meeting was our outstanding 2002 results. Nestlé USA surpassed our Real Internal Growth (RIG) stretch goal, ending the year with a fantastic 4.2% RIG! This is our fifth consecutive year of achieving RIG of 4% or better — which is an amazing accomplishment by any standard. Importantly, our EBITA (Earnings Before Interest, Taxes & Amortization), which is how we measure profitability, was up 27% vs. last year.

I believe that these outstanding results were achieved through phenomenal teamwork by all of our business units and support functions — including the support we receive from Carlos E. Represas, our team leader in Zone Americas. There is nothing we cannot accomplish when we all work together as a high-performance team!

At the State-of-the-Company meeting I also introduced the concept of Shared Service Centers as an important part of the new "Nestlé in the USA" organization. We will begin our analysis for Shared Service Centers in mid-2003. The results of this analysis will be the basis for our plan to create Shared Service Centers to support the business units and enable them to focus their energy on the consumer. Although I showed some concepts for how the organization might look, please remember that we are at the very early stages of this process. Things almost certainly will change once we complete the business case analysis. I talked about Shared Service Centers so that you would have an idea — directionally — of where we are moving as an organization.

We have another challenging year in 2003! I ask you all to stay focused on our key initiatives (use the 2003 *Blueprint for Success* to set your priorities). Also, please give your complete support to the BEST/GLOBE team as they gear up for our Wave 2 "go-live" on April 7. It is critical that we minimize business interruption during this transition to our new common systems.

Keep up the great work!

Joe
Joe Weller
Chairman & CEO

247

What's On My Mind
A Word from Joe

As of July 1, Nestlé USA changes from being an individual operating company to a parent company. This new structure means some kind of change for all of us.

For me, the new structure means that I will be less involved in the day-to-day operations of our business — that's now the responsibility of Brad Alford, Stephen Cunliffe and Pat McGinnis. My role will be one of accountability for the total Nestlé USA results vs. the responsibility for how each business unit meets its goals.

We've grown so much in the past few years — thanks to the dedication and effort of each of you — that it's difficult for any one person to be involved in the day-to-day operations of several large businesses. With our restructure, I will rely on the excellent, experienced leadership of Brad, Stephen and Pat. Ultimately, of course, I remain accountable for delivering excellent results for Nestlé USA to our parent company in Vevey, Switzerland.

Since 1990, we've had excellent growth in Sales and return on invested capital. The problem has been our profit margins — otherwise known as EBITA (Earnings Before Interest, Taxes and Amortization). In 1990, our EBITA was 7.5%. In 2002, we've increased it to 11.8%. We're going in the right direction, but we're simply not getting there fast enough to stay competitive. As we've improved, our competitors have gotten better as well. The industry average is now 15.5%, with key competitors like Hershey and Kraft well above that mark.

It is impossible to significantly improve our EBITA with our current business model. That's a key driver behind our new business model, which has independent, highly focused business units focused on our consumers. A critical piece of our new business model is the Nestlé Business Center shared services business unit, led by Dan Stroud.

The Shared Services business case begins July 7 in Glendale, Calif. We don't yet know what kind of cost savings and service improvements we'll be able to achieve — that's the role of the business case team. They will be looking beyond the easy answer and challenging themselves by asking two questions: "Is it good for our consumer? Is it cost-effective for Nestlé?"

I know this will be a major change for our organization and for each of us individually. It will be painful at times, but it is also a positive opportunity for each of us to grow, learn, and succeed as we go through the change process. As always, I'm relying on your support through the exciting and challenging months ahead.

Joe

Joe Weller
Chairman & CEO

Joe Weller

WHAT'S ON MY MIND

A WORD FROM JOE

You've heard me talk about "Nestlé. Good Food, Good Life" and you've seen it appear where appropriate on our company materials and letterhead — the new design of *Nestlé Times* is a good example. "Nestlé. Good Food, Good Life" is our worldwide corporate sentiment reflecting our commitment to be a respected and trustworthy food, nutrition and wellness company.

"Nestlé. Good Food, Good Life" captures the essence of what we do everyday when we come to work — making food a pleasurable experience in people's lives. It also communicates the nutritional goodness of food, whether that's through quality products, delicious flavors, or healthy ingredients.

And who better to do all this than the world's largest food company? Nestlé has a century-long, worldwide commitment to nutrition research, education, and awareness that allows us to provide for emerging nutrition, health and wellness needs of consumers from all demographics and lifestyles.

Nestlé USA is positioned very well for "Nestlé. Good Food Good Life." Our broad portfolio of products gives consumers many food choices that make good living possible. For example, **Stouffer's Lean Cuisine** is the #1 calorie- and portion-controlled frozen entrée business in the U.S. In addition, we offer sugar-free products such as **Nestlé Turtles** and **Nestlé Nips**. Other products are available in fat-free or low-fat versions, including **Nestlé Nesquik, Buitoni, Nestlé Coffee mate** and **Nestlé** Evaporated Milk. Of course, many products are packed with vitamins and minerals like **PowerBar, Nestlé Carnation Instant Breakfast**, and **Kerns** nectars. That's not to say there is no room for indulgent treats. Candy consumed in moderation is part of a healthy lifestyle that includes a balanced diet and exercise. Of course, Nestlé Purina PetCare has embraced the idea of healthy and happy pets since the beginning.

Good nutrition, health and wellness are the business of each of us at Nestlé and will help us fulfill our greatest ambition: to become a vital ingredient in lives lived to the fullest.

Joe Weller
Chairman & CEO

WHAT'S ON MY MIND
A WORD FROM JOE

Our Shared Services initiative will have a huge influence on the future success of Nestlé in North America — it is absolutely the right thing to do for our business! Moving to a business model with a shared services organization will help improve profit margins and enable our operating companies to stay focused on their consumers and customers.

We have a fantastic opportunity to leverage our combined size and design an organization that will deliver shared support services to Nestlé operations across North America more efficiently and effectively — and at a significantly reduced cost. This will significantly increase our ability to stay competitive in a very tough industry.

This is an important initiative that will have a powerful impact on our business, and it's only natural that it's a hot topic of discussion around the office. In place of rumors, however, I'd like to share some facts about Shared Services.

- Purchasing is the first area to move into the Design phase because the Shared Services business case told us that it was by far the biggest opportunity to leverage our combined size and gain savings — Nestlé in North America spends about $9 billion annually on purchased goods and services. This is a major undertaking and will affect everyone who buys goods and services on behalf of Nestlé.

- I've heard a variety of rumors speculating on the location of the Nestlé Business Services organization. The fact is, we just don't know yet. We plan to begin the process of looking at our needs and possible locations in late 2004. There are many possible options, including a single location, multiple locations (maybe even utilizing existing Nestlé sites), or some kind of "virtual" organization. It is much too early to speculate on these or any other scenarios. Once we determine our needs, we will then be able to choose the optimal locations to meet them.

  When a decision has been made, we will communicate this information as quickly as possible. I know this is one of the most urgent questions we all want answered — and I'm counting on your continued patience as we go through this process.

We are still in the early stages of the Shared Services initiative, and we simply do not yet have the answers we're all waiting for. Not knowing can be uncomfortable and frustrating, but misinformation and rumors only add to that frustration. The best advice I can give is to stay focused on doing your part to help achieve our business goals.

The industry is changing, our company is changing, and our individual roles are changing (including mine!). I believe that embracing change with an open mind makes the process easier and more rewarding.

In the midst of all these changes, I encourage each of you to take time to enjoy the holidays with family and friends. It's a good time to recharge and gear up for a fast start in 2004!

Happy holidays,

Joe Weller
Chairman & CEO

P.S. If you have a question about Shared Services, you can submit it on the Nestlé Business Services site on the *Nestlé Very Best Web* intranet.

Joe Weller

A WORD FROM JOE

I would like to congratulate each of you on your teamwork, passion and efforts this past year. In 2003 we faced serious challenges and associates at each of our operating companies (Nestlé Brands, Nestlé Prepared Foods, and Nestlé Purina PetCare Companies) rose to the occasion. Together we exceeded our profit goals in all three operating companies. Nestlé Brands and Nestlé Purina PetCare exceeded plan and for Nestlé USA overall we had Real Internal Growth (RIG) of 3%.

I am particularly proud that Nestlé Brands Company and Nestlé Prepared Foods Company together once again exceeded 4% RIG, achieving 4.5% RIG in 2003. These two companies, which formerly made up Nestlé USA, just celebrated their 6th consecutive year of 4+% RIG. There's no major competitor here in the U.S. that can match that accomplishment.

Now, as we move forward through the first quarter of 2004, it's key that we all become familiar and focused on our Blueprint goals for the year. The *Blueprint for Success* is an important tool that helps all Nestlé associates stay aligned and focused on our business priorities, and fulfills our vision to be the very best food company in the U.S.

This year, Nestlé USA and its operating companies each have their own *Blueprint for Success*. Each operating company's Blueprint focuses on business-specific objectives to help them meet their long-term goals.

The Nestlé USA Blueprint provides overall direction to the organization through broad-based and high-level initiatives. While the Nestlé USA Blueprint plays an important role in providing the framework for an aligned organization, it complements, but does not supersede, the operating companies' individual Blueprints.

I'm excited about the year ahead and feel confident that we can grow our businesses while we improve our profit margins. I encourage each of you to work within your teams and use your Blueprints as a tool for teamwork and alignment. Together we can achieve outstanding performance in 2004.

Joe
Joe Weller
Chairman & CEO
Nestlé USA

251

WHAT'S ON MY MIND
A WORD FROM JOE

We recently had the opportunity to host the Nestlé S.A. Board of Directors and Executive Board here in the U.S. As you'll see from this issue of the *Nestlé Times*, they toured four great Nestlé cities – Glendale, Fort Worth, St. Louis and Solon – to learn more about our current businesses, future initiatives, and to meet our dedicated associates.

The Board members are key leaders of our company and it was a privilege to showcase our business to them. The feedback I have received on their visit is excellent and that is a direct compliment to your commitment and hard work!

I'm pleased to report our fourth quarter performance is strong. You all are doing a great job and we are in the home stretch. I ask that you keep focused on your company Blueprints and let's put "the pedal to the metal" in bringing home the results for 2004.

As we approach 2005, we must prepare our goals for the new year. We are creating the initiatives for the 2005 Nestlé USA *Blueprint for Success*, and I know that Brad Alford, Stephen Cunliffe and Pat McGinnis are working on their operating company Blueprints as well. The Blueprints for each operating company and Nestlé USA include business-specific objectives to help us stay aligned and focused on our priorities. Stay tuned, as we will share the new Blueprints soon.

I want to thank you for your dedication and passion for your work. During this fun and busy time of year, I hope each of you will take time out for yourself to enjoy the holiday season with family and friends.

Happy holidays,

Joe Weller
Chairman & CEO

Joe Weller

A WORD FROM JOE

As we approach the second half of the year, I would like to thank all of you for your teamwork and commitment to the *Blueprint for Success*. Because of your continued focus on our 2005 initiatives, we are on track to meet our Sales, Real Internal Growth (RIG) and Organic Growth goals. Our results so far this year are favorable and all three Nestlé USA businesses are on track to meet or exceed our goals.

This strong first half performance is impressive and hasn't been easy in light of some challenges all of our businesses are facing. One key issue is the increasing cost of commodities. Commodities are cyclical and we are in an up cycle. This of course affects all businesses including competitors, and even though we anticipated this change in pricing, it still impacts our cost structure. For example, if you think about it, commodity pricing for energy affects almost every aspect of our business — everything from product packaging, fuel for transportation, to energy to run our plants. We need to find a way to manage this pressure of commodity costs and still ensure profitability.

Our first half performance has been a real team effort. Here are some key initiatives that have contributed to our success.

First, hats off to Nestlé Prepared Foods Company for a successful product launch with SPA CUISINE™ meals from STOUFFER'S® LEAN CUISINE® — the launch results are even better than anticipated! The category is growing and STOUFFER'S LEAN CUISINE is gaining share in the nutritional frozen meals category.

Also I would like to mention that the trade category acceptance of the new HOT POCKETS® brand and LEAN POCKETS® brand SUBS line has been terrific. If you haven't already, I encourage all of you to try this new product.

Next, Nestlé Brands Company has seen consumption of NESCAFÉ® TASTER'S CHOICE® significantly increase after its starring role on *The Apprentice* TV show. This is another great example of how innovative marketing campaigns can be affective.

The PowerBar Product Development team took advantage of the recent "carb" craze and hit the ground running with fantastic products to fulfill our consumers' needs. Now we are facing our next challenge with this diminishing trend, however we are optimistic about the appeal of the new POWERBAR® TRIPLE THREAT™ energy bars.

And, Nestlé Purina PetCare Company has done a fantastic job during the first half of the year and is exceeding all of its goals. They made a conscious effort to launch new products early in the year. They successfully leveraged their dry pet food expertise and launched PURINA® FANCY FEAST® Dry Cat Food. PURINA® BENEFUL® HEALTHY RADIANCE® Dog Food was also launched first quarter leveraging the interest in nutrition and health for dogs.

Also, I'm pleased with the focus of the Hispanic Initiative this year. This issue of the *Nestlé Times* includes an insert on this initiative, which I urge you all to read.

These are just a few highlights of our successful start to 2005. In my mind the second half is all about focus. I think we must continue to focus on our Blueprint initiatives and keep the momentum going. I'm confident your commitment to teamwork, alignment, passion and balance will again result in a strong year-end performance.

Joe

Joe Weller
Chairman & CEO

Endnotes

Chapter 6

[1] John Kotter, *Leading Change,* Harvard Business School Press, 1996, 7.

[2] Ibid.

Chapter 7

[1] Jon R. Katzenbach and Douglas K. Smith, *The Wisdom of Teams: Creating the High-Performance Organization,* Harvard Business School Press, 1993, 9.

[2] Ibid, 3.

Chapter 8

[1] John Kotter, *Leading Change,* Harvard Business School Press, 1996, 25.

[2] Ibid.

[3] Ibid.

Chapter 9

[1] Jim Hunter, *The Servant: The Simple Story About the True Essence of Leadership*, Prima Publishing.

[2] Mike Huckabee and John Perry, *Character Is the Issue: How People with Integrity Can Revolutionize America*, Broadman & Holman Publishers, 1997, 43.

Chapter 10

[1] "Fight Cancer! Reduce Heart Disease! Live Longer!" *Forbes*, February 16, 2004, 28.

[2] Ibid.

Index

Joe Weller